The Arras Campaign

The Arras Campaign

Andrew Rawson

Pen & Sword
MILITARY

First published in Great Britain in 2017 by
PEN AND SWORD MILITARY
an imprint of
Pen and Sword Books Ltd
47 Church Street
Barnsley
South Yorkshire S70 2AS

ISBN 978 1 47389 291 0

Printed and bound in England by
CPI Group (UK) Ltd, Croydon, CR0 4YY

Typeset in Times by CHIC GRAPHICS

Pen & Sword Books Ltd incorporates the imprints of
Pen & Sword Books Ltd incorporates the imprints of Pen & Sword
Archaeology, Atlas, Aviation, Battleground, Discovery,
Family History, History, Maritime, Military, Naval, Politics,
Railways, Select, Social History, Transport, True Crime,
Claymore Press, Frontline Books, Leo Cooper, Praetorian Press,
Remember When, Seaforth Publishing and Wharncliffe.

For a complete list of Pen and Sword titles please contact
Pen and Sword Books Limited
47 Church Street, Barnsley, South Yorkshire, S70 2AS, England
E-mail: enquiries@pen-and-sword.co.uk
Website: www.pen-and-sword.co.uk

Contents

Regiments

Regiments in Alphabetical Order	Abbreviations Used
Argyll & Sutherland Highlanders Regiment	Argylls
Bedfordshire Regiment	Bedfords
Black Watch Regiment	Black Watch
Border Regiment	Borders
Buffs (East Kent) Regiment	Buffs
Cambridgeshire Regiment	Cambridgeshire
Cameron Highlanders Regiment	Camerons
Cameronians (Scottish Rifles) Regiment	Scottish Rifles
Cheshire Regiment	Cheshires
Coldstream Guards	Coldstreamers
Connaught Rangers	Connaughts
Devonshire Regiment	Devons
Dorsetshire Regiment	Dorsets
Duke of Cornwall's Light Infantry	DCLI
Duke of Wellington's (West Riding) Regiment	Duke's
Durham Light Infantry	Durhams
East Lancashire Regiment	East Lancashires
East Surrey Regiment	East Surreys
East Yorkshire Regiment	East Yorkshires
Essex Regiment	Essex
Green Howards (Yorkshire) Regiment	Green Howards
Gloucestershire Regiment	Gloucesters
Gordon Highlanders	Gordons
Grenadier Guards	Grenadiers
Hampshire Regiment	Hampshires
Herefordshire Regiment	Herefords
Hertfordshire Regiment	Hertfords
Highland Light Infantry	HLI
Honourable Artillery Company	HAC
Irish Guards	Irish Guards
King's (Liverpool) Regiment	King's
King's Own (Royal Lancaster) Regiment	King's Own
King's Own Scottish Borderers	KOSBs
King's (Shropshire Light Infantry) Regiment	KSLIs
King's Own (Yorkshire Light Infantry) Regiment	KOYLIs
King's Royal Rifle Corps	KRRC
Lancashire Fusiliers	Lancashire Fusiliers

Leicestershire Regiment	Leicesters
Lincolnshire Regiment	Lincolns
London Regiment	Londoners
Loyal North Lancashire Regiment	Loyals
Leinster Regiment	Leinsters
Manchester Regiment	Manchesters
Middlesex Regiment	Middlesex
Monmouthshire Regiment	Monmouths
Norfolk Regiment	Norfolks
Northamptonshire Regiment	Northants
North Staffordshire Regiment	North Staffords
Northumberland Fusiliers	Northumberland Fusiliers
Oxford and Buckinghamshire Light Infantry	Ox and Bucks
Rifle Brigade	Rifle Brigade
Royal Berkshire Regiment	Berkshires
Royal Dublin Fusiliers	Dublin Fusiliers
Royal Fusiliers	Royal Fusiliers
Royal Inniskilling Fusiliers	Inniskilling Fusiliers
Royal Irish Fusiliers	Irish Fusiliers
Royal Irish Regiment	Irish Regiment
Royal Irish Rifles	Irish Rifles
Royal Munster Fusiliers	Munsters
Royal Scots Regiment	Royal Scots
Royal Scots Fusiliers	Scots Fusiliers
Royal Sussex Regiment	Sussex
Royal Warwickshire Regiment	Warwicks
Royal Welsh Fusiliers	Welsh Fusiliers
Queen's (Royal West Surrey) Regiment	Queen's
Queen's Own (Royal West Kent) Regiment	Queen's Own
Scots Guards	Scots Guards
Seaforth Highlanders	Seaforths
Sherwood Foresters (Notts and Derbyshire)	Sherwoods
Somerset Light Infantry	Somersets
South Lancashire Regiment	South Lancashires
South Staffordshire Regiment	South Staffords
South Wales Borderers	SWBs or Borderers
Suffolk Regiment	Suffolks
Welsh Regiment	Welsh
Welsh Guards	Welsh Guards
West Yorkshire Regiment	West Yorkshires
Wiltshire Regiment	Wiltshires
Worcestershire Regiment	Worcesters
York and Lancaster Regiment	York and Lancasters

Introduction

The Arras campaign is a poor relation to others in the Great War because it is sandwiched between two campaigns which are given wider coverage. They are also much longer campaigns. Arras follows the British Expeditionary Force's first major campaign, the Somme campaign, the campaign which started with a disastrous first day, which introduced the tank to ground warfare, and which ended in winter mud. The fighting switched to Field Marshal Douglas Haig's preferred battlefield only a month after Arras finished: Flanders. That campaign is connected with the name Ypres and it ends with another slog across the muddy wastes around Passchendaele.

A quick look at what books are available on Arras confirms the lack of material on the campaign. It is over twenty-five years since Jon Nicholls' book on Arras, *Cheerful Sacrifice*, was published. There has been little since.

This one concentrates on the British Army's experience during the first five months of 1917 rather than politics, the German view or personal experiences of the men who fought and died. It starts with the plans for the spring, plans which are disrupted by the German decision to withdraw. They had spent months preparing a defensive line on the ground of their choosing and they invited the Allies to attack it.

The campaign story starts with the slow withdrawal from the Somme wasteland, followed by the rapid move back to the Hindenburg Line. Along the way there were many rearguard actions as the Germans conducted a scorched earth policy designed to delay the Allies. The stages of the Arras campaign, starting on 9 April and ending on 3 May, all get equal attention no matter how large or small. The same applies to the prolonged action at Bullecourt, south-east of Arras.

The information came from many sources but the backbone of the narrative comes from the single *Military Operations, France and Belgium* volume on the campaign. It is one of the twenty-eight Official Histories on the Great War and was compiled by Captain Cyril Falls under the direction of Brigadier General Sir James Edmonds. The first volume was printed in September 1939, just as Great Britain went to war for the second time in the twentieth century.

The 'Battleground' series of books, which are part narrative and part travel guide, has several volumes dedicated to the early 1917 campaign. The quality of information varies from limited to overwhelming but they all contribute something, sometimes confirming and sometimes contradicting the Official History. I say 'contradicting' because the official version often smoothed over the reasons why attacks failed by omitting the mistakes, problems or bad luck which prevented success.

A lot of information comes from the numerous divisional histories and regimental histories which were published on behalf of units before the Official History came out. The quality of information varies enormously, with some giving the bare details of a unit's accomplishments while others are virtually a copy of the daily unit war diary. But most provided more interesting detail than the Official History. They usually gave explanations of what went right and what went wrong, although, naturally, units tend to blame the actions of others, rather than their own.

Virtually all the regimental and divisional histories can be accessed for an annual or individual fee at militaryarchive.co.uk. You can also access medal rolls, army orders, army lists and get assistance with locations, biographies, awards and photographs of individuals. Joining the archive gave me prolonged access to all this for the same cost of a day visiting the London archives. If you are interested in printed histories and medal rolls, this is the website for you.

So why is there little information from the war diaries in the National Archives held at Kew? In my experience, they often say little about a battalion's experience on the day of battle because the war diarist is fully occupied, both physically and emotionally. And sometimes material you would expect to find has been removed or lost.

I also had to judge on the level of detail at which to pitch the information. Too shallow and there is nothing new to learn; too deep and the detail becomes overwhelming. So this is not an exhaustive account of the withdrawal to the Hindenburg Line and the Arras campaign, but it is a comprehensive one of the British Expeditionary Force's experience during the spring of 1917.

I have also bucked the Army trend of describing deployments and events from right to left. I have chosen to write the narrative to suit the situation.

Nearly sixty maps have been included to increase the reader's understanding of the battle. 'A picture is worth a thousand words' and I believe the same goes for maps. Time after time in military books we read pages while relying on a few small-scale maps, and they do little to help. My inspiration was Noah Trudeau's *A Testing of Courage*, a book about Gettysburg in the American Civil War. Having read books and watched documentaries on this three-day battle, I was still confused. Trudeau's book uses large-scale maps every few pages, illustrating the development of the action day by day and sometimes hour by hour. It helped me understand the unfolding battle when I visited Gettysburg. I wanted to do the same for the spring of 1917.

The Official History maps are sometimes cited as good examples, but the level of detail and clarity diminishes rapidly over the course of the campaign. Some maps are small-scale, some cover many days fighting, some are devoid of all but the main terrain features. The overriding theme with the Official History maps seemed to be inconsistency.

In this book there is often a map for each corps on each occasion there was an attack with a gain or loss of ground. A few which did not work geographically use one map to cover two or more corps, while two maps are used to cover a corps action. Trench map extracts have been used as the topographical background because they are well known to anyone with an interest in the First World War. Their grid system is 1,000 yards for each large square and 100 yards for each minor graduation. One advantage of a trench map is that the terrain is often the same today as it was a century ago. Contours, roads, watercourses and woods have not altered while villages have changed little; only the trenches have gone. It means the maps can be used to help locate places on the battlefield.

The symbols have been kept as simple as possible. Front lines before the battle commences are marked in solid lines while ground captured is marked by a line of dots. Corps boundaries are marked by a line of dashes and dots. Arrows are often used to indicate the direction of the advance. The location of each division and brigade is marked by their number but battalions are not shown because they would clutter the maps and obscure topographical information. Battalions usually leapfrogged each other every few hundred yards and it would be impossible to chart their progress on maps of this scale. It is quite easy to estimate a battalion's position by checking the text and the maps together.

This is not a comprehensive study of the campaign. It would be twice the length if it was. So what has been left out? There is no talk of politics and little opinion on the relationship between Lloyd George's War Cabinet, General Sir William Robertson, the Chief of the Imperial General Staff and Haig's GHQ. But there are explanations about the meetings between the British and the French politicians; their areas of agreement, their arguments and their compromises.

The same goes for the relationship between Field Marshal Haig, Marshal of France Joffre and General Nivelle as they argued over strategy, dates and commitments. There is also little information on the German units involved in the battles but there is some information on their defensive arrangements, their tactics and their impact on the British attacks.

You will not find narratives from personal diaries, letters or printed histories either. They usually follow a depressing theme of mud, blood and a desire to be somewhere else. The few quotes given were chosen for their eloquence in writing, their pride in the men's determination and their dark humour.

There are few mentions of casualties unless they were disproportionately high or low because records are incomplete and it would be inappropriate to mention some units and not others. Casualties were always high and both sides suffered.

So what will you find? There is the reasoning behind each attack and its objectives. There is discussion on the bombardments, the tactics, the weather and the terrain. There are the reasons behind the successes and failures of each attack. The men who made a difference are often mentioned; the men who lead the assault waves or the bombing teams, those who cut the wire and led the survivors into the German trenches, those who stopped the counter-attacks and those awarded the Victoria Cross.

The British Army faced many tactical problems, some natural, some man-made, and they tried to solve them. We see how they tried different methods and how they learned from their mistakes. The staff, the artillery, the infantry, the engineers and Royal Flying Corps all had a part to play in learning their own lessons and then coordinating new ideas. The problem was it cost thousands of casualties to discover the errors and solve the problems. But the cadre of survivors kept trying and they kept teaching the replacements.

Two important things become apparent. The first is that in 1917 it was more difficult and costly to capture a position rather than to sit tight and defend one. The second is that all commanders, from company up to divisional and corps level, kept trying to get it right. They did not blindly follow orders. They suggested ideas and questioned orders. Sometimes their superior officers amended their instructions and sometimes they did not. So much had to be arranged and done, so much could go wrong, and there were so many opportunities for bad luck to intervene. The coordination of the infantry advance and the artillery bombardment had to be carried out with precision if the attack was to stand any chance of success. Commanders often recognised mistakes, made improvements and tried new techniques and tactics to improve their chances of success; they did not always work. They sometimes drew the wrong conclusions and sometimes they just got it wrong.

I would like to thank David and Julie Thomson, of Number 56 Bed and Breakfast in La Boisselle, for being my host during my visit to the battlefield. Although their establishment is on the Somme, it is only 25 miles from the centre of Arras. I would also like to thank Professor John Bourne for providing information on the BEF's generals.

This is the fourth book in a series on the British Expeditionary Forces campaigns on the Western Front in the Great War. Researching the events of the spring of 1917 has fulfilled a long standing ambition of mine: to increase my understanding of this seminal conflict. Particularly as my great-uncle was mortally wounded on 13 April, near Guémappe. He was serving with the 8th East Yorkshires, as part of 3rd Division, and is believed to be buried in Tilloy British Cemetery, Tilloy-lèz-Mofflaines. I have enjoyed writing about the withdrawal to the Hindenburg Line, the Arras campaign and the battle for Bullecourt and I hope you enjoy reading about them.

Andrew Rawson 2016

Chapter 1

War or Peace?
October to December 1916

Initial Plans for 1917

Discussions about the spring 1917 offensive had begun while the Somme offensive was coming to an end. Colonel Renouard of the French Operations Bureau explained the French plans to Brigadier General Davidson, head of the Operations Branch at the British Expeditionary Force's (BEF) General Headquarters (GHQ), in October 1916. General Joseph Joffre, commander-in-chief of the French armies on the Western Front, intended to broaden the offensive either side of the devastated Somme area and wanted the British to attack on a 16-mile front between Vimy and Bapaume while the French advanced on a 20-mile front between the rivers Somme and Oise.

On 1 November 1916, Joffre, and his British counterpart, General Sir Douglas Haig, agreed to coordinate their offensive efforts on the Western Front the following spring.

The Somme offensive was at an end when Haig attended a meeting at the French Grand Quartier Général (General Headquarters) in Chantilly. He was accompanied by General Sir William Robertson, Chief of the Imperial General Staff, and the Director of Military Operations, Major General Frederick Maurice. Joffre was concerned that Germany and her allies were proving to be unexpectedly resilient.

Following a meeting at the War Office, a letter asking for a British attack in Flanders to be included in the plans for 1917 was sent to the French on 1 December. They asked because the Admiralty wanted to stop German ships and submarines operating out of Ostend and Zeebrugge attacking cross-channel shipping. Joffre's reply suggested a main attack, supported by two surprise attacks to pin down reserves on the Aisne and in Upper Alsace. He also suggested a landing on the Belgian coast to engage German reserves.

The Allies met again on 6 December and they agreed that there had to be coordinated offensives on all fronts in 1917. At least they agreed in theory. In practice, the Russians had little offensive power while the French were considering increasing their efforts in Macedonia. Robertson was against sending more British troops to the Mediterranean because it was difficult to supply them.

The British Expeditionary Force on the Western Front was going to increase from 56 to 63 infantry divisions during the early part of 1916; it also had 5 cavalry divisions. The number of heavy British artillery pieces was going to increase from 1,150 to 1,500 during the same period. British industry was also on a war footing, capable of producing the huge numbers of weapons and ammunition required to support the BEF.

The French armies were tired and Joffre was looking to Great Britain to do more. Haig believed his armies could be ready to attack at Arras by early February but wanted to wait until the weather had improved and suggested early May. They compromised by deciding to launch a combined British and French offensive on the Western Front at the end of February.

The Allied Forces in Early 1917

Many lessons had been learnt during the Somme campaign. The artillery could now fire barrages which 'crept' forwards at set speeds and the infantry were experienced at staying close to them. It was well known that 'hugging the wall of exploding shells' was the safest way to cross no man's land. There had been innovations with the types of barrages, with fake barrages, practice barrages and different combinations of shrapnel and high explosive. A new fuse which exploded on contact rather than according to a timer had just been introduced. It increased the effectiveness of barrages, particularly against barbed wire.

Steps had also been taken to make the field artillery more flexible during the Somme campaign, so batteries could stay in line longer. A quarter of batteries had been formed into army field artillery brigades, leaving each division with two mixed brigades, armed with 18-pounder and 4.5-inch howitzer batteries. These new brigades could be deployed where the action was.

Infantry tactics had also been tried and tested, with companies usually advancing in two waves around 75 yards apart, each on a frontage of 200 yards. Each company deployed its platoons in two lines, around 20 yards apart, and the men were trained in specific tasks. The riflemen and bombers manoeuvred against enemy positions while the Lewis gunners and rifle bombers gave covering fire. It was also standard procedure to deploy 'moppers up' to locate and search dugouts while other groups carried equipment and ammunition forward to help hold captured positions.

Tanks had first been used on the Somme on 15 September 1916 and there had been many teething problems. There were still seventy Mark Is in operation and another fifty improved Mark IIs were due to be delivered in January. Experimental Mark IIIs would never be deployed while the promised Mark IVs, with their thicker armour and improved engine, would arrive after the spring offensive.

The impact of the weather on offensive operations had been studied for some time and meteorological stations across France forwarded regular reports to GHQ. Experiments had been tried out during 1916 to test the effects of the weather on artillery accuracy. Studies showed that air temperature, wind speed and barometric pressure all affected the range of shells. GHQ issued range corrections related to weather on a daily basis, starting in January 1917.

The Royal Flying Corps (RFC) had also increased its number of squadrons in France to thirty-six. There would have been more, but twelve squadrons had been retained in England to stop Zeppelin airships dropping their bombs. A lot of work had been done on improving the cooperation between the artillery and the RFC during the Somme campaign. The number of artillery spotting planes equipped with wirelesses had been doubled and each corps established setup teams to work closely with its dedicated squadron. They were kept busy checking aerial photographs for targets and damage so they could mark up maps to distribute to the artillery batteries.

Political and Moral Factors
Herbert Asquith resigned as Great Britain's Prime Minister on 5 December 1916 and David Lloyd George was welcomed as his replacement. He formed a War Cabinet which advocated offensives in other theatres, in opposition to the War Office's plans for a spring attack on the Western Front. But Lloyd George could find little support for his plans to send troops to Macedonia, Egypt, Italy or Russia.

The French Prime Minister, Aristide Briand, had planned to demote Joffre until he threatened to resign. Briand then had to reform his government on 13 December with General Hubert Lyautey as his Minister of War. He also formed a War Committee presided over by President Raymond Poincaré. Joffre still remained commander-in-chief of the French Armies but his role was reduced to that of the government's technical adviser and a coordinator with the Allies.

Joffre's position was further devalued when General Robert Nivelle took command of the Armies of the North and North-East. Then on 21 December, Joffre's role was undermined even more when Nivelle was allowed to liaise with the government and its allies. He resigned five days later and was created a Marshal of France. Haig was promoted to field marshal around the same time.

But who was Nivelle? He was an artillery officer described as 'an articulate and immensely self-confident gunner'. He had risen from the rank of colonel to command a corps' artillery in a short time. He had taken control of Second Army during the battle of Verdun and became famous for issuing the order, 'they shall not pass' – *'Ils ne passeront pas!'* – in June 1916. Nivelle then conducted several surprise counter-attacks around the city. This led to him being promoted ahead of the three Army Group commanders and everyone hoped he would go on to replicate his success on a much larger scale.

The Germans Propose Peace

As the Somme campaign came to an end, the Chief of the General Staff, General Paul von Hindenburg, and his Quartermaster General, General Erich Ludendorff, conceded it was unlikely the Axis Powers could win a victory on land. Germany's armies were not large enough to conduct offensive warfare, so all they could do was defend while looking for another way to win the war.

The Allied naval blockade was stopping foodstuffs and essential supplies reaching Germany. Rationing had been in place since early 1915 while the Hindenburg Programme had put every man between 17 and 60 years of age on essential war work. It was estimated that unrestricted submarine warfare against merchant ships could starve Great Britain into submission in a matter of months. But the risk was it could bring the United States of America and its massive resources into the war if its ships were sunk. The gamble was, could Great Britain be forced to the peace table before America could put an army into the field?

The defeat of a Romanian attack in the autumn of 1916 left the Central Powers in a confident position. On 5 December 1916 they asked to discuss peace with the United States and the Holy See in Rome. They did not expect a positive reply:

Should our enemies refuse to enter peace negotiations, and we have to assume that this will be the case, the odium of continuing the war will fall on them. War weariness will then grow and generate new support for the elements that are pushing for peace. In Germany and among its Allies, too, the desire for peace has become keen. The rejection of our peace offer, the knowledge that the continuation of the struggle is inevitable thanks alone to our enemies, would be an effective means of spurring our people to utmost exertion and sacrifice for a victorious end to the war.

An ambiguous proposal was submitted a week later but it was, as expected, turned down. The refusal would be used to justify launching the submarine campaign.

On 18 December, President of the United States of America Woodrow Wilson proposed opening talks which would 'determine how near the haven of peace, for which all mankind was longing, might lie'. The Central Powers asked for a meeting to exchange views; the Allied governments refused.

Hindenburg, Ludendorff and Admiral Henning von Holtzendorff pressured Kaiser Wilhelm II to begin the unrestricted submarine campaign and he finally issued the order on 9 January. Germany's *Unterseeboots*, or U-Boats, would begin attacking merchant ships on 1 February. The United States had already warned that it would cut relations with Germany if its ships were attacked and the German Ambassador in New York was handed his passport as a symbolic gesture. The U-Boat campaign was an immediate success. Nearly 500,000 tons of shipping were sunk in February and March; over 850,000 tons would be lost in April. It seemed as if the German plan could work.

There was another development when a telegram sent by the German Foreign Office to their ambassador in Mexico was intercepted and deciphered by British intelligence in January. It suggested an alliance between Germany and Mexico if America went to war against Germany. A month later the telegram was given to the United States ambassador and it enraged public opinion across the United States. The telegram would be named after the German Foreign Secretary, Arthur Zimmermann. On 2 April, President Wilson told the joint houses of Congress that he believed 'it would suffice to assert our neutral rights with arms, our right to use the seas against unlawful interference'. It was not, and the United States formally declared war four days later.

Great Britain and France had also been handed a peace proposal by the Austrian ambassador. Emperor Franz Joseph had died on 21 November 1916 and his son Charles inherited the title and became supreme commander-in-chief of the armed forces. He thought the Austro-Hungarian army was unfit for war and he wanted to sue for peace; a separate peace from Germany if necessary. Charles dismissed his Chief of the General Staff, Field Marshal Conrad von Hötzendorf, and he instructed his brother-in-law, Prince Sixte de Bourbon Parma, an officer in the Belgian Army, to work on his behalf. Charles gave Prince Sixte a letter for President Raymond Poincaré on 24 March 1917. In it he offered to try to get the provinces of Alsace and Lorraine returned to France. He also suggested restoring all possessions to Belgium and giving Serbia access to the Adriatic. But the negotiations failed and the letter would drive a wedge between Germany and Austria when it became public knowledge in April 1918.

Chapter 2

Plans for the Spring
January to March 1917

General Nivelle's Plan

Nivelle had visited Haig on 20 December knowing that he was about to replace Joffre as the French commander-in-chief. He explained how he intended to break the German front along the Aisne with three French armies. Nivelle also asked for Haig's cooperation by taking over twenty miles of French trenches astride the River Somme. He also wanted the British to engage German reserves between Arras and Bapaume while a French army pinned them down between the Somme and Oise rivers. The British could launch their own offensive at Arras as soon as the Aisne front had been broken. The two attacks would destabilise the salient based around Compiègne, tearing a hole over 100 miles wide in the German line.

Nivelle was concentrating on the long term prospects but Haig was focusing on the short term situation. He believed the Somme offensive had exhausted the Germans and he wanted to keep up the pressure on the British front. But his army would be weakened if it took over the French trenches. Haig eventually agreed to take over 10 miles of trenches but he wanted the French to take them back if their offensive failed so he could attack in Flanders. Nivelle was irritated that Haig was even considering his offensive could fail.

Haig had to back down when Nivelle visited him four days later. After arguing his corner, he agreed to relieve more of the French line, south of Somme, and he agreed to do it by the end of March. On 2 January 1917 Nivelle explained he wanted a three-stage battle but Haig protested at such a long-drawn-out campaign. He had suggested two weeks of preliminary attacks, followed by the main offensive, giving the British time to clear the Belgian coast in the summer. Haig wanted the French to take back their trenches so he could be ready to attack on 1 May but Nivelle refused.

At the same time, the politicians were having their own say at the Inter-Allied Conference in Rome. Prime Minister Lloyd George was refusing to send any more divisions to Salonika but he was proposing to lend over 250 heavy guns to Italy and wanted France to do the same. Prime Minister Briand and his Minister of War General Hubert Lyautey were unenthusiastic; so was the chief of staff of the Italian Army, General Luigi Cadorna.

Another conference in London opened on 15 January and this time Haig and Nivelle were invited. Finally a compromise was agreed over the relief of the Somme sector. They also agreed that the French would begin their offensive around 1 April, as Nivelle had wanted.

The Plan of Operations

Nivelle had appointed General Ferdinand Pont as his chief of staff. General Franchet d'Espèrey replaced General Ferdinand Foch as commander of the Group of Armies of the North and General Édouard de Castelnau briefly replaced d'Espèrey as commander of the Group of Armies of the

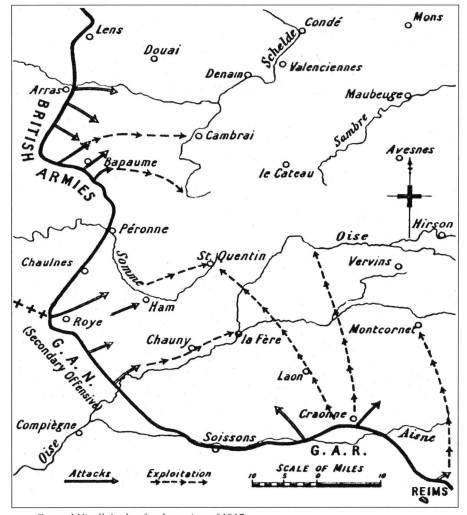

General Nivelle's plan for the spring of 1917.

East. Nivelle chose to take the Seventh and Eighth French Armies under his direct command.

Nivelle had to move his GHQ to Beauvais, north-east of Paris, three weeks later because Premier Briand wanted to move on from Joffre's regime. General Ferdinand Foch was given command of a new army group bearing his name while General Joseph Micheler was appointed Nivelle's assistant and was given command of the Group of Armies of the Reserve. General Phillipe Pétain remained in command of the Group of Armies of the Centre but he was against Nivelle's ambitious plans for the spring.

Nivelle wanted the British to attack between Arras and Bapaume while the French struck between the Oise and the Avre rivers with twenty divisions. The main offensive would follow between Vailly-sur-Aisne and Berry-au-Bac, seizing the infamous Chemin des Dames ridge. It would open with 15 divisions and increase to 30 infantry and 7 cavalry divisions.

But Nivelle soon changed his mind. The 28 divisions of Micheler's Group of Armies of Reserve would advance north, between the Aisne–Oise canal and Rheims, looking to destroy the German armies in the open. Another 12 infantry and 5 cavalry divisions would then widen the gap as the British continued their advance towards Cambrai.

The Calais Conference
Supplying the Somme campaign had stretched the railways in north-east France beyond their limits. The civilian railway expert Sir Eric Geddes had been appointed Director General of Railways and Inspector General of Transportation in September 1916 so he could sort out the transport situation. The French now wanted the British to manage the railways they were using and GHQ knew they would struggle to supply its armies during an offensive.

Geddes had a series of problems to deal with over the winter. A grounded steamer closed Boulogne harbour for several weeks in December. The canals froze in January stopping the barges moving, while the February thaw meant that wheeled traffic cut up the muddy roads. The incidents proved that many railway lines needed to be doubled up if GHQ was going to supply an offensive in the Arras area.

On 24 January Haig told Nivelle the BEF needed 35,000 tons of supplies a day during an offensive. It would require around 200 trains to carry them. Ways of improving railway traffic were discussed on 29 January and Nivelle was confident the figure could easily be raised to 28,500 tons a day. Haig disagreed. He told Robertson about the 'highly unsatisfactory' French plans and warned of 'very heavy casualties with inadequate results' on 14 February. Geddes also thought the French were being over-optimistic about the railway situation. The Chief of the French Mission at GHQ, Brigadier General Pierre des Vallières, upset everyone when he suggested the British attack would be too narrow and too shallow to achieve the desired outcome.

Nivelle visited Haig's headquarters in Montreuil on 16 February. They agreed the attack would not begin until the British railway requirements had been met, and agreed to aim for 10 April. The generals then met the politicians and transport experts in Calais on 26 February. The French suggested that the British could be more efficient in how they used their trains but they also agreed that the BEF had to rely on trains for everything. The outcome of the meeting was that the French would send more trains to the British zone.

Nivelle wanted the BEF to attack east and south-east of Arras. Haig wanted to capture Vimy Ridge, north-east of the town, to cover his flank. But he did not want to attack the new fortified line under construction south-east of Arras, the line soon to be known as the Hindenburg Line.

Lloyd George suggested Nivelle should exercise military authority over Haig but Robertson said he would resign before agreeing to such an arrangement. So they agreed the French would direct the spring offensive while the British would give their total cooperation.

The agreement was signed in Calais on 27 February but its terms were soon being tested. The following day Nivelle asked Haig how he would deal with the instructions issued to his armies. He also asked for Lieutenant General Sir Henry Wilson to lead the British mission at his headquarters. Haig and Robertson mistrusted Wilson as an intriguer but he was a favourite of Lloyd George and was appointed on 17 March.

Haig was concerned about the consequences of the German withdrawal towards the Hindenburg Line. He was also concerned his plan to attack in Flanders might be sidelined now he had to answer to the French. Nivelle was also troubled about the British commitment to his plans. But Haig and Nivelle sailed to England on 13 March and signed the agreement in London. Although a settlement had been made, the War Office was far from happy with it.

The War Cabinet interviewed Field Marshal Haig for the last time before the spring offensives began on 14 March. He explained his plans for a spring attack in Arras followed by a summer offensive in Flanders. But three days later the Allied plans were thrown into disarray because the Germans withdrew as fast as they could to the Hindenburg Line. The fortified line had been known about for some time and prisoners and documents had suggested the withdrawal was imminent.

The German retreat released British divisions so Haig could extend his offensive front. First Army could now capture Vimy Ridge while Third

Army advanced east of Arras. Fifth Army now had the devastated 1916 Somme battlefield behind its front, so the plan was for it to attack the Hindenburg Line at Bullecourt at a later date.

The Allies were in agreement, on paper at least, but there was trouble ahead. Nivelle had to consider replacing a French offensive north of the Oise with an attack on the Hindenburg Line. Meanwhile, the unpopular General Hubert Lyautey had been shouted down in the French Chamber on 15 March 1917 and no one else wanted the post of Minister of War. Prime Minister Aristide Briand resigned five days later, following disagreements over the Nivelle offensive. His replacement, Prime Minister Alexandre Ribot, appointed Paul Painlevé as his Minister of War, an opponent of Nivelle's optimistic forecast for the spring offensive.

Chapter 3

A Horrible and Loathsome Place
Withdrawal from the Somme

The BEF's Winter Instructions

Haig issued his general orders for the winter after hearing the outcome of the Chantilly military conference. He wanted the trenches to be improved so they could be held by as few men as possible, allowing him to withdraw divisions for training. He also wanted regular bombardments and raids all along the front to keep the Germans under pressure. Haig issued specific instructions after hearing Nivelle's plans for the spring. Fifth and Fourth Armies would continue minor operations to make the Germans think the Somme was still the chosen battlefield. But Fourth Army also had to take over twenty miles of French trenches. Meanwhile, First and Third Armies would prepare to attack north and east of Arras by 15 March at the earliest and 1 April at the latest.

Operations on the River Ancre, 11 January to 14 February

Fifth Army spent the winter holding a ten-mile sector on the Somme. Lieutenant General Sir Walter Congreve's XIII Corps held the north bank of the River Ancre while Lieutenant General Sir Charles Woollcombe's IV Corps held the south bank. General Hubert Gough wanted to capture the ridge north-east of Beaumont Hamel but the winter weather interfered with offensive operations and the men found it a struggle to survive in the muddy, water-filled trenches.

The men of 7th Division were just some of those who thought it was 'a horrible and loathsome place in which to live and fight'. The Germans captured Hope Post, north-east of Beaumont Hamel, on New Year's Day and the 9th Devons recaptured it four nights later. Major General George Barrow wanted to capture Muck Trench early on 10 January and the 2nd Border Regiment had to carry duckboards so they could cross muddy patches in no man's land. They reached Muck Trench and took over 140 prisoners who were relieved at being allowed to leave a trench which was deep in mud and water.

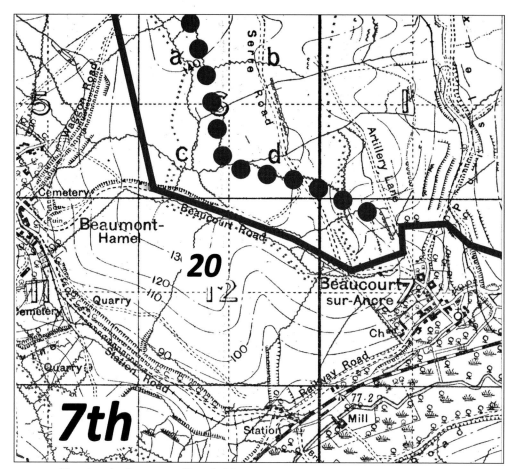

Clearing the Beaumont Hamel ridge.

A Frozen Battlefield

Life was a little easier when the cold weather froze the mud and water but it made it difficult to dig trenches without using explosives and it was impossible to erect wire in no man's land. The lull in the fighting allowed changes to be made at corps level. North of the Ancre, V Corps took over XIII Corps while II Corps relieved IV Corps on the opposite bank.

V Corps, Beaucourt, 10 and 11 February

Lieutenant General Sir Edward Fanshawe wanted 11th Division to extend its hold on the north bank of the Ancre. Two 5th Dorset and 11th Manchester companies advanced early on 10 February through thick fog north of Beaucourt. Unfortunately the Dorsets overlooked a large dugout and the Germans came out and attacked them in the rear, forcing them to retreat.

It was 7th Division's turn next and the infantry advanced through thick fog at 6.37 am on 11 February after a ten-minute barrage. Two companies each of the 22nd Manchesters, 1st South Staffords and 21st Manchesters plodded behind what was possibly one of the slowest-moving barrages of the war, advancing only ten yards every minute. Munich Trench had been obliterated, so 91 Brigade had to link shell holes together to form a new line. Brigadier General Cumming's men came under heavy shellfire when the fog cleared mid-morning but they held on while the 6th Green Howards and the 6th York and Lancasters occupied an abandoned trench north of Beaucourt.

II Corps, Grandcourt, 3 to 13 February
63rd Division, North of the Ancre
Major General Cameron Shute organised a surprise attack along the north bank of the Ancre at 11 pm on 3 February. The Nelson Battalion covered the left flank as the Hawke and Hood Battalions crawled across the snow-covered ground under a bright moonlight.

Lieutenant Commander Shelton led the Hawke's left into Puisieux Trench but Sub-Lieutenants Blackmore and Wilkes veered right and became mixed up with the Hood Battalion alongside the Ancre. Lieutenant Commander Monro had been wounded, so an unlikely replacement stepped forward to reorganise them. The previous commander, Lieutenant Commander Asquith, had been sent on staff duties but he had tricked his way into joining his battalion by pretending to be an artillery observer. He made sure River Trench was secured but a strongpoint was still holding out in the centre of 189 Brigade.

Counter-attacks were stopped and Brigadier General Philips sent reinforcements forward during the evening. But Asquith was wounded leading the Drake Battalion so Sub-Lieutenant Lunn became lost and his men were cut off. Sub-Lieutenant Bowerman would eventually silence the strongpoint and secure the rest of Puisieux Trench the following morning. The Hood Battalion held on along the river bank and discovered that the Germans had abandoned Grandcourt during the night.

At 11 pm on 7 February Lieutenant Colonel Boyle and Captain Bryant were killed as the 1st HAC captured Baillescourt Farm and cleared the sunken road north of the farm, capturing over eighty prisoners.

32nd Division, Ten Tree Alley, 10 to 13 February
Major General Reginald Barnes was instructed to clear Ten Tree Alley, south of Serre. The 11th Border Regiment and 2nd KOYLIs overran the trench, taking over 200 prisoners, while the 16th Northumberland Fusiliers covered their flank. A counter-attack early the following morning was halted but the 17th and 16th HLI were driven out of the west half of the trench on 13 February. The Borders and the KOYLIs had to return to the line to recapture their objective.

<u>18th Division, Grandcourt</u>
The 10th Essex occupied Folly Trench, south-east of Grandcourt, during the night of 10/11 February.

II Corps, Miraumont, 17 and 18 February

Fourth Army began taking over the French front astride the River Somme during the second half of February. Fifth Army helped by taking control of I Anzac Corps, north of Gueudecourt. Haig wanted Gough to advance astride the Ancre and he asked for his plans. He wanted to capture Hill 130, overlooking Miraumont from the south side of the river. The Butte de Warlencourt and Gueudecourt, on his right flank, would be captured on 1 March, followed by Serre a week later on his left flank. He hoped Miraumont and Loupart Wood, in his centre, would fall a few days later.

Lieutenant General Sir Claud Jacob had to capture Hill 130, overlooking the Ancre, to force the Germans to evacuate Miraumont. The new 106 fuse would be used to demolish the wire because it made shells explode as soon as they touched the ice-covered mud.

The infantry were expecting to advance in waves over the frozen ground at 5.45 am and the creeping barrage speed had been planned for the same circumstances. However a sudden thaw during the night created slush and sloppy mud while fog cloaked the battlefield. To make matters worse, two deserters had warned the Germans of the advance and their artillery and machine gun fire hit the deployment area before zero hour.

The artillery observers failed to notice the creeping barrage was firing short and it was difficult to distinguish between the exploding British and German shells in the fog. Many men became disorientated and many ankles and knees were twisted in the mud. Up ahead Very Lights and rockets lit up the mist and some said it looked like 'Brock's Benefit', an annual fireworks display put on by the Brock Firework Company at Crystal Palace.

<u>63rd Division, North of the Ancre, 17 February</u>
The Germans were not prepared for the attack on the west bank of the Ancre and the 1st Royal Marines and Howe Battalion cleared most of their objective, while the Anson Battalion advanced along the river bank. The Marines suffered over 400 casualties, many of them in a four-hour battle for one strongpoint north of Grandcourt, but they captured nearly 600 prisoners. The Germans tried to retake the strongpoint from the 1st Marines the following day but Major Ozanne brought down accurate artillery fire on the position. He sat in his dugout relaying instructions to Brigadier General Prentice with a phone to each ear throughout the engagement.

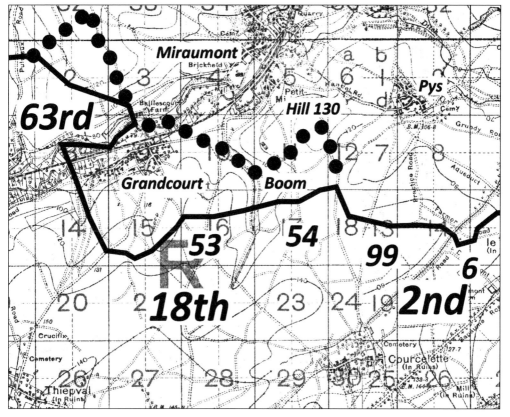

The taking of Grandcourt and Boom Ravine.

18th Division, Hill 130, 17 February

On 53 Brigade's front, the 6th Berkshires pushed through gaps in the wire to clear Coffee Trench but the 8th Suffolks moved down the wrong side of the Grandcourt road until Captain Ashdown realised the mistake and led them into Grandcourt Trench. In 54 Brigade's sector, the 11th Royal Fusiliers had been unable to see the exploding shells of the creeping barrage in the mist because the guns were firing at such a low trajectory over Hill 130, so they were pinned down in front of the wire. The advance restarted after the Suffolks silenced three German machine guns in Boom Ravine and they reached the Grandcourt–Petit Miraumont road. The Germans manned Grandcourt Trench as the 6th Northants cut a way through the entanglement; the few who reached the trench could not fight because their weapons were clogged with mud, so they had to fall back to the West Miraumont road. They then found themselves under fire from South Miraumont Trench, where the 11th Royal Fusiliers should have been covering their left flank.

2nd Division, South of Pys, 17 February

In 99 Brigade's sector, the 11th Royal Fusiliers and 1st KRRC were enfiladed by machine gun fire from their right, where the 2nd South Staffords should have been holding Gallwitz Trench. Most of the KRRC's officers were hit while the support waves were pushed to the right because 18th Division had lost direction. They ended up in the wrong place and then a counter-attack drove them back. The 22nd Royal Fusiliers followed up, clearing Boom Ravine, but its left flank lost direction until Captain Powell realised the error. He led them back towards the West Miraumont Road and then withdrew them. But Captain Simmons did not realise the mistake and led his men 'into the blue' where most were cut off and never seen again. Corporal Wilmott used his Lewis gun to cover the survivors as they withdrew.

Major Walsh was mortally wounded and Captain Evans was hit leading the rest of the 22nd Royal Fusiliers. Lance Sergeant Palmer cut through the wire and his men captured a trench where the Germans 'fought like tigers'. They stopped seven counter-attacks before they were driven out in a battle 'fought splendidly and cleanly'. Palmer collected grenades and helped them retake the trench when he returned; he was awarded the Victoria Cross while the rest of his party received other gallantry awards.

The 2nd South Staffords lost all but one officer south of Pys because the German machine guns were trained on the few gaps in the wire. Only the right company reached Desire Support Trench and they had been driven out before a wounded officer reached Brigadier General Walsh's headquarters with the news.

Lieutenant General Claud Jacob was disappointed by the results of the attack. Although Boom Ravine had been taken, Hill 130 was still in German hands and he did not have the coveted observation post over the Ancre. The attack had cost II Corps over 2,700 casualties for an advance of no more than 1,000 yards.

Fourth Army, Astride the Somme

General Henry Rawlinson had extended his front as far south as the Amiens–Roye road by the end of February, leaving Fourth Army holding an extra twenty miles of trenches. He had also had to attack tactical points to make the Germans think the Somme campaign would be renewed as soon as the weather and ground conditions became acceptable.

XIV Corps, Le Transloy, 27 January to 8 February

The first attack was made towards Le Transloy by 29th Division on 27 January. Major General Sir Beauvoir de Lisle had organised a double barrage by his field artillery to catch the Germans out. Half the batteries bombarded the German front line for four minutes before they were joined by the other half shelling the area in front of the trenches. A minute later they both moved forward. The plan was the Germans would leave their dugouts as soon as the first barrage advanced, only to be caught by the second line of exploding shells.

Brigadier General Bray's men moved quickly across the frozen ground and while part of the 1st Border Regiment and the 1st Inniskilling Fusiliers took the enemy by surprise, a machine gun post pinned down the Borders' left flank. A wounded Sergeant Edward Mott ran forward and grabbed the gunner, allowing his comrades to continue the advance. Bray's men had captured over 350 prisoners but they found it difficult to dig into the frozen ground as they consolidated the captured position.

I Anzac Corps, 1 February, Gueudecourt

Major General William Holmes was supposed to capture Stormy Trench, north of Gueudecourt, but a cold snap was interfering with 4th Australian Division's plans. Colonel McSharry reported that the freezing temperatures were affecting the mortar ammunition. Some shells were falling short while others were bouncing off the icy mud. Lieutenant General William Birdwood had to instruct the corps' heavy artillery to cut the wire, even though their shells would cut up no man's land.

The 15th Australian Battalion made a surprise attack from Grease and Shine Trenches on the evening of 1 February. Major Mundell's men took many prisoners on the left but Captain Dunworth's men were stopped by wire on the right. The artillery did not see the SOS signals through the mist until it was too late, when the Germans attacked Mundell's men before dawn. The battalion suffered nearly 150 casualties, including many men missing from Mundell's company.

It was 5th Australian Division's turn next on 4 February. Major General Talbot Hobbs was instructed to capture Finch and Orion Trenches, east of Gueudecourt. An artillery relief was due, so twice the number of field guns would be available to fire in support. The men would also carry as many bombs as possible. Each bomber would carry 20 bombs while 80 carriers would carry 24 each; even the riflemen would have bombs stuffed into their pockets. Each of 13th Australian Battalion's companies would be carrying around 2,000 bombs across no man's land. There would also be another 1,000 rifle grenades available.

The Germans abandoned the two trenches shortly before the attack, so Lieutenant Colonel Durrant's men assembled in Shine Trench and attacked Stormy Trench under a full moon on the night of 4 February instead. Lieutenant Bone's company caught the Germans in their dugouts but Captain Murray was delayed finding a gap in the wire, so his men faced a tough fight for the trench. Private Stephens recalled the danger and excitement of crossing no man's land:

> *The barrage had for one minute been swishing and banging low and close when someone said "Now!" There was a bustle and I found myself in no man's land jostling someone to get around a shell hole... We crouched in our advance, moving slowly, picking our way, with the shells shrieking over us and bursting only a few yards in front of us... The wire! We were up against it, but the shells weren't finished. They had made a good mess of it as I stepped from loop to loop. No the shells weren't finished yet, they were bursting behind me... and then there was a straight line of intermittent flashes in front. At that moment I slid and scrambled down a steep bank and found myself in the German trench.*

Private Stephens would be killed in the battle for Bullecourt a few weeks later.

Stormy Trench had been taken but the fight for the maze of trenches surrounding it raged throughout the night. Captain Harry Murray time and again rallied his men to stop the counter-attacks, living up to his nickname 'Mad Harry'; he would be awarded the Victoria Cross. Stormy Trench was held but it had cost 13th Battalion around 350 casualties.

XV Corps, Sailly-Saillisel, 8 February

Major General Philip Robertson was instructed to carry out a third attack against a trench overlooking Sailly-Saillisel. Again the cold weather caused problems for 17th Division and it took 52 Brigade three weeks to dig a jumping-off trench in the frozen mud. The men had to tie sandbags around their boots so they could walk across the frosty ground and they were showered with ice and frozen mud every time a shell exploded nearby.

Brigadier General Goodman had chosen the 7th Green Howards to attack and the plan was to do away with a preliminary barrage and rely on a double creeping barrage like the Australians had used. Colonel Fife's men advanced at 7.30 am but there were problems. The guns were worn out so they were firing short, while the cold weather was again causing some shells to detonate prematurely. Captains Wilkinson and Huffington both confirmed they had captured the objective but the British shells continued to explode in no man's land amongst the support companies and the ammunition carriers. Despite the issues, Fife was able to report his men were holding what became known as Green Howards Trench. It brought Fourth Army's attacks to an end for the time being.

Chapter 4

Operation Alberich
The Withdrawal Begins

Building the Hindenburg Line

The Battle of the Somme was in its final throes when British observation planes spotted new digging at several locations south-east of Arras. A more detailed reconnaissance was ordered and on 9 November observers reported a new ten-mile length of trench running south-east from Neuville-Vitasse past Fontaine-lès-Croisilles and Bullecourt to Quéant. It was a surprising discovery because it was over ten miles behind the German front line.

The GHQ Intelligence Summary for 8 November included a report from a Russian prisoner who had escaped across no man's land. His French interrogators had learnt there were 2,000 Russians working on fortifications in the Saint Quentin area, thirty-five miles south of Quéant. The prisoner spoke of wire entanglements, trenches and dugouts protected by concrete. Again the work was being carried out far behind the German front line.

The two work sites were part of the *Siegfried Stellung* or Siegfried Position, named after one of the characters in Richard Wagner's operatic performance *The Nibelung Ring*. The British would later refer to it as the Hindenburg Line, naming it after General Paul von Hindenburg, the German Chief of the General Staff since 29 August 1916.

GHQ Intelligence did not make a connection between the two pieces of information for several months. While it is easy to be critical with the benefit of hindsight, there were reasons why the correct conclusions were not drawn. The section of trench in the north was opposite a quiet sector, where there were no British plans to attack and so no need to investigate. More trenches opposite Fifth and Fourth Armies' front were even further behind the German lines. Instead GHQ was using its limited resources to study those trenches which were closer to the front line or in active sectors. The instructions suited the Royal Flying Corps for two reasons. Their pilots did not like flying long range missions in their outdated machines against the new Imperial German Army Air Service's Albatross DIII planes. The winter snow, rain and mist also made long distance aerial reconnaissance missions dangerous.

On 2 January Nivelle told the French Armée de l'Air to cooperate with the RFC as they investigated any references to new defences. Prisoners were interrogated and agents' reports were studied but little was seen over the course of the month even though construction work was continuing apace. Trenches were being dug in short sections and were eventually connected into one long line stretching eighty-five miles from Neuville-Vitasse to the River Aisne east of Soissons.

The RFC did what it could to keep an eye on the Hindenburg Line but it was 26 January before GHQ's Intelligence Summary mentioned a defence line between Arras and Laon. Nivelle talked about stepping up efforts to investigate the reports but the French Armée de l'Air would not start flying detailed observation missions over the Hindenburg Line until the Germans began to withdraw in March.

Piece by piece the British observers noted the ever growing belts of wire and trenches. They reported new trenches between Drocourt and Vitry-en-Artois, 10 miles north-east of Arras, at the end of January and defences near Quéant, 10 miles south-east of the city, at the beginning of February. Two more sections of trenches were spotted on 15 February south of Vitry and the other near Bellicourt, ten miles east of Péronne. The extension of Fourth Army's line south meant that the RFC had a new area to survey and they were soon reporting that the defensive system went as far south as Saint Quentin. By 24 February GHQ knew the full extent of the Hindenburg Line. It was just in time because the Germans were already withdrawing astride the River Ancre.

Flying reconnaissance missions was dangerous because of the efficiency of the German fighter pilots. Manfred von Richthofen's fighter squadron Jasta 11 and their Albatross D111s were based at the nearby Douai aerodrome. Its pilots would shoot down thirty-six planes between 22 January and the end of March and it was the beginning of April before the RFC were able to take low level, detailed photographs of the Hindenburg Line. The aerial observers also noticed another line around ten miles east of Arras. The Germans called it *Wotan Stellung* or the Wotan Stellung, Wotan being another character in *The Ring*; the British called it the Drocourt–Quéant Switch.

The Withdrawal Begins
The first signs of a local withdrawal were noticed during the last week of February. Messages telling the wireless stations between Achiet-le-Petit and Bapaume 'to dismantle and be prepared to move with all material and not to leave anything behind' were intercepted on the 20th and 21st. Fifth Army told I Anzac Corps but Lieutenant General Birdwood's staff thought they

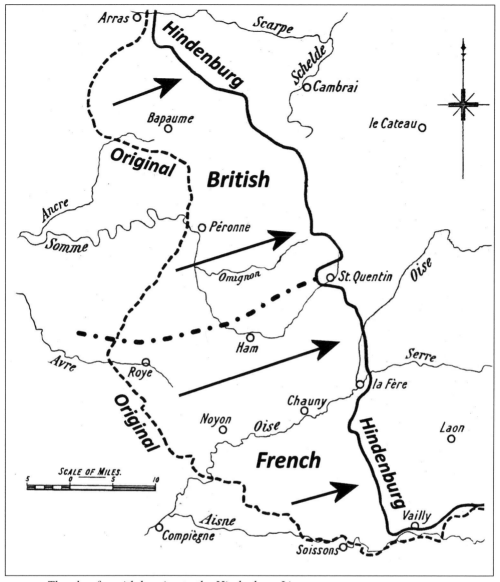

The plan for withdrawing to the Hindenburg Line.

were being told 'just on the chance of there being something in it', so they did not pass on the information to the Australian divisions. On 22 February patrols went out into no mans' land and while they could see little in the fog, they could hear the Germans making plenty of noise. The following day their machine guns and mortars were quieter than normal but the artillery was more active. One observer noted, 'The German front appeared to be almost dead. The known points from which machine guns usually fired were silent.'

Brigadier General Bennett complained that his patrols could not hear any movement whatever in the enemy lines. 'They should have endeavoured to enter the enemy trench.... The cause for this omission I put down to the effects of trench warfare.' Several battalion commanders sent out patrols to check out the strange occurrences but they failed to report anything to their brigade headquarters. It was 5pm on 24 February before V Corps told Fifth Army that the German trenches around Petit Miraumont had been abandoned. It concluded that 'a certain withdrawal of the enemy's forces has taken place or is about to take place.'

The interrogation of captured prisoners gave clues that a withdrawal was underway and fires and explosions were seen in German-held territory when the fog cleared. Meanwhile, the British 'were stationary, nobody knowing quite what had happened and wondering where the Boche had gone to. All through the day the horizon was marked with high, rolling columns of black and yellow smoke from the burning villages, and at night the whole sky was red.'

The Germans were withdrawing to the Siegfried Stellung, using three trench lines, around five miles behind their front, to cover the movement. GHQ initially thought they would withdraw in stages but a captured document revealed the full extent of a rapid withdrawal. The Germans named it Operation Alberich, a daring move named after a malicious dwarf who appeared in Wagner's *Ring*. The question was, could they pull it off?

The New Fortifications
The fortified line between Neuville-Vitasse and Quéant was a standard line of wire and trenches because it had been built in range of the British artillery. But it was far more sophisticated further south, where it had been built beyond the range of the British guns. The first trenches had been dug on forward slopes but after consideration it was decided they could be destroyed by a heavy bombardment.

Ludendorff advocated using a defence in depth. Only a few troops would hold the front line and they would disorganise the advancing troops so the supports could back them with counter-attacks. Starting in February 1917, a second trench system was built on reverse slopes about 2,500 yards in front of the original line. Each system had a double line of trenches spaced 200 yards apart supported by observation posts which could direct artillery and machine gun fire against a breakthrough.

An outpost trench was added 600 yards in front later on, increasing the defensive zone up to a depth of three miles in places. Strongpoints were often laid out in a chequerboard pattern so they could give supporting fire and they were usually connected by trenches. Concrete bunkers had been built at surface level for machine gun teams while the infantry could shelter in concrete shelters built under the parapets. Deep dugouts had also been built to house headquarters, communication centres and medical facilities.

The trenches were all protected by wide entanglements, erected in irregular patterns with gaps to funnel enemy troops into the sights of waiting machine guns. Each one was around fifty yards deep and corkscrew pickets had been used to tie the wire down.

German construction companies built the emplacements but Russian prisoners and Belgian civilians had been drafted in to do the manual work. The work had been carried out without interference but the hard part was about to begin. The Germans had to withdraw their artillery and infantry from under the Allies' noses and move them back over sixty miles in places; and they had to do it all in bad weather. Ludendorff was aware of the effect it would have on his troops. 'The decision to retire was not reached without a painful struggle. It implied a confession of weakness bound to raise the morale of the enemy and lower our own. But as it was necessary for military reasons, we had no choice, it had to be carried out.'

The only consolation was that they could choose when to stand and fight and when to withdraw. They were also going to destroy everything they could: roads, railways, houses, dugouts, wells, everything.

The Ancre Valley, 21 February to 4 March
I Anzac Corps, Gueudecourt, 21 and 22 February
Late on 21 February, troops of 12 Australian Brigade bombed along Stormy Trench, north of 4th Australian Division's sector, which covered Gueudecourt. They captured thirty-two prisoners and not one of them mentioned a withdrawal. Elsewhere patrols could see little in the fog thrown up by the morning thaw, but they could hear parties working and came under sniper and machine gun fire if they tried to investigate. Everyone was reporting a normal situation; nothing indicated the Germans were about to withdraw.

II Corps, 22 to 24 February
On 18th Division's front, Lieutenant Lucas led a party of the 7th Queen's Own through a British barrage on the afternoon of 22 February. He returned to report there were no Germans on the ridge south of Miraumont, so Major General Richard Lee gave Brigadier General Price instructions to occupy it. Patrols went forward through the mist the following morning and found burning dugouts in an abandoned South Miraumont Trench.

The 7th Buffs and the 7th Queen's moved slowly along the east bank of the Ancre on 24 February. They occupied South Miraumont Trench and

Captain Clapperton then cautiously led his company of Buffs through a deserted Petit Miraumont. Price then heard that the Germans had also evacuated Miraumont and Pys.

The mystery was solved when a German soldier suffering from trench foot (a painful ailment caused by standing in water for prolonged periods) was taken prisoner. During his questioning he gave a piece of information which 'fell like a thunderclap both on leaders and on troops'. He said 'that Miraumont had been vacated on the night of 22 February, and that the Germans were withdrawing to a line of trenches at Cambrai, 22 miles back'.

It suggested that around 100 miles of trenches between Arras and Soissons was about to be abandoned and every staff officer understood the motive behind the withdrawal. The Germans would be moving back to a shorter line (thirty miles shorter), creating a new reserve. But it would also dislocate the British and French attacks planned for early April. The Anzac Corps' chief of staff, Brigadier General White, summed up the situation with the words, 'I am afraid it is a very clever thing the Germans have done.'

V Corps, 24 February
7th Division, Serre
Three patrols of the 21st Manchesters skirted around Serre, because it was under British artillery fire, and Colonel Norman watched as they crossed the Serre ridge. Nobody fired on them. During Brigadier General Cumming's tour of the front line he 'found a most unusual and abnormal hush; everything was so curiously and suspiciously peaceful that they did a little patrolling on their own but still found everything quiet. Indeed they were inclined to suspect a trap.'

62nd Division, Miraumont
Everything was too quiet on the west bank of the Ancre so 187 Brigade's major, Captain Hoare, decided to investigate. He walked past the outposts and out onto the hill above Miraumont without a shot being fired at him. Major General Sir Walter Braithwaite agreed to occupy the high ground after he reported the situation and Brigadier General Taylor sent the 2/4th York and Lancasters forward. They saw no one.

The patrols returned before midday but Lieutenant General Edward Fanshawe did not hear about the situation until 4 pm when he immediately issued orders to send out patrols during the night. All four of V Corps' divisions had to be ready to send advanced guards forward between Serre and Miraumont the following morning. They did so, finding Pendant Alley and Beauregard Way deserted in the fog.

I Anzac Corps, 24 February

3rd Australian Division, Gueudecourt

During the evening of 23 February a large number of flares were seen above the German line but no one realised they were being used to coordinate the withdrawal. Patrols soon found that Sunray Trench and Stormy Trench had been abandoned while the German artillery was shelling Maze and Hook Trenches; both supposed to be occupied by their own infantry.

The situation was being repeated all along the line but only Lieutenant Colonel Jacob thought to inform his brigade headquarters when a 10th Australian Battalion patrol entered an empty Hook Trench. It had been empty for twenty-four hours before the Australians realised. News of a withdrawal around Petit Miraumont, on V Corps' front, reached I Anzac Corps headquarters late on the afternoon of 24 February. Brigadier General White telephoned all the Australian divisions and Birdwood declared he wanted to occupy all abandoned ground 'without hesitation' when he received the confirmation message.

The 22nd and 21st Australian Battalions entered an abandoned Gallwitz Trench on 2nd Australian Division's front but Lieutenants Cozens and Murray were killed as they led their troops around the outskirts of Warlencourt. In 1st Australian Division's sector, 7th and 8th Australian Battalions engaged a rear guard in Bayonet Trench until Colonel Jess ordered his company commanders to drive it out. Captain Bowtell-Harris initially reported that 'a cat couldn't get through' the wire but some bombers eventually entered the trench, forcing the Germans to withdraw. South of Le Barque, 48th Australian Battalion cleared a long length of Stormy Trench for 4th Australian Division. On the right, 30th Australian Battalion occupied Sunray Trench but the Germans still held Le Transloy in front of 5th Australian Division.

By dawn on 25 February, it was clear the Germans had abandoned a large amount of territory astride the Ancre; they had fallen back over two miles in places. Gough told Lieutenant Generals Fanshawe, Jacob and Birdwood to push forward strong patrols to find the new German position. It did not take them long.

V Corps, Serre, 25 February

The 8th Gloucesters became disorientated in the fog on 19th Division's front and had to regroup along the Hébuterne road, north-west of Serre. The 1st South Staffords became scattered in the fog as they fought their way through Serre in 7th Division's sector. Meanwhile, 63rd Division advanced to Beauregard Dovecote strongpoint and Gudgeon Trench, north of Miraumont.

II Corps, 25 February

Lieutenant General Jacob instructed a continuation of the advance astride the Ancre. The 7th Buffs occupied Pys on 18th Division's front but shellfire stopped a patrol entering Irles. Meanwhile, the 2nd HLI occupied Grundy Trench, to the east, but they became too disorientated in the mist and could not report their position to 2nd Division for some time.

I Anzac Corps, 25 February

Brigadier General Gellibrand had been instructed to capture Malt Trench, on 1st Australian Division's front. The Australians suffered a lot of casualties from artillery and machine gun fire when the fog suddenly cleared and both the 18th and 20th Australian Battalions were pinned down in Barque Switch Trench. On the right, the 9th and 10th Australian Battalions advanced too far beyond Le Barque in the mist and then fell back to Oat and Wheat Trenches when they realised their mistake. Gellibrand ordered another attempt in the afternoon in the belief that he only faced scattered outposts; it only resulted in more casualties. One German observer noted that the 'Tommy was entirely strange to the war of movement; the result was heavy losses for him'. The same applied to the Diggers.

V Corps, Puisieux, 26 and 27 February

A patrol of the 18th Durhams entered an abandoned Gommecourt Park and village in front of 31st Division, so 46th Division was invited to take over the sector. But neither the 16th West Yorkshires nor the 10th East Yorkshires could advance towards Rossignol Wood and Captain Jones was killed leading his East Yorkshires' company towards Berg Graben, a trench south-east of the wood. As 31st Division dug in along the Gommecourt–Puisieux road, 19th Division occupied Rossignol Trench alongside. Early the following morning the 16th West Yorkshires sent a company into Gommecourt Wood but only one platoon returned; the rest had been captured.

On 26 February, 7th Division advanced across a crater field towards Puisieux. The 2nd Border Regiment cleared the west half of the village but Captain Anscombe was wounded leading the 1st Welsh Fusiliers forward. Most of Second Lieutenant Montgomery's men were hit trying to capture the church, so the survivors had to withdraw. The 2nd Warwicks found Puisieux had been abandoned when they moved through the ruins the following morning.

On V Corps' right, 62nd Division had reached Gudgeon Trench, north of Miraumont. Gough was disappointed with the slow advance. It was giving the Germans time to prepare their first line of defence between

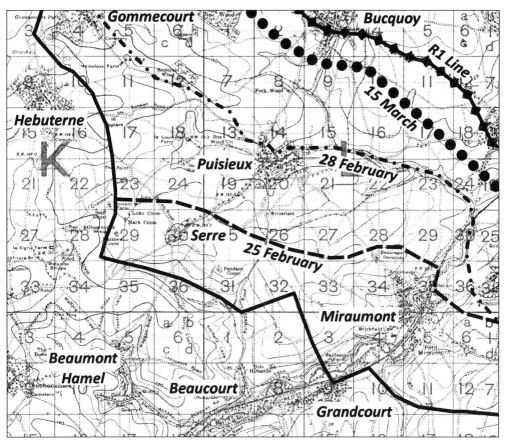

V Corps' advance to the R2 Line, west of the Ancre.

Bucquoy and Achiet-le-Petit: the *Reserveleitung 1 Stellung* or Reserve Line 1 Position (R1).

II Corps, Irles and Loupart Wood, 26 February

The first advance by 63rd Division was stopped in front of Gudgeon Trench, north of Miraumont, but a second barrage convinced the rearguard to abandon it during the afternoon. In II Corps' centre, 18th Division was pinned down by machine gun fire in front of the R1 Line, north-east of Irles. A company of the 7th Queen's discovered that Irles was occupied the following morning and it had to fall back. On 6 March, the 8th Suffolks captured Resurrection Trench, west of Irles. But there were problems in 2nd Division's sector, where it was impossible to reach Grévillers Trench.

I Anzac Corps, Le Barque, 26 February

The Australians were more cautious after being caught out the previous day and they waited for the barrage to start creeping forward. But Major General

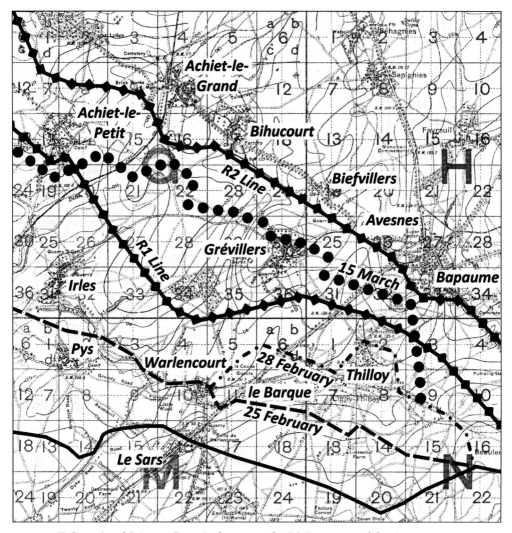

II Corps' and I Anzac Corps' advance to the R2 Line, east of the Ancre.

Harold Walker cancelled an advance over the top because the gunners overshot their target and 1st Australian Division's bombers moved forward instead. On 3 Australian Brigade's front, Lieutenant Hart's bombers entered Malt Trench during the afternoon. Bombing parties tried in vain to clear the same trench facing 5 Australian Brigade's sector during the night and the Germans left before dawn, leaving a sign which said something like, 'If we did not want you here, you would not be here'.

Brigadier General Bennett had instructed the 12th Australian Battalion to creep towards Le Barque during the evening, without the benefit of an artillery barrage and most of the garrison was taken by surprise. The only fighting was on the left, where Captain Newland's men triggered a tripwire which fired a flare into the night sky. By dawn the village was clear and the Germans had abandoned the east half of Malt Trench.

The following day, 11th Australian Battalion cleared Thilloy and established a line close to the R1 Line. An aerial observer reported that the north-west end of Malt Trench was empty, but 19th Australian Battalion found the Germans waiting for them. It would take 2nd Australian Division two days to clear it.

II Corps, Irles and the Lady's Leg, 10 March
Winter weather returned with another frost on the night of 3 March and it then snowed on the night of 4 March. The men had no braziers and fuel was scarce, so they spent the nights shivering in the trenches. Many suffered with colds and the regular sneezing and coughing meant it was unsafe to send out patrols. Those lucky enough to stay in a dugout had to endure the poisonous fumes given out by their coke fires while they tried to warm up their food and tea. But it was no better when the morning thaw came. Melting ice filled the trenches with muddy water and covered the roads in slush.

Gough had told Haig he would attack the R1 Line around 13 March but II Corps still had to take Irles and Grévillers Trench, in the centre of Fifth Army's front. The heavy artillery of V Corps and I Anzac Corps would assist on each flank, giving each division the support of eighty howitzers. Gough had wanted to attack on 5 March but the artillery faced a difficult time cutting the wire.

Zero hour was set for 10 March but Lieutenant General Jacob kept hearing that there were few gaps in the three belts of wire: 'the first about eight feet deep and waist high; the second similar to the first and the third higher and stronger than the first two, having an apron in front'. To make matters worse, there was a thaw during the night, turning the frozen ground into thick, oozing mud. Then a thick fog formed over the battlefield before dawn.

The field guns began shelling the German trenches at zero hour and the infantry spent six minutes crawling across no man's land to find that all three belts of wire had been smashed. They rose to charge the moment the guns lengthened their range at 5.15 am and killed or captured many Germans before they could bring their machine guns into action.

Howitzers shelled the south-west corner of Irles while the 10th Essex secured the north end. The 8th Norfolks' left swerved in the darkness, missed the gap in the wire and ran into the entanglement covering the south-east corner of Irles. Prisoners later reported the village had been empty until one hundred men had been sent back to defend it. Meanwhile, Captain Morgan crossed an obliterated Grévillers Trench without realising it, but the Norfolks' right flank recognised it and dug it out. On the right, the 8th Suffolks captured Irles Trench and then shot at the village garrison as they tried to escape.

The 1st KRRCs and 1st Berkshires cleared the rest of Grévillers Trench, under fire from Loupart Wood, on 2nd Division's left. Companies of the 23rd Royal Fusiliers advanced either side of Lady's Leg while Lewis guns and Stokes mortars fired into the ravine; the survivors were then encouraged to surrender.

Lewis gun sections established an outpost line in craters made especially for them by II Corps' 6-inch howitzers. By nightfall both Major Generals Richard Lee and Cecil Pereira were able to report they were close to the R1 Line in front of Loupart Wood. They had taken over 400 prisoners for the cost of only 250 casualties.

Withdrawal from the R1 Line, 11 to 13 March
Prisoners had suggested that the German High Command planned to withdraw to the R2 Line and then to the Hindenburg Line. They were currently herding civilians into selected villages so that the engineers could booby-trap or demolish the rest. Wagons were busy taking stores and ammunition to the rear while anything that could not be moved was being burnt or destroyed. All unnecessary troops were being pulled out of the line while batteries were being reduced to a couple of guns; the rest were being sent to the rear.

The withdrawal from the R1 Position began opposite II Corps during the night of 11 March but British patrols did not enter the empty trenches until the following night. Early the following morning, the 13th Essex entered the R1 Position north-west of Loupart Wood, while Lieutenant Kynaston led the 1st King's through the wood. Meanwhile, 2nd Australian Division had pushed patrols through Grévillers towards the R2 Position during the night.

But the Germans had not gone far. The 7th Bedfords came under fire from the R2 Position when they advanced beyond Achiet-le-Petit on 18th Division's front on 13 March. Stretcher bearer Christopher Cox rescued four Bedford men under fire and then helped to bring in the wounded of other battalions. He continued his work for two more days; he would be awarded the Victoria Cross.

An important document, dated 5 March, had been sent back to 2nd Division's headquarters. It made it clear that the Germans planned to withdraw quickly from the R2 Position to the Hindenburg Line. The move would be made over three 'Marching Days' and 13 March was going to be the first day.

V Corps, Bucquoy, 13 March

Lieutenant General Fanshawe had planned to capture Bucquoy on 15 March. Then on the afternoon of 13 March he brought the attack forward to that night, despite protests from both his division commanders. Major General William Thwaites had been told the wire was intact and the Germans were on high alert. Brigadier General Campbell's troops were training at Souastre, eight miles behind the front line, when they were told. The 1/5th South and the 1/5th North Staffords spent the evening marching along busy roads in the rain and then learnt that the pipe-pushers (tubes filled with explosives) they planned to use to cut the wire were not available. It was the same story on 7th Division's front, where Major General George Barrow had wanted the attack postponed until dawn.

The barrage was ineffective because the gunners had not had time to register their targets and the observers could not adjust the barrage because clouds were hiding the moon. The Staffordshire men advanced on time, after a hurried deployment, but none of them could get through the wire. The 22nd Manchesters and the 2nd Queen's were still deploying south of Bucquoy at zero hour.

The men were forced to crawl through the few gaps in the wire so that the mud clogged their weapons. The Manchesters' right company and a few of the Queen's under Captain Foster got through but they had to withdraw after throwing all their bombs. The hasty attack had achieved nothing for the cost of over 570 casualties. It had been a waste of lives because the Germans were about to evacuate Bucquoy and withdraw to the R2 Position.

Fourth Army

The Germans were withdrawing in front of Fifth Army but were holding fast in front of Fourth Army between Le Transloy and the River Somme. Rawlinson issued orders to his three corps commanders on 17 February, telling them to capture observation points on 27 February. He later had to postpone two attacks and cancel the third, due to the bad weather. Meanwhile, Fourth Army was still taking over the French trenches, as IV Corps extended its line as far south as the Amiens–Roye road.

XIV Corps, 28 February

The 12th KRRC lost direction as they advanced east of Lesboeufs, in front of 20th Division. They did not capture Ersatz Point.

Major General Sir Beauvoir de Lisle wanted to secure an observation post for 29th Division east of Sailly-Saillisel. Smoke filled no man's land as two creeping barrages moved towards Palz Trench. One company of the 1st Lancashire Fusiliers and the 1st Dublin Fusiliers' left discovered that the trench mortars had not cut the wire, but the Dublin Fusiliers still entered Palz trench. They bombed along it until they had to stop and build a block while the Lewis gunners cleared mud from their weapons. Many Germans surrendered to the 2nd Royal Fusiliers on the right but they had to consolidate Potsdam Trench because they could not clear their objective.

A heavy bombardment preceded a German bombing attack down Bayreuth Trench during the early afternoon while snipers picked off the Royal Fusiliers' bombers. The Germans were eventually stopped short of the junction of Weimar and Palz Trenches. The Royal Newfoundland Battalion would fight for possession of Weimar Trench for several days.

XV Corps, Fritz and Pallas Trenches, 4 March
An attack between Bouchavesnes and Moislains by 8th Division was postponed until 4 March. Major General William Heneker's plan was to clear Fritz and Pallas Trenches before advancing towards Rancourt. The heavier howitzers benefited from a new sound-ranging instrument which was better at locating enemy batteries while the 6-inch howitzers smashed the wire with shells armed with the 106 impact fuse. The men formed up in the mist in no man's land in silence. They chewed on the gum issued to stop them coughing as they lay in the mud; there had been no time to dig an assembly trench. Heneker only wanted five minutes of preliminary bombardment so that the trenches would be preserved for consolidation.

Snow fell just before the assault at 5.15 am. Captain Fergusson led the 2nd Northants forward while some of the 1st Worcesters went as far as Bremen Trench. Fritz Trench was consolidated but enfilade fire hit the Northants' left flank. The Germans then counter-attacked from the wood north-west of Moislains. Lieutenant Colonel Sherbrooke sent two companies of the 1st Sherwood Foresters forward to reinforce Pallas Trench while the rest ferried bombs to the front line. After the fifth counter-attack, Lieutenant Colonel Buckle reported that the 'Hun is shelling like hell but has had a bellyful of fighting and is beat'.

The 2nd Berkshires' first wave had followed the oblique slope of the hill in the darkness but Captain Scobell kept the support companies moving on the correct compass bearing. They crossed Pallas and then Fritz Trenches and some went as far as Bremen Trench, returning after dropping gas bombs into the dugouts. They were soon joined by Major Griffin's 2nd Lincolns, who had been busy mopping up.

A barrage hit Lieutenant Colonel Haig's Berkshires during the afternoon and Brigadier General Coffin sent the 2nd Rifle Brigade to reinforce them.

Early the following morning the Germans recaptured 300 yards of Fritz Trench. Lieutenant Parsons was killed and Captain Hanbury-Sparrow was wounded trying to take it.

The Rifle Brigade relieved the Berkshires and they were improving Fritz Trench when Second Lieutenant George Cates' spade hit a buried bomb. He placed his foot on it as it started to burn and the explosion killed him. Cates' sacrifice saved his comrades; he was posthumously awarded the Victoria Cross.

Before dawn the following morning the Germans counter-attacked the Berkshires. A wounded Captain Hanbury-Sparrow lost part of Fritz Trench but it was retaken when Captain Cahill organised a rifle grenade barrage from Pallas Trench to cover Lieutenant Prest's charge. Artillery bombardments and machine gun barrages stopped later attacks. Heneker was able to report Fritz and Pallas Trenches had been taken with over 200 prisoners for the cost of 1,100 casualties.

The Withdrawal from the R2 Position
The German withdrawal began near Rancourt and two people claimed they discovered it first. Captain Brand of the 1st Scots Guards went alone to investigate fires in St Pierre Vaast Wood early on 14 March. He returned to report an empty front line trench. Lieutenant Cropper, a forward observing officer for the Guards artillery, also crossed no man's land with an infantry patrol and found the same thing. Patrols spent the afternoon carefully searching abandoned trenches all along the line.

The 1st Scots Guards encountered no one as they moved cautiously through St Pierre Vaast Wood the following morning but the 1st and 2nd Irish Guards were stopped by long-range artillery and machine gun fire north of the wood. It was clear that the Germans were carrying out a fighting withdrawal: 'One cannot say we caused them to leave one position an hour before they intended. They inflicted on us a considerable number of casualties.' They were also leaving 'little or nothing behind'.

At dusk on 14 March, the Guards informed Colonel Jack of the 2nd West Yorkshires that Drossen Trench was empty. Second Lieutenants May and Hall took patrols forward east of Rancourt and confirmed the 'astounding news'. Captain Palmes led the West Yorkshires' advance the following morning.

But the Germans were determined to hold onto the trenches around Sailly-Saillisel, opposite 20th Division, for another forty-eight hours. Snipers and machine guns then covered the withdrawal as British patrols cautiously explored the abandoned trenches. The German rear guards had finally evacuated the R2 Position on 16 March, making it the first Marching Day opposite Fourth Army. They would withdraw as fast as they could to the Hindenburg Line.

Chapter 5

Everything of Value had been Destroyed
The Withdrawal Continues

General Nivelle wanted the Group of Armies of the North to attack two weeks before the main offensive on the Aisne. General Franchet d'Espèrey had instructions to break through between Roye and Lassigny, on the British right, and then advance east. Preparations were in progress when it became clear the Germans were withdrawing and Franchet d'Espèrey wanted to catch them on the move. But Nivelle thought they were only withdrawing a short distance and would only allow a limited attack, beginning with a three-day bombardment on 17 March.

The French infantry waited while observers reported the Germans were destroying stores and bridges behind their lines. Then their patrols discovered abandoned German trenches on the night of 12 March. Four nights later Franchet d'Espèrey ordered an advance but the Germans were already across the River Avre. The opportunity to catch them on the move had been wasted. All the French could do was follow them to the Hindenburg Line.

Meanwhile, Haig met Allenby, Gough and Rawlinson to discuss the consequences of the German withdrawal. The shortening of the line meant they would have more divisions in reserve to counter-attack while they tried to break though. The front was moving fast and the advance guards were pushing forward around the clock while the main bodies followed in stages.

Third Army, 17 to 28 March
Observers reported that the German artillery was shelling its own trenches at Monchy-au-Bois, 10 miles south-west of Arras, early on 17 March. Major General Hew Fanshawe ordered 58th Division to check them out and then occupy them. Patrols continued to push east, looking to keep in contact with the Germans but they saw no one for over two miles.

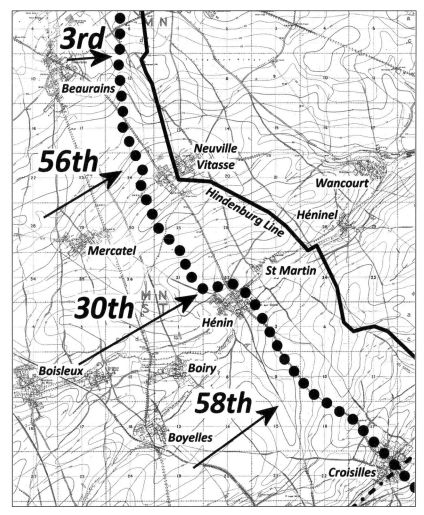

Third Army's advance to the Hindenburg Line.

The Germans had to move fast because they had no R3 Position opposite Third Army and Fifth Army had already crossed the R2 Position. Gough was looking to attack their exposed flank when he ordered the Lucknow Cavalry Brigade to cut behind the Germans facing Third Army. But the Germans had already withdrawn, leaving 58th Division to search an abandoned R1 Position.

There was little movement on Third Army's left, where 3rd Division was east of Arras, but 56th and 30th Divisions reached the Arras–Bapaume road, near Beaurains, on 19 March. Meanwhile, 58th Division occupied Boiry-Becquerelle and Boyelles, six miles south of Arras, in touch with Fifth Army. Allenby had already withdrawn XVIII Corps due to the

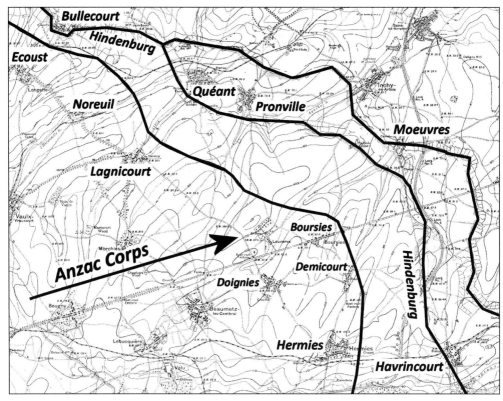

The southern part of Fifth Army's advance to the Hindenburg Line.

contraction of his front but he warned Generals Snow and Fanshawe to approach the villages in front of the Hindenburg Line with care.

Fifth Army's Advance, 17 to 28 March
I Anzac Corps, 17 to 21 March

Early on 17 March, Captain Scott of 19th Battalion discovered that the Germans had evacuated the R2 Line covering Bapaume. So 5th Australian Division occupied Avesnes on the north-west outskirts of Bapaume. Lieutenant Colonel Clark ordered 30th Australian Battalion to advance after hearing Corporal King's patrol had entered the R2 Line but Lieutenant White ran down the road so he could claim he was the first man to enter Bapaume. Captains Barbour and Cheeseman then led their men into the burning and abandoned town. On the far side, they could see columns of troops and transport heading across the green fields into the distance.

The following day, 21st Australian Battalion took the rear guard defending Vaulx-Vraucourt by surprise, driving it back towards Lagnicourt. On the right, 59th Australian Battalion outflanked Frémicourt and then

Beugny, under fire from the German rear guards. Meanwhile, 2nd Australian Division encountered more resistance along the Cambrai road but patrols pushed beyond Lebucquière to the south. Major General Nevill Smyth had intended to advance cautiously to avoid unnecessary casualties, but Brigadier General Gellibrand decided to make an unauthorised attack to cut off Noreuil, north of the road, early on 20 March.

On the left, 21st Australian Battalion was delayed by German outposts waiting on the Longatte spur on the cold, dark night. Captain Jones turned towards the village too early and the rest of the battalion followed just as it was getting light. They walked straight into the sights of the machine gun teams guarding Noreuil. On the right, Lieutenant Colonel Bateman had given his company commanders the impression that 23rd Australian Battalion was supposed to capture Lagnicourt, rather than just draw fire from the main attack. Consequently, Captain Rossiter led his troops too close to the village and they were pinned down by machine gun fire.

Gellibrand had to report that the two battalions had been forced to withdraw having suffered over 325 casualties. Early on 21 March, Brigadier General Elliott's column of Australians occupied an abandoned Beaumetz-lès-Cambrai and then had to spend the next two days fighting off counter-attacks. It was clear the Germans were not giving up without a fight.

II Corps, Achiet-le-Grand to Croisilles, 17 to 18 March
North-west of Bapaume, II Corps started moving on 17 March, after hearing the Australians had advanced through and beyond the R2 Position. On the left, 18th Division moved through Bihucourt and into Achiet-le-Grand. The 7th Bedfords were then shelled as they cleared the village while machine gun fire from Gomiécourt stopped them advancing any further for a while. On the right, 17th Middlesex led 2nd Division through Biefvillers into Sapignies. Lieutenant General Jacob warned the advanced guards to be cautious but 2nd Division had reached Mory by nightfall on 18 March.

Major General Richard Lee had not had time to organise enough artillery to support 18th Division's attack on Croisilles so he decided to try to rush it instead. The 6th Northants approached the village early on 20 March, while the Yorkshire Dragoons moved around the flanks. The 29th Lancers moved around the north-west side of the village, while a squadron of the King's Dragoon Guards approached Ecoust to the south-east. No less than fifteen machine guns and half a dozen field guns opened fire and Lieutenant Colonel Turner called off the Northants' attack to avert a disaster. It was the

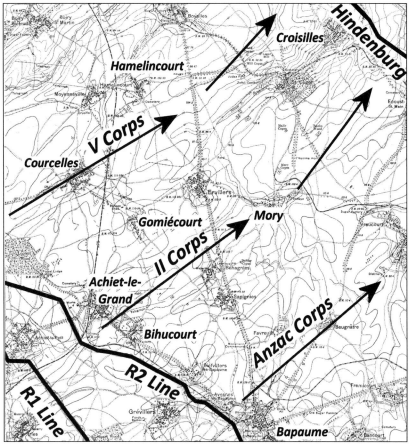

The northern part of Fifth Army's advance to the Hindenburg Line.

first sign that the Germans planned to hold the villages in front of the Hindenburg Line; they would become known as the outpost villages.

V Corps, Bucquoy to Hamelincourt, 17 and 18 March

All three of Lieutenant General Fanshawe's divisions crossed the abandoned R2 Line on 17 March and the soldiers marvelled at their advance across the green, open fields. As 46th Division passed through Essarts and Ayette, 7th Division moved through Bucquoy, Ablainzevelle and Courcelles-le-Comte, and 62nd Division passed through Achiet-le-Petit and Gomiécourt. The good weather was drying the roads out but Fanshawe's request for tanks to spearhead his advance was denied because they were being readied for the Arras offensive. Instead the Lucknow Brigade and the 29th Lancers moved north to try to cut off the retreating Germans. They were stopped by machine gun fire east of Hamelincourt on 18 March so they turned east, finding rear guards holding Croisilles, Ecoust, Noreuil and Lagnicourt the following day.

A Difficult Advance

Haig was pleased with Fifth Army's progress but he was concerned about the ability of the advance guards to defend themselves. Gough increased them to brigade sized groups so they could fend off small counter-attacks. He also instructed the main bodies of his divisions to build fortifications between Ablainzevelle and Bapaume, ready to stop any large counter-attacks.

Late on 20 March, Gough told Birdwood and Fanshawe to capture the outpost villages as quickly as possible. But it was going to be difficult to haul their artillery forward because the Germans were carrying out a 'scorched earth' policy, destroying everything in their wake. The only reason some buildings were still standing was because booby traps had failed to detonate. Engineers removed over 700 lbs of explosive from the cellars of one chateau alone.

The Germans had been busy booby-trapping everything to make the British and Australian soldiers as wary as possible. They went to enormous lengths to make an array of devices, ranging from ingenious to crude. Explosives had been buried along the roads, ready to detonate if a vehicle drove over them. They had blown craters which had to be filled in or bypassed. Barricades and trees had been dragged across the roads and many were wired up to explosives. Most of the bridges had been demolished but some were left partially damaged, so the engineers would repair it unaware that a delayed-action mine had been dug into the structure.

Dugouts were particularly deadly places, no matter how tempting it was to get out of the bad weather. Camouflage covering the entrance could be wired to explosives while sandbags blocking the door could be tied to a stick of grenades. Loose handrails, protruding nails or uneven floorboards could all be booby-trapped, ready to explode if they were hammered or pushed back into place. The cold, damp weather meant that men would do anything to light a fire but detonators were sometimes found carved into lumps of coal, discarded chimney stoves were wired up to charges and chimneys were lined with explosives. Discarded souvenirs, books or useful tools were often attached to detonators ready to explode if they were picked up. Tempting rum jars, set to explode if they were checked, were a common item.

The largest booby trap detonated on the night 25 March. Engineers had already removed one mine from Bapaume town hall and it had been declared safe. But an ingenious delayed action fuse used acid to corrode the spring holding the striker. The huge explosion killed many Australian troops sleeping in the cellars. Another mine would explode near Béhagnies four months after the Germans set it. It was down to the tunnelling companies of the Royal Engineers to make the rear areas safe; it would take them many weeks to complete their work.

I Anzac Corps, Lagnicourt, 26 March

Lieutenant General Birdwood decided 2nd Australian Division would capture Lagnicourt on 26 March. Major Robinson had difficulty getting 26th Australian Battalion into position in the darkness until the barrage started. Captain Cooper then followed the explosions around the north side of the village while Captain Percy Cherry rushed the Germans holding a huge crater in the centre. Lieutenant Bieske took over when Lieutenant Hamilton was wounded. Cherry noticed that the Germans were firing yellow flares to help pinpoint Australian positions for the German artillery during the counter-attack. So he found some yellow flares of his own and fired them away from his position to confuse the enemy gunners. A shell killed Cherry soon afterwards; he was posthumously awarded the Victoria Cross.

V Corps, Ecoust, 28 March

Major General George Barrow had wanted 7th Division to attack Ecoust on 28 March but his gunners had not had time to cut the wire. Instead the artillery hit Croisilles and failed to either cut the wire or subdue the machine gun teams. At 5.45 am the 1st South Staffords were pinned down west of the village but Captain Duguid led some of the 22nd Manchesters through the wire. Too few made it and they had to withdraw.

General Barrow wanted to try again with help from Third Army's VII Corps. Unfortunately, Gough did not want to wait until 30th Division had relieved 58th Division because it would give the Germans time to relieve their troops. The same two battalions attacked on 29 March and this time they initially had more success. Second Lieutenant Curry was stopped on the 1st South Staffords' right and while Captain Dickens entered the village on the left, his company was surrounded and taken prisoner. The 22nd Manchesters cut through the wire only to become isolated in the German trenches beyond. They would hold on for thirty-six hours before they were forced to withdraw.

Fourth Army, 17 to 28 March

Fourth Army's left faced the Tortille stream but the cavalry crossed the Canal du Nord where it went through a tunnel around Ytres. Meanwhile, patrols found suitable crossings for field artillery over the Canal du Nord at Moislains, six miles to the south, on 18 March. Fourth Army's right faced the River Somme and the canal running parallel to it. Every bridge had been destroyed or damaged while rear guards covered all the causeways.

The engineer-in-chief, Major General Rice, sent engineers forward to assess what was needed at each crossing. A corps' chief engineer then sent the appropriate bridging material forward and Fourth Army's engineering companies supervised the work at each site. There was always a lack of local material because the Germans had either destroyed or removed everything of use.

Infantry clambered over the damaged bridges to establish bridgeheads and the engineers could then begin clearing tree trunks, slabs of ice and other debris from the watercourses. They sometimes built dams or used explosives to create new river channels to improve the water flow. Pontoons could then be launched and rafts could be built to carry the rest of the men and the field artillery across. The engineers worked around the clock, lighting bonfires at night to illuminate the bridging sites.

III Corps, 15 to 20 March
48th Division, Péronne
A deserter told the 1/6th Gloucesters that his comrades were withdrawing from Péronne on the evening of 15 March and a lot of Very lights over the town confirmed something was happening. Patrols checked out the canal and Lieutenant Byard entered the German trenches early the following morning; all he found was a solitary sniper guarding them. Further south, the 1/5th Gloucesters found the trenches around La Maisonette deserted the following night. Captain Condon was the first man to report that the withdrawal had started opposite III Corps.

Six pontoons and two rafts were towed into position during the hours of darkness and a floating bridge was ready by noon on 17 March. A company of the 1/8th Warwicks crossed during the evening and they covered the engineers as they built a sturdier bridge for the artillery to use. The Warwicks found Péronne to be 'very much damaged' and with 'hardly a building left standing'. They were then kept busy evacuating hundreds of civilians across the river while the 1/4th Gloucesters checked out the town's southern suburbs. Every bridge was down but the divisional engineers would build six footbridges, three medium bridges and a heavy duty bridge in just nine days.

1st Division, Brie
A rearguard delayed the 1st Gloucesters at Villers-Carbonnel while the 10th Gloucesters and 2nd Welsh came under fire when they approached the River

Somme at Brie on 16 March. The infantry completed a temporary footbridge two days later, allowing Lieutenant Forbes to form a bridgehead with the Gloucesters. They kept guard while the engineers worked around the clock to bridge the watercourses. The main St Quentin road was opened to wheeled traffic early on 20 March but something stronger was needed so the heavy artillery could cross.

The engineers built a dam and used explosives to create a new water channel. They also dismantled the damaged bridge and reused the material to build a new one, using bricks from demolished houses to create the approach ramps. A bridge for heavy traffic was opened on the afternoon of 28 March, five days earlier than promised.

IV Corps, 18 to 20 March
32nd Division, Voyennes

The 1st King Edward's Horse and the corps' cyclists reached the Somme canal opposite Offoy on 18 March. A patrol of the 16th Northumberland Fusiliers crossed the Somme canal via a damaged bridge and approached the houses. All was quiet until Lieutenant King was welcomed by the 'village harlot' and she reported that the Germans had left a few hours before. The bridge was repaired the following day and Voyennes bridge, two miles to the north-west was opened to wheeled traffic late on 20 March. It meant III Corps was across the Somme on a thirteen-mile front; it had taken only three days to cross.

Summary

The withdrawal programme had not included a prolonged stand on the R3 Position. There were only two marching days opposite Fourth Army's left and they ended on 17 March. It stopped after three marching days opposite the right. After four weeks of moving back in stages, the Germans were behind the Hindenburg Line, leaving the British out in the open fields with no trenches or wire.

On 19 March cavalry patrols moved to the Tortille stream but the Guards Division was not impressed with their efforts. It reported, 'the cavalry on our front usually withdraws at night and seldom reports anything which our infantry patrols have not discovered several hours earlier.' The following day, Fourth Army's outpost line was across the Tortille at Manancourt. Although 8th Division entered Nurlu, the spring weather had turned the ice into liquid mud, slowing traffic to a crawl.

Fourth Army had advanced to a line 6 miles east of Bapaume on the left, 7 miles east of Péronne in the centre and 8 miles west of St Quentin on the right. Outposts were established all along the front while platoon-sized strongpoints were built and connected together. The rest of the infantry were busy repairing the roads while the engineers worked to bridge the rivers and canals.

Every mile had brought about new problems on the roads. There were fallen trees to be moved and craters to be filled in or bypassed. Road repairs involved scraping off the mud, digging new drains and creating a surface with timber beams. Shell holes had to be cleaned out and filled by hand while the largest ones had to be crossed by trestle bridges. The endless columns of horse-drawn vehicles were cutting the roads to pieces and there was not enough stone or labour to repair all the damage. But Rawlinson had to keep pushing to keep up with the French to the south.

Chapter 6

The Outpost Villages
The Withdrawal Ends

Third Army
VII Corps, 2 April
30th Division, Hénin-sur-Cojeul

Captains Field and Smith had led the 2nd Green Howards into Hénin-sur-Cojeul during the night of 30 March but they had been forced to withdraw. Lieutenant Colonel Edwards tried again the following morning and this time Captain Smith led his company around the north side of the village, blocking the road to St Martin-sur-Cojeul. Lieutenant Bright and Captain Field were delayed advancing towards the south-west side of the village and they lost the barrage. Captain Baron reinforced the pinned-down companies and they pushed through the village, followed by two companies of the 19th Manchester who searched the houses and cellars. A company of the 2nd Wiltshires joined the fight but it still took nine hours to clear the village and Captain Field was killed during the final battle for the Mairie (the village hall). Brigadier General Goodman was delighted to hear the final outpost village had fallen and said that 'the news was so unexpected that he fell off his chair with surprise!'

21st Division, Croisilles

Major General David Campbell did not have any villages to clear and he had plenty of heavy artillery. Brigadier General Rawling's 62 Brigade reached the road between St Martin-sur-Cojeul and Croisilles without any difficulty apart from where the 13th Northumberland Fusiliers could not clear the east end of Croisilles on the right flank. A counter-attack allowed the garrison to escape towards Fontaine-lès-Croisilles as 7th Division closed in from the south.

Fifth Army

Gough wanted to secure the outpost villages in front of the Hindenburg Line before the attack began at Arras. Lieutenant General Fanshawe's V Corps was to capture Croisilles and Ecoust-St-Mein while Lieutenant General Birdwood's I Anzac Corps was to capture Noreuil, Louverval and Doignies. Following the occupation of Lagnicourt, 4th Australian Division relieved 2nd Australian Division on I Anzac Corps' left but 5th Australian Division stayed in line.

V Corps
Fanshawe had been given extra artillery batteries but he still wanted to surround Croisilles rather than attack it frontally. His plan was to involve 21st Division, which belonged to Third Army, advancing past the north flank while his own 7th Division would bypass it to the south.

7th Division, Croisilles, 2 April
Major General Herbert Shoubridge had replaced General Barrow and this time the artillery had enough time to cut the wire. The plan was for the heavy howitzers and guns to continue shelling Ecoust and Croisilles until twelve minutes after zero while the infantry advanced between them.

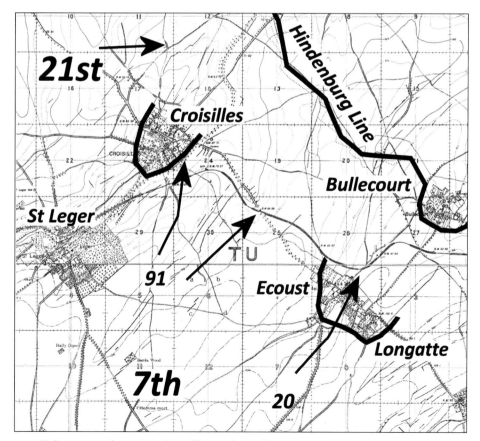

V Corps attack against Croisilles on 2 April.

Brigadier General Cumming wanted three of his battalions to advance in line but an early bright moon meant the assembly was delayed. Another problem was that one battery had arrived late and the gunners had not had time to register its guns. So shells fell behind the 2nd Queen's and 21st Manchesters but landed ahead of the 1st South Staffords, causing some confusion at zero hour.

The Queen's formed a flank facing Croisilles and put down suppressive fire on the strongpoint called the Tooth. Two Manchester companies and the Staffords crossed a fortified embankment covered in brambles and barbed wire and the Manchesters turned to face the village while the Staffords reached the railway between the two villages. Lieutenant Robinson led the Manchesters along the banks of the Sensée and they began clearing Croisilles, but 21st Division had failed to advance north of the village, allowing the garrison to escape.

On 20 Brigade's front, Lieutenant Colonel Thorpe faced the double village of Ecoust and Longatte. The 9th Devons headed for the two gaps in the wire, on the road crossings, only to find they were both covered by machine guns. Captain Inchbald and Lieutenant Bellamy were killed but their men kept going until they reached the railway embankment north of Ecoust.

The 8th Devons overran the machine gun teams waiting outside the wire and the Lewis guns then supressed the rest of the German machine guns behind it. It allowed Captain Duff and Lieutenant Perkins to lead their men through the single gap in the wire. Private Owen silenced the machine gun covering the main street and Second Lieutenant Cornelius then led the fight for the village. Meanwhile, the 2nd Gordons had struggled to get through Longatte. The 9th Devons fired from the railway embankment when the Germans finally fled. As the men defended the village in a blizzard, a badly injured Captain Duff returned to the Devons' headquarters and announced, 'who says the 7th Division is sticky now?' He was referring to criticism over the division's failure to capture Croisilles a few days earlier.

I Anzac Corps
5th Australian Division, Noreuil and Doignies, 2 April
Major General Hobbs had decided to attack Noreuil at 5.15 am but machine gun fire pinned 51st Australian Battalion down as they moved past the north side of the village, until Lieutenant Earl crept forward and silenced three crews with his pistol. Major Christie's men were then forced to take cover in a shallow trench because the Lagnicourt–Bullecourt road was under machine gun fire.

Captains Armitage and Churchill-Smith rushed the barricades south of Noreuil but the artillery barrage had failed to supress the Germans in front of 50th Australian Battalion. Lieutenants Jose, Bidstrup and Hoggarth were killed while Sergeant Wilson's men were pinned down along the Lagnicourt road. Fortunes changed when Private O'Connor shot the machine gunner behind one barricade and six men rushed the post as Private Jørgen Jensen threatened to kill the group of forty Germans with the two grenades he was holding in his hands. They surrendered and Jensen then stood on the barricade and waved his helmet to warn nearby British troops not to fire on his prisoners. Jensen was awarded the Victoria Cross.

Meanwhile, Captain Todd's company had wheeled too early on the right flank and his men were pinned down by machine gun fire. Then disaster struck. Lieutenant Edwards had too few men to clear the village and the Germans killed or captured them all before withdrawing. They stumbled on Todd's men and shot them all before escaping. Brigadier General Glasgow had to report that the capture of Noreuil had cost over 600 casualties.

Hobbs had instructed Brigadier General Hobkirk to attack astride the Cambrai road before dawn. Lieutenant Colonel Woods was moving 55th Australian Battalion into position ready to advance into Doignies when a dog alerted the Germans. So Captain Stutchbury's company moved quickly into the village and, while they took the garrison by surprise, many escaped.

It was dawn by the time 56th Australian Battalion attacked Louverval chateau and they approached from the front by mistake rather than from the flank. Lieutenant Colonel Scott's men came under machine gun fire and eight officers were hit as they struggled through the wood. But their men persevered and captured the chateau. Counter-attacks were stopped later in the day but the attack had cost over 400 casualties.

<u>1st Australian Division, Boursies and Hermies, 8 and 9 April</u>
Major General Harold Walker began with an advance from Louverval onto the high ground north of the road during the early hours of 8 April. Two companies of the 12th Australian Battalion were pinned down north of the road but Captain James Newland led some men along the road to Boursies mill. Meanwhile, two companies of the 10th Australian Battalion were spotted south of the road and while Captain McCann and many others were hit, Captain de Courcy-Ireland and the survivors were pinned down.

Early on 9 April 1st Australian Division renewed its advance along the Cambrai road but the company of the 12th Battalion was pinned down until Captain Newland's bombers charged Boursies mill. The Germans recaptured the position later that night but Newland was 'leading men here, urging men there, arranging for ammunition, directing reinforcements to

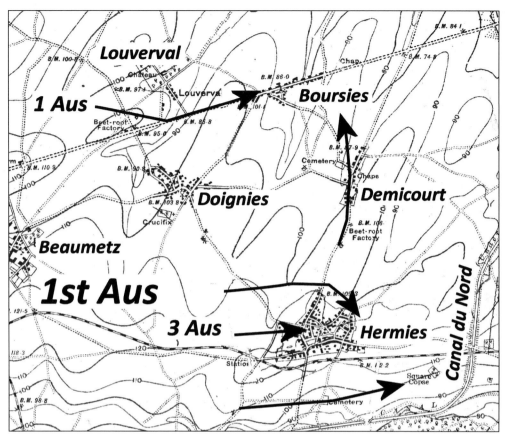

I Anzac Corps attack on Boursies and Hermies on 8 and 9 April.

weak spots and instilling confidence'. It was the first of many of Newland's deeds which would lead to him being awarded the Victoria Cross.

Lieutenant Colonel Milligan's 2nd Australian Battalion approached from the north-west, looking to close off the escape route from Hermies. A random flare set fire to a heap of straw, illuminating the advancing troops so Lieutenant Robins kept advancing while Lieutenant Mann led the charge into the east end of the village, finding the garrison sleeping in the cellars. Lieutenant Millar's company was pinned down facing the north-west corner of the village until Lieutenant Laver took the German position from the rear.

Lieutenant McMaster and Lieutenant MacDougal were hit leading 3rd Australian Battalion from the west but Corporal Ewart silenced a machine gun, allowing the rest of Lieutenant Colonel Moore's men to enter the village. To the east of the village, 2nd Australian Battalion established outposts to cut off the garrison's retreat. Private Bede Kenny rushed forward when a machine gun pinned down his platoon and he killed the officer and captured the crew. His actions closed off the Germans' escape route and

Hermies was in Australian hands along with over 200 prisoners by dawn. Kenny was awarded the Victoria Cross.

Brigadier General Lesslie was told that the Germans had abandoned Demicourt. Again the information was wrong and Lieutenant Colonel Stacy's 1st Australian Battalion came under machine gun fire as they approached. It took until noon to clear Demicourt and Boursies. By nightfall on 9 April the Germans were behind the Hindenburg Line all along Fifth Army's Line. It was now time to start planning how to break through the formidable obstacle.

Fourth Army

Fourth Army was pushing towards the Hindenburg Line but Rawlinson knew it was too weak to attack it. He was determined to capture the outpost villages but the advanced guards soon discovered that the Germans intended to delay the advance for as long as possible.

A mixed force of a 1/4th Oxfords company, two 18th Bengal Lancers squadrons and two armoured cars captured Roisel while the Canadian Cavalry Brigade took Equancourt on 26 March. They found hundreds of hungry civilians in the villages: 'their health was consequently very bad but their morale was excellent'. They were soon on the way to the rear in lorries and looking forward to a hot meal.

Armoured cars drew fire from weapons firing armour-piercing bullets as they drove towards Villers-Faucon the following day. But the 8th Hussars galloped around the flanks and sealed off the escape route, forcing the rearguard to surrender. The Canadian Cavalry Brigade used the same tactics against Saulcourt. There was also a race to secure the trench covering Guyencourt but Lieutenant Fred Harvey ran ahead of his men, vaulted over the wire, shot a machine gunner and captured his gun. Lord Strathcona's Horse were then able to clear the village. Harvey was awarded the Victoria Cross.

The advance was carried out in stages with XV Corps and III Corps advancing on 30 March on Fourth Army's left and centre. Then IV Corps pushed forward to the River Omignon on the right flank over the next two days. The advance resumed on the left and in the centre on 4 April with the right pushing forward the following day.

XV Corps, 30 March

<u>20th Division, Ruyaulcourt</u>

Sleet had blown into the faces of the 7th KOYLI as they advanced towards the north side of Ruyaulcourt after dusk on 28 March. The 7th DCLI had stumbled into a low wire entanglement hidden in the crops as they approached from the south and they had to withdraw after failing to cut through. The 12th King's had more success in Neuville-Bonjonval but they still took all night to clear the village. The following night the 7th Somersets found that Ruyaulcourt had been abandoned.

On 30 March, 59 Brigade occupied the high ground south-east of Neuville-Bonjonval. During the afternoon Captain Slade and Lieutenant West led the 11th Rifle Brigade towards Metz-en-Coutre under fire from Havrincourt Wood and they then had to endure shellfire as they dug in. Lieutenant Colonel Cotton asked for three minutes of artillery fire on the wood but the shells fell short. So Captain Slade silenced the machine gun himself with help from the 10th Rifle Brigade. Brigadier General Browne-Clayton instructed Colonel Cotton to check out Metz-en-Coutre the following night but his patrol was spotted as it moved across the snow-covered ground and it had to withdraw. The 10th Rifle Brigade was also unable to enter the village the following night.

8th Division, Heudicourt, 30 March

Major General Heneker ordered a night approach and a dawn attack. On the left, 2nd Berkshires rushed Fins while the 2nd Rifle Brigade and 1st Irish Rifles occupied Sorel. Heudicourt was surrounded on three sides by 23 Brigade but the garrison held out. Brigadier General Grogan then ordered an attack against Revelon with the field artillery and machine guns using observed fire controlled by light signals.

Snow delayed the early afternoon attack but the Rifle Brigade and Irish Rifles were pinned down by machine gun fire until Lieutenant Brown's Lewis gun team silenced it. Second Lieutenants Adams and Southall had been wounded so Lieutenant Colonel the Hon. Brand led the Rifle Brigade through Dessart Wood. Although Lieutenant Colonel Lloyd's Irish Rifles could clear the area to the south east, Lieutenant Colonel the Hon. Thynne could not advance far beyond Guyencourt and neither could XV Corps' cavalry patrols.

Lieutenant Colonel Hall's 2nd Middlesex entered Heudicourt from the west at 4.30pm while Lieutenant Colonel Sutherland's 2nd Devons approached from the south-east. Captain Clayton's company of the Middlesex then closed in on Revelon and met the Devons. The British correctly concluded that the Germans were concentrating their troops in villages while ignoring the ground around them. It made them easy targets for the gunners and simple for the infantry to surround.

III Corps, 30 March

48th Division, Epéhy, Ronssoy and Lempire

The British field artillery had not been warned about an attack against St

Emilie, so the 1/4th Gloucesters advanced without a barrage. All they had was Second Lieutenant Hall's machine gun firing from a sugar refinery on the flank. Lieutenant McCelland, Captain Hall and Lieutenant Gardiner were hit leading the advance and the German machine gun teams kept their men pinned down until the 200-strong garrison evacuated the village.

Major General Robert Fanshawe organised a surprise attack against Epéhy on 48th Division's front on 1 April. On the left, the 1/6th Warwicks advanced against the north side of the village as the 1/6th Gloucesters and 1/7th Worcesters moved through the south end. The village was easily cleared but the Germans were waiting for the Midland men along the railway line to the east.

IV Corps, 1 and 2 April
32nd Division, Savy, 1 April
The 11th Border Regiment and 17th HLI attacked Savy at dawn on 1 April but they faced a tough fight until the Germans withdrew. It then took time to move the field guns forward and it was 3 pm before two Lancashire Fusiliers battalions approached Savy Wood after a miserable two-mile slog through snow, hail and wind, under long-range machine gun fire. Lieutenant Colonel Harrison deployed the 15th Lancashire Fusiliers to cover the north-west side while Lieutenant Colonel Abercrombie led the 16th Lancashire Fusiliers though the wood. Meanwhile, the 2nd Inniskilling Fusiliers came under fire from Epine de Dallon on the right.

63rd Division, Holnon, 2 April
Major General Shute wanted to capture Holnon and Francilly-Sélency, east of Holnon Wood, but he had to wait until dawn on 2 April because the horses struggled to haul the field guns across the muddy fields. One commentator noted that Brigadier General Seymour's instructions had a vital flaw: 'It was explained that the villages could be distinguished by the fact that one possessed a spire and the other a tower, but as neither village was more than about eight feet high, this information was not of much assistance in finding our objectives.'

The 1st Dorsets, the 2nd Manchesters and the 15th HLI moved north at 5 am and they cleared the two villages in less than an hour. The Manchesters had two notable successes. Second Lieutenant Taylor captured six machine gun teams in a quarry, while a wounded Captain Glover captured a battery of six field guns after it had fired at his men over open sights.

The following night Major Fred Lumsden, Lieutenant Ward and Lieutenant Trappes-Lomax led an artillery party forward to rescue the German guns. The horse teams were in the middle of limbering up when a group of Germans rushed the infantry guards and blew out the breach of one gun. They were driven off and the gunners eventually rescued all the guns, including the damaged one; Lumsden was awarded the Victoria Cross.

The attack allowed 32nd Division to contact 61st Division on the far side of Holnon Wood, only the advance had taken too long and the Germans had already left. Early the following morning, 61st Division's left pushed forward to Bihecourt and Maissémy on the River Omignon.

XV Corps, 4 April
20th Division, Metz-en-Coutre
Heavy snow interfered with the artillery bombardment so Brigadier General Browne-Clayton's attack on Metz-en-Coutre was delayed until 4 pm on 4 April. The barrage was split into two parts, with half the guns following a fixed programme while the rest responded to signals. The Germans were taken by surprise and white flares told the gunners when to extend their range so the infantry could move quickly through the village.

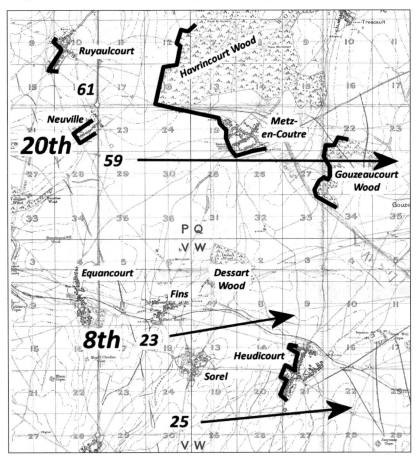

XV Corps capture of Metz-en-Coutre and Gouzeaucourt Wood on 4 April.

The KRRC trudged through the slush and mud towards Metz-en-Coutre. Lieutenant Colonel Priaulx's 11th KRRC cleared the village but Lieutenant Colonel Ley's 10th KRRC lost many men, including Captain Egerton Leigh, moving across the fields to the south-east. Lieutenant Colonels Troughton and Cotton then coordinated an attack to capture a trench north-west of the village. The 10th Rifle Brigade were hit by machine gun fire from Havrincourt Wood until a patrol silenced the weapon. Meanwhile, Captain the Hon. Bertie led the 11th Rifle Brigade to the objective, which would become known as Green Jacket Ridge.

8th Division, Gouzeaucourt Wood
Brigadier General Coffin's men advanced towards Gouzeaucourt Wood at 2 pm on 4 April, delayed by the same snow storm. The 2nd Rifle Brigade cut through the wire on the south-west edge but the 2nd Berkshires were pinned down negotiating the wire on the north-west edge. Lieutenant Colonel Haig spotted the Germans assembling to counter-attack, so he called upon the 2nd Lincolns to reinforce his men and they held their positions. The wood was evacuated when it was clear Metz had been taken, allowing Captain Cahill's company to occupy the north end.

III Corps, 5 April
48th Division, Ronssoy and Lempire
There was another surprise attack by 48th Division against the twin villages of Ronssoy and Lempire on 5 April. This time the Germans were expecting the 1/5th Gloucesters, 1/4th Ox and Bucks and 1/4th Berkshires and artillery fire hit their assembly area. The advance began at 4.55 am and it took time to clear the houses one by one, with the infantry signalling the artillery when they needed it. Ronssoy was the last of the villages in the Somme Department to be cleared by British troops in the spring of 1917.

IV Corps, 5 April
59th Division, Fresnoy-le-Petit
Major General Colin Mackenzie had planned to attack Fresnoy-le-Petit at 10 pm on 5 April. Patrols reported it had been evacuated so the bombardment was called off. However, the two companies sent to occupy the village found it was occupied and were unable to dislodge the garrison. The Gloucester and Worcester men made another attack the following night, this time supported by artillery, but they failed to break through the wire in the centre of the village. A simultaneous attack on the north bank of the Omignon was also stopped by wire. A third attempt to clear Fresnoy succeeded on the night of 7 April. Two days later 61st Division was able to

advance astride the Omignon stream, forcing the Germans to evacuate le Verguier, allowing 59th Division to enter it.

Fourth Army Summary

Fourth Army had now closed up to the Hindenburg Line and Rawlinson was able to instruct his artillery to shell it as Third and First Armies attacked to the north. But there were still many problems to solve because the Germans had caused considerable damage to the road network behind his front. The morale of the troops had risen as they advanced across open country after months of huddling in wet, muddy trenches. They had been quick to use the tactics of open warfare but they sometimes reverted to their old ways:

> *The maintenance of forward movement depends on the determination and power of direction of sections, platoons, companies and battalions. The habit of digging a trench and getting into it, or waiting for scientifically arranged artillery barrages before advancing, must be discarded. A slow advance will give time for the German reinforcements to arrive – the greater the rapidity of an advance the more is resistance likely to lessen. A few sticky company commanders may not only delay the whole operation but will also cause unnecessary casualties by giving the enemy time to reinforce.*

But once again the British and Australian infantry had to dig, this time in front of the Hindenburg Line. The men suffered as they tried to find shelter from the bad weather but the animals suffered more as they carried their heavy loads with only reduced rations to eat.

Chapter 7

Artillery Conquered and Infantry Occupied
Planning the Offensive

First Army's Infantry Plan

First Army's objective was to capture the huge escarpment north of Arras; the formidable Vimy Ridge. It ran north-west to south-west for over four miles and the Germans held the summit. The slope behind the British and Canadian line fell gently west and south-west towards the River Scarpe. But the ground behind the German line fell quickly around 75 metres down to the Douai plain below.

Taking the ridge was no easy task because the Germans had held it since October 1914. The French had failed to capture the summit in the spring and autumn of 1915 and their two offensives cost over 150,000 casualties. A German counter-attack in May 1916 recaptured a lot of the lost ground and the ridge then became a mining area as tunnellers fought to gain control underground.

The German line ran from Notre Dame de Lorette south-east to Ecurie and was based around a network of caves which had been connected by tunnels dug under the trenches. The artillery batteries were protected by concrete casemates below the crest where they were hard to hit.

Haig's memorandum on 17 November 1916 had instructed First Army to 'prepare an attack on the Vimy position, to secure observation over the Douai plain and assist the advance of the Third Army on its right'. General Sir Henry Horne received definite orders on 2 January 1917 and he in turn submitted his plan of operations on the last day of the month.

Lieutenant General the Hon. Sir Julian Byng's Canadian Corps would advance between Givenchy-en-Gohelle and Ecurie to clear the summit of Vimy Ridge. A later attack would capture Hill 120 (known as the Pimple) at the north end of the ridge while Lieutenant General Arthur Holland's I Corps cleared Bois en Hache at the east end of the Lorette ridge.

The reorganisation of First Army's front began when I Corps took over the Canadian Corps' left flank at the beginning of March. The arrival of

24th Division on the Souchez stream allowed 1st and 2nd Canadian Divisions to move to the south end of Vimy Ridge, so the four Canadian divisions were side-by-side, in numerical order from right to left. Byng had also been given the 5th British Division and while one brigade was attached to the 2nd Canadian Division, the rest was held in corps' reserve.

Byng gave Horne the Canadian Corps 'Scheme of Operations' on 5 March. They soon learnt that the bombardment would begin on 20 March with the offensive opening on 8 April. Byng added the dates to his plan and Horne confirmed First Army's order of battle on 26 March.

The Canadian Corps had held Vimy Ridge for six months. Aerial observers had photographed the trenches so accurate maps could be drawn, and raids had taken prisoners to glean more information. A model of the ridge was built at First Army headquarters so it could be studied by officers and non-commissioned officers alike. They in turn could pass on what they had learnt to their men during lectures and practice attacks.

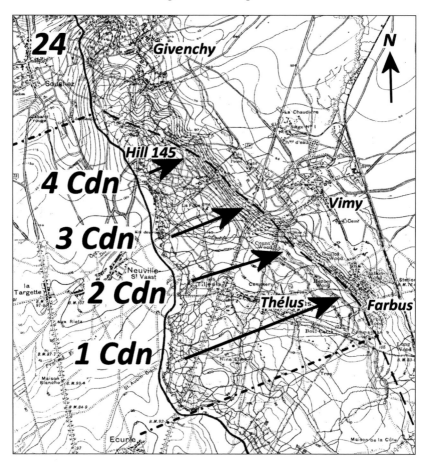

First Army's plan to capture Vimy Ridge on 9 April.

Each division had to advance a different distance with 4th Canadian Division moving less than half a mile on the left while 1st Canadian Division had to go five times that distance on the right. All four divisions would advance 750 yards, while clearing three trenches, in just thirty-five minutes, and then there would be a pause on the Black Line for forty minutes. The 4th and 3rd Canadian Divisions would then move to the Red Line, their final objective beyond the crest of the ridge.

Meanwhile, 2nd and 1st Canadian Divisions would advance 400 yards to the *Zwischen Stellung*, or Intermediate Position, also code-named the Red Line. The advance to Blue Line involved clearing Thélus, Hill 135, Bois de Bonval and the Count's Wood. A British brigade would join 2nd Canadian Division's left, completing the third part of the advance after 5 hours and 20 minutes.

Both divisions would reach their final objective at 7 hours and 48 minutes after zero hour. The Brown Line covered the German Second Position which ran through Farbus Wood, the Bois de la Ville and the south part of the Bois de Bonval. All four Canadian divisions would end their advance along the German position below the summit of Vimy Ridge.

Third Army's Infantry Plan
Third Army planned to advance east of Arras with ten divisions. Both XVII and VI Corps had to advance 600 yards to the Black Line astride the River Scarpe in 36 minutes and then halt for 84 minutes. On the right, VII Corps would wait because it already held on the Black Line, following the recent short withdrawal to the Hindenburg Line. The three corps would take around sixty minutes to move another 1,000 yards to the Blue Line. They would then wait for 3 hours and 40 minutes while the field artillery moved forward to cut the wire in front of the Brown Line. Third Army would then advance another 1,500 yards to the Point du Jour Line north of the Scarpe and the Feuchy–Wancourt Lines south of the river. They would reach what was code-named the Brown Line eight hours after zero hour.

Three reserve divisions were poised to pass through the assault divisions and advance to the Green Line another 3,500 yards to the east. It was the first time the BEF had tried to 'leapfrog' divisions during a battle. They would seize Fampoux, Monchy-le-Preux and Guémappe, increasing Third Army's advance to 4½ miles. The three divisions of the Cavalry Corps were waiting to move beyond the Green Line as soon as the infantry cleared it. Lieutenant Colonel Pretor-Pinney summed up the urgency of the advance with the following words to the men of the 13th Rifle Brigade: 'Gentlemen, we will take Monchy or die!'

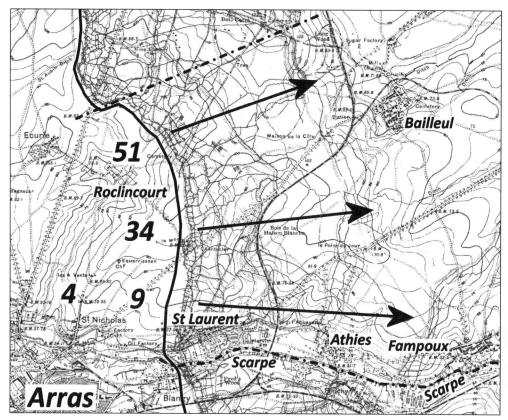

XVII Corps planned advance north of the River Scarpe on 9 April.

First Army's Artillery Plan

General Horne tabled his artillery plan on 8 February. He wanted improved coordination between field artillery and the machine guns, and closer liaison between the heavy artillery and the infantry divisions. Observers were instructed to forward their reports as fast as possible so they could be acted on quickly.

The Canadian Corps' mantra was, the 'artillery conquered and the infantry occupied'. First Army had been reinforced with artillery and while I Corps had 132 heavy guns and howitzers, the Canadian Corps had 245. There were 102 field guns and howitzers with I Corps while the Canadian Corps had another 618. First Army had spent three months stockpiling over 42,500 tons of ammunition and the plan was to deliver another 2,500 tons a day during the battle.

First Army and Canadian Corps intelligence units catalogued and assessed targets so they could be bombarded in turn. The list included strongpoints, roads, light railways and ammunition dumps. It was recognised that the field artillery could not destroy the entanglements covering the Blue Line and Brown Line, so medium howitzers where tasked with creating gaps using shells armed with 106 fuses which exploded on contact with the ground. Horne had emphasised the need for effective counter-battery work, and aerial photography had located around 85 per cent of the 212 batteries facing First Army. Isolated batteries were silenced first and groups of batteries were then hit with high explosive and gas shells.

Half of First Army's artillery started shelling targets on 20 March while the rest remained silent and hidden. The rest joined in on 2 April, starting what the Germans called the 'week of suffering'. One Canadian observer said that the shells were pouring 'over our heads like water from a hose, thousands and thousands a day'. Nine camouflaged field batteries remained silent on the Canadian Corps' right until the 9 April. They had been deployed close to the front line, ready to cover the final stages of 2nd and 1st Canadian Divisions' advance on the right.

Villages and tracks were shelled and the RFC's observers could see where the men walked during the night because they left footprints in the snow. The Canadian Machine Gun Corps fired overhead barrages during the hours of darkness, forcing the Germans to use the communication trenches. Ration parties often took so long to get to the front line that the food was cold or spoiled. Morale fell even further when the trench mortars joined in; the large calibres hit the trenches while the rest destroyed the wire.

Over one million rounds would be fired at Vimy Ridge; a total weight of 50,000 tons of ammunition. The combination of shelling and rain turned the German trenches into a muddy moonscape of water-filled shell holes. The infantry dared not go into the open during the day; they stayed in their dugouts as trenches collapsed and filled with mud and water. They often struggled to carry out repairs during the night.

The Canadians carried out several nights of raids before the attack. The largest was made against Hill 120 on 31 March, involving 600 men of the 10 Canadian Brigade. A soldier returned with a document entitled 'Experience of the Recent Fighting at Verdun' which advocated a mobile defence within a deep fortified zone. It suggested building strongpoints and machine gun posts to break up the British and Canadian attacks. A counter-attack could then drive the disorganised advancing troops back once they were low on ammunition. It was a successful tactic but there had not been time to build enough strongpoints on Vimy Ridge to make it work.

One fact noted in the raids was that the Germans, like the Canadians, had relied on their tunnels and deep dugouts to protect the infantry during the bombardment. Most of the entrances were in the first system of trenches so Byng decided to do away with the usual intensive bombardment before zero hour. He did not want to the Germans to know when zero hour was. His plan was for the Canadians to advance quickly, posting guards at the dugout entrances, trapping as many as possible underground.

Third Army's Artillery Plan

General Allenby had wanted a surprise attack preceded by a forty-eight-hour hurricane bombardment followed by a rapid advance. The batteries would fire as fast as possible with one in three resting at any one time so the gunners could rest.

Haig made it clear he was against Allenby's idea on 12 February. He doubted the trench mortars could cut the wire or that the heavy artillery could silence enough German batteries in such a short time. He also believed the short bombardment would not reduce German morale sufficiently. Finally he thought that the intense rate of fire would wear out the gunners and their guns alike.

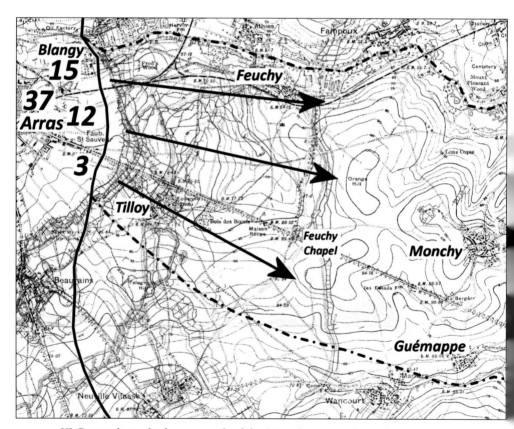

VI Corps planned advance south of the River Scarpe on 9 April.

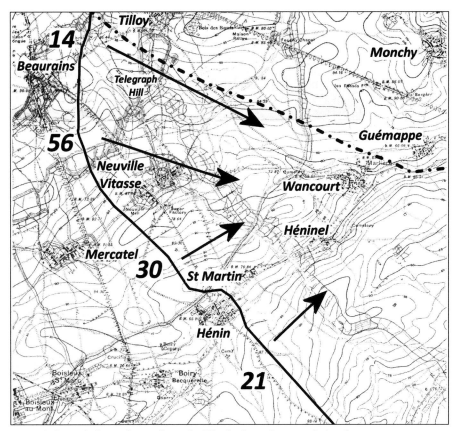

VII Corps' planned attack on the Hindenburg Line on 9 April.

Allenby was not giving up on his plan and he carried out practice barrages which proved it neither damaged the guns nor exhausted their crews. They proved that nearly half the wire could be cut in two days. He also suggested that the enemy's morale would be at its lowest after forty-eight hours of intense shelling; any longer and the men became desensitised to it. He also argued that a prolonged bombardment gave the German high command time to move up reserves and relieve demoralised units.

GHQ's Chief of Artillery, Major General Noel Birch, disagreed with Allenby. While it might be possible to cut a wire entanglement under test conditions, it took longer to observe the ongoing damage and repair process in no man's land. He was also concerned that many of the heavy artillery batteries had inexperienced crews who were going to be in their first large-scale offensive. They would need more time to destroy their targets than experienced gunners. Birch was also aware that the field artillery had insufficient stocks of shells armed with the 106 impact fuses which were ideal for destroying the wire. Most of the batteries would have to fire shells armed with time delay fuses, and the most experienced of crews found it difficult to hit distant targets with them.

Third Army's new artillery commander, Major General Robert Lecky, agreed with Birch so Allenby had to concede. The artillery plan would be extended to six days to give time to destroy the wire. The heavy artillery would also rely more on map fire, hammering enemy batteries until they had been destroyed.

Third Army had 1,134 field guns and 586 heavy howitzers and guns; an artillery piece for every 12 yards on its 12-mile front. They were divided as follows:

858 18-pounders	276 4.5-inch howitzers
144 60-pounders	220 6-inch howitzers
24 6-inch guns	84 8-inch howitzers
94 9.2-inch howitzers and guns	15 12-inch howitzers and guns
5 15-inch howitzers	

The Engineers

One important lesson learnt during the Somme campaign was that an army had to keep its logistics in good order. This involved dozens of tasks which the Royal Engineers had to organise. Everything from roads and railways, communications and water supplies, to ammunition dumps and medical facilities had to be built and maintained.

Haig, after issuing instructions to his army commanders following the Chantilly Inter-Allied military conference at the beginning of December 1916, then gave the army's chief engineers a list of tasks they had to complete. The Royal Engineers and the Royal Canadian Engineers supervised dozens of major building projects in the weeks before the offensive. Existing roads had to be kept open and that involved stockpiling hundreds of tons of stone and timber while another five miles of road had to be built. Horses had to haul hundreds of wagons to the dumps so they could be unloaded and return before dawn. Every day labourers repaired the roads in a constant battle with the cycle of frost, thaw and rain.

Every night the light railway companies alone delivered 830 tons of supplies across the tramways. Opposite Third Army, Major General Kenyon wanted to lay 50 miles of light railway and have another 50 miles ready to link to the German system.

Battery positions had to be built and many of them needed timber bases to stop the guns and shells sinking into the mud. The engineers also had to erect dozens of portable bridges so the field artillery could cross the trenches once the advance had begun. Most of the villages around Arras were in ruins and it took an enormous effort to find or build enough accommodation for the 100,000 men of Third Army. There was also a need for hundreds of depots, medical units, repair shops and maintenance facilities. Hundreds of storage facilities had to be built to hold all the food, ammunition and equipment. Miles of pipeline had to be laid so that water could be pumped to storage ponds for the men and the animals to drink.

The Underground War

British tunnellers had spent the summer of 1916 winning the battle under Vimy Ridge. The Royal Canadian Engineers had taken over the sector towards the end of the year and First Army's Controller of Mines, Lieutenant Colonel Williams, immediately started to plan the work.

The 172nd, 176th, 182nd and 185th Tunnelling Companies began digging or extending fourteen tunnels ranging from 250 metres to 1,700 metres long. There was Coburg, Gobrun, Blue Bull, Vincent, Tottenham, Cavalier, Grange, Goodman, Lichfield, Zivy, Bentala, Douai, Barricade and Souchez Tunnels. Not all would be used during the attack but they all had rooms equipped as headquarters, dressing stations and stores. They also had

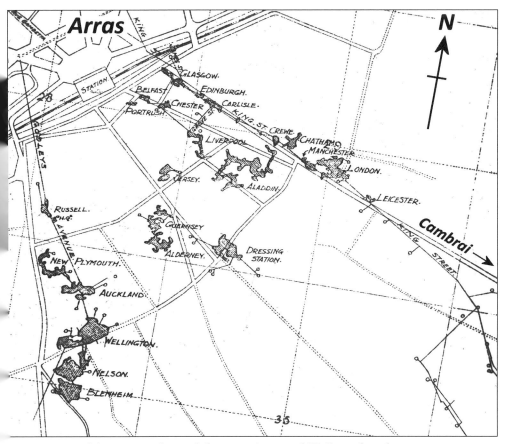

Map of the caves and tunnels between Arras and VI Corps front line.

electricity, water and telephones and some even had tramways. The tunnels would be used to protect the men during artillery bombardments and Zivy Cave, east of Neuville St Vaast, had enough room to house an entire battalion.

Third Army made use of the tunnels the people of Arras had dug in the chalk beneath their city over the centuries. Large cellars beneath Grande and Petite Places were cleared out so that 13,000 men could live underground. Caves were connected so they could house another 11,500 men. They were joined together by the Crinchon sewer which ran around the city. The Saint Sauveur tunnel connected the caves under the Cambrai road and ended in five exits in 3rd Division's line near Tilloy-lèz-Mofflaines. The Ronville tunnel joined the caves under the Bapaume road and ended in exits under the original British line near Beaurains. Between them they could provide underground accommodation for 24,500 men.

Most of the extra digging was carried out by the New Zealand Tunnelling Company. The engineers then installed lighting, water, beds and toilets. Many men would spend the week before the battle waiting in the underground 'boves' for zero hour. It was a surreal world which was 'damp, smelly, gritty and unhealthy'. But life went on:

8 April, Easter Day. The eve of the battle… We had Holy Communion this morning in the cellar which we use as a mess. The altar was built of ammunition boxes covered with sand bags. The candlesticks were whisky bottles and outside the endless roar of the bombardment.

The Tanks

The tunnelling war under Vimy Ridge had left a string of craters in no man's land, making most of First Army's front unsuitable for tanks. Allenby had only been given eight and Byng had given them to the 2nd Canadian Division. Major General Henry Burstall suspected they would get bogged down, so neither the infantry nor the artillery plans made many provisions for them.

Meanwhile, Third Army had been given forty tanks of 1 Brigade of the Heavy Branch, Machine Gun Corps (renamed the Tank Corps in July 1917). Eight tanks were allocated to XVII Corps and sixteen each to VI and VII Corps. Colonel Baker-Carr had instructions to let his tanks follow the infantry through the first trench system. They would catch up on the Black Line and join the advance to the Blue Line. They were expected to cut the wire beyond the range of the field artillery as well as help the infantry deal with strongpoints.

The tanks would meet at rallying points and four tanks would then leave VII Corps for VI Corps. If all went well eighteen tanks would advance to Chapel Hill and then turn north and south to clear the Brown Line. The surviving tanks would then move towards Monchy-le-Preux and the Green Line beyond. It was a tall order for Colonel Baker-Carr's crews and they would have to depend on their maintenance teams to bring supplies to them.

The Royal Flying Corps

The Royal Flying Corps' tasks fell into three broad categories. Ninth Wing had seven squadrons of scout planes and fighters to drive the German pilots from the skies above First and Third Armies. The air offensive began on 5 April but the German planes were often superior and many British pilots were shot down.

No 8 (Naval) and No 40 Squadrons attacked observation balloons and fought the German planes flying over First Army's front. Meanwhile, No 2 and No 16 Squadrons had been observing and taking aerial photographs of the trenches on Vimy Ridge for weeks. Nos 25 and 43 Squadrons were busy carrying out long and medium range reconnaissance missions but they also had to protect the planes flying short-range reconnaissance missions. No 1 Kite Balloon Squadron also kept a close watch on the German positions on Vimy Ridge.

Twelfth Wing was detailed to carry out reconnaissance and photography missions up to the Brown Line on Third Army's front. A squadron had been allocated to each corps and the pilots made short-range reconnaissance missions, cooperated with the artillery, and took photographs of the results. They would also report on the infantry's progress during the advance. Thirteenth Wing deployed five squadrons and some would carry out long-range reconnaissance and photography missions beyond the Brown Line. Others would keep enemy planes away from the reconnaissance patrol planes. Some would attack observation balloons while others would carry out night bombing raids deep into enemy territory; No 100 Squadron was detailed to carry out night raids. There was also a company of observation balloons and each corps had two balloons.

Communications

The Somme campaign had proved that reliable and robust communications were essential. Around 1,500 miles of underground cables and 1,100 miles of overhead lines had been installed to make sure everyone could keep in contact. Underground cables were used when possible because they were better protected than overhead ones. Many were installed in tunnels under Vimy Ridge where they were safe from artillery fire and traffic. All of First

Army and most of Third Army were holding well-established positions and each corps had several cable routes connected to the infantry and artillery brigades. Each division also had connections to the battalions and batteries.

It was easy to see across the flat, open slope so the forward artillery observers could signal directly to their batteries by day and by night. Five receiving stations had also been set up to receive messages from the front. The German withdrawal to the Hindenburg Line on VII Corps' front required new overhead lines for 30th and 21st Divisions. They would have to communicate with power buzzers which used ground induction to send messages to amplifiers. Each division also received two trench wireless sets to help them out.

The Bombardment

The bombardment began at 6.30 am on 4 April, code-named V Day, and fifteen minutes later gas was released all across XVII and VI Corps' sectors. The following day Nivelle told Haig that the Aisne attack was going to be delayed by forty-eight hours.

The creeping barrage was practised for the first time on 6 April, X Day, so the gunners could get used to the timetable; it was also hoped it would confuse the Germans. The assault was supposed to begin on 8 April, Z Day, but the poor visibility meant it had been difficult to cut the wire. So Haig took advantage of the French delay to add an extra day to the British bombardment.

During daylight hours, all but the largest calibres of artillery fired extended destructive barrages. The heavy guns only fired short, irregular salvoes, to increase the harassment to the enemy. Frequent pauses were held to allow the aerial spotters to fly over, inspect the damage and take photographs. The German rear areas had been divided into small zones and each one had a definite target. It was a simple innovation which speeded up the reporting process (compared to using map references) and it also improved security. It meant that each battery was always aiming at a specific target.

Batteries of 2-inch trench mortars concentrated on the wire in no man's land while the 18-pounders fired at the rest of the wire in front of the Black Line. A combination of 18-pounders, 4.5-inch and 6-inch howitzers hit the second and third trench systems. The 60-pounders targeted nearby billets, communication trenches, light railways and tracks. The 6-inch guns shelled distant billets, communication centres, ammunition depots, railheads and potential headquarters. The 8-inch, 9.2-inch and 12-inch howitzers targeted the enemy batteries and distant trenches. Some 12-inch batteries tried to destroy strongpoints while the huge 15-inch howitzers aimed at distant villages and bridges. All the heavy and siege artillery turned their attentions to counter-battery work the day before the attack. The field guns fired short, intense barrages against the wire and the trenches during the night, trying to catch repair teams and carrying parties working in the open. Heavier guns fired at the roads and villages, aiming to hit transport columns and relieving troops. Harassing fire was fired in two zones to try to catch troops moving in the open. The 18-pounders and 4.5-inch howitzers hit the inner zone while the 60-pounders and 6-inch howitzers shelled the outer zone. At dusk on 8 April, the 4.5-inch howitzers and 60-pounders switched to firing gas shells at the enemy batteries, command posts, communication centres and dugouts. They switched to tear gas shells just before zero hour.

The Assembly
Tens of thousands of soldiers left their billets late on 8 April, under bright moonlight, and marched around three miles to their assembly positions. Many would have remembered it was Easter Sunday but there had not been time to attend church. The sky soon became covered in clouds, and snow filled the air as men followed the lines of stakes covered in luminous paint which marked the tracks through the battery positions. Some deployed in shallow trenches while others lay down in and around the many craters in no man's land. Many of the support troops would wait in the tunnels, gathered in underground chambers as the gunfire rumbled overhead.

Openings had been made in the wire on Vimy Ridge so the Canadian soldiers could file through. Patrols reported plenty of gaps in the German entanglements. By 4 am 30,000 men had deployed on a 4-mile front and half of them were only 100 yards from the German lines. So far the alarm had not been raised but they had to lie in the mud for ninety nerve-racking minutes as the snow continued to fall.

Allenby's staff had organised the movement of ten divisions along Third Army's eleven-mile front. A lot of lessons had been learnt about staff work during the battle of the Somme and arrangements were now much smoother and more efficient. The men were also self-assured thanks to their rigorous training and 51st Division's schedule was typical. They had been walking back and forth across a full-scale taped-out course to learn what they had to do. Men carrying signal flags and pipers represented the barrage while drummers represented the enemy machine guns. Major General George Harper emphasised the following key points:

1. Use envelopment; hold the enemy front and attack their flank
2. Maximum use of mechanical weapons and the minimum use of infantry

3. Troops had to advance in depth

4. A leader without personality will achieve nothing

He was determined that his men would fight 'with their wits and not by a mere display of seeing red and brute courage'.

The Final Moments

German signal centres were targeted during the final phase of the preliminary bombardment and most of their telephone lines were destroyed before zero hour, leaving the front line troops reliant on runners to get their messages through. The guns on Third Army's front lengthened their range beyond the Black Line area ninety minutes before zero to confuse the Germans. Thirty minutes before zero the guns switched back to their original targets while the heavy howitzers re-registered their targets.

The gunners behind First Army's front slackened their rate of fire as zero hour approached, rather than increasing it as was customary. Then at 5.30 am every battery on First Army's front fired three minutes of rapid fire, hammering the first German trench with shrapnel and high explosive. Smoke was used but there was no gas because of an unfavourable wind. Two mines were detonated near Hill 145 and rockets were fired into the sky above Vimy Ridge, calling for help from the artillery. Little came because the heavy artillery was firing on the enemy batteries while the medium heavy artillery was hitting observation posts and communications. The German batteries had to fire their SOS barrages blindly into the snow-filled sky.

The Canadian guns fired two rounds a minute as they lengthened their range by 100 yards every three minutes. Machine guns fired 400 yards ahead of the advance to catch any reserves moving forward or anyone retreating. Meanwhile, the German artillery batteries were targeted by gas shells, so the horses could not haul the guns to safety.

On Third Army's front, the 18-pounder batteries fired salvoes of shrapnel to warn the infantry the barrage was about to creep forward. They then switched to firing 50 per cent shrapnel and 50 per cent high explosive, lengthening their range by 100 yards every four minutes, with each gun firing two rounds a minute. The 4.5-inch howitzers and 6-inch howitzers continued to shell the support trench until the creeping barrage reached it.

The night before the attack, Haig had told Robertson that he had never seen his subordinate commanders so satisfied with the preparations. Everyone was optimistic for the attack. The artillery had prepared the ground, now it was time for the infantry to seize it and hold it.

Chapter 8

Advancing as if on Parade
First Army – 9 April

Canadian Corps, 9 April

As the barrage intensified at zero hour, the first of many waves of Canadian troops advanced towards the German front trenches even before the guns extended their range. It was difficult to see where they were going across the muddy moonscape. But the wind was blowing snow in a north-east direction across the ridge which virtually blinded the German lookouts until the Canadians were on top of them. In many cases it was too late to warn their comrades hiding in the dugouts.

<u>4th Canadian Division, Hill 145</u>

Major General David Watson's men had the shortest distance to travel but they also faced the highest point on Vimy Ridge, Hill 145. They had dug their assembly trenches close to the German line while six shallow tunnels (called Russian saps) had been dug under no man's land ready to be opened up into communication trenches.

On the division's left, 12 Canadian Brigade had to link up with I Corps. Smoke screened the advancing troops from the Pimple. Two mines were detonated under the German trench, killing most of the German garrison, and the rest ran when they saw the Canadians coming towards them through the snow. The 73rd Battalion captured the first trench in only seven minutes and they then occupied a communication trench, contacting troops from 24th Division in Gunner and Kennedy Craters.

In the centre, 72nd Battalion overran the first trench but they then lost the barrage and were pinned down. Bombers worked around the flank and cleared the second trench, allowing some men to reach the third trench. But the smoke was clearing and the sky was brightening, allowing the German machine gun teams on the Pimple to stop the rest reaching the final objective.

The 38th Battalion cleared the first trench on the right but they were delayed negotiating the crater field beyond, giving the Germans time to exit their dugouts. Captain MacDowell and Privates Kobus and Hay silenced one machine gun nest and chased the crew away. They then found a dugout full of men and MacDowell bluffed them into thinking he had a large group of men with him. Two officers and seventy-five other ranks climbed out to discover they had been tricked. One German prisoner grabbed a rifle only to be shot as the weapon was wrestled from him. MacDowell was awarded the Victoria Cross for his exploits.

The smoke started to clear as 78th Battalion passed through 38th Battalion and while the first wave was hit by machine gun fire from Hill 145 on the right flank, a few made it to the second trench. The support companies were approaching Givenchy-en-Gohelle when a counter-attack overwhelmed them but the Lewis gun teams stopped the Germans breaking through. Brigadier General MacBrien was able to report that the crest was secure but he could not reach the final objective until Hill 145 had been captured on his right.

In 11 Canadian Brigade's sector, 87th Battalion's left came under fire as they emerged from Tottenham Tunnel. The artillery had destroyed a strongpoint but the Germans had rebuilt it. The artillery commander wanted

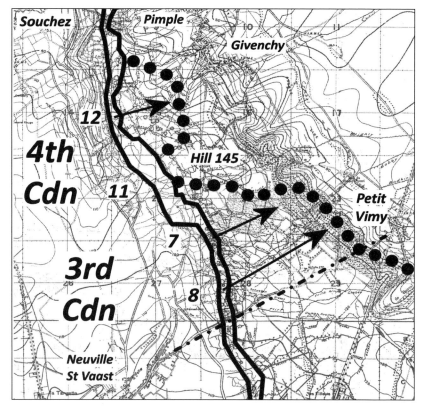

As 4th Canadian Division struggled to capture Hill 145, 3rd Canadian Division advanced to its objective.

to destroy it again but the infantry commander refused because he intended to use it as a defensive position. It was a mistake and many Canadians were cut down by machine gun fire in front of the wire. Meanwhile, 102nd Battalion crossed the smashed wire, surprised the Germans in their dugouts and advanced to the summit.

The support battalions were moving up and 75th Battalion carried some of 87th Battalion forward towards the crest but the rest fell back in the face of fierce machine gun fire. Some came under fire from the German held area on their flank and then from the rear as men emerged from dugouts. It meant 75th Battalion's right company struggled to leave its assembly trenches, giving the Germans time to man their second trench. Brigadier General Odlum heard that his left had been pinned down and 54th Battalion had to withdraw when its exposed flank came under attack. But 102nd Battalion was on objective, preventing the artillery from shelling the trench again. It would be cleared by 87th Battalion's bombers during the early afternoon.

A plan was put together to seize the west side of the summit and 46th and 47th Battalions were sent forward to reinforce the position. Brigadier General Odlum cancelled 11 Canadian Brigade's ten-minute bombardment but left it too late to tell the infantry. The Germans were as surprised as the Canadians by the lack of artillery fire when the advance began at 6.45 pm. Two companies of the 46th Battalion captured craters along the Souchez road on the left and then approached the summit of Hill 145 from the west. To the south, 85th Battalion had emerged from two tunnels to clear the craters around Bois Carré before heading up the east slope. The loss of Hill 145 significantly reduced the amount of accurate German artillery fire across the north end of Vimy Ridge.

3rd Canadian Division, Bois de la Folie

Major General Louis Lipsett's division had to advance from the trenches north-east of Neuville St Vaast and through a wooded area on the south side of Hill 145. Many troops had assembled underground and they climbed the steps out of Grange and Goodman tunnels into the front trench before heading across no man's land. In 7 Canadian Brigade's sector, the 42nd Battalion, the Princess Patricia's Canadian Light Infantry (PPCLI) and the Royal Canadian Regiment overran the garrison of the first trench only to come under fire as they moved past the École Commune. The bombardment had obliterated many landmarks, troops sometimes became disorientated in the snow and smoke, and some ran into their own barrage.

The Black Line was taken by 6.25 am and the west edge of Bois de la Folie was reached an hour later. Lewis gunners and patrols led 7 Brigade down the wooded slope only to come under fire from snipers and machine gun teams hidden in the undergrowth. On the left a 42nd Battalion patrol found no one guarding a track down the slope but they could not exploit it because 4th Canadian Division was struggling to clear Hill 145. A defensive flank had to be established back to the original front line and the PPCLI took over part of their line. The only counter-attack against 7 Brigade's right was stopped by the Royal Canadian Regiment and Brigadier General Macdonell was able to report that his troops were consolidating a line through Bois de la Folie.

It was a similar story in 8 Canadian Brigade's sector where the 4th, 2nd, and 1st Canadian Mounted Rifles (CMR) advanced quickly across the ridge. In the centre, the 2nd CMR trapped 150 Saxons in Schwaben Tunnel and then overran the ruins of La Folie Farm. On the right, teams from the 8th Machine Gun Company inflicted many casualties as they led the 1st CMR across the ridge. One team shot at the staff of a battalion headquarters as they tried to escape along a muddy communication trench towards Bois de Bonval. They then stopped a group of Germans assembling to counter-attack. Many troops missed the battered third trench in the swirling snow and smoke.

Bois de la Folie was reached and again the Canadians descended the escarpment. A counter-attack against the 4th CMR was stopped on the left flank while troops from 2nd Division drifted into the path of the 1st CMR on the right. But Brigadier General Elmsley was soon able to report that his men were digging in close to the edge of the wood, overlooking Petit Vimy.

2nd Canadian Division, Thélus

Major General Burstall had been allocated eight tanks but he suspected they would struggle to cross the muddy battlefield. The plan was to advance north-east, through Thélus village and across Hill 135, to Bois de Bonval on the far side of the ridge.

On the left, 26th and 24th Battalions followed the creeping barrage and they found most of the Germans hiding in their dugouts. On the right, 19th Battalion overran the enemy trenches but 18th Battalion came under fire from two machine guns in Zwischen Stellung. Lance Sergeant Ellis Sifton bayoneted one team and then prevented the Germans re-entering the trench until his comrades arrived. Sifton was killed but he was posthumously awarded the Victoria Cross. As the advance continued, aeroplanes flew low sounding their klaxon horns to warn the infantry below to signal their progress. The men on the ground tried to signal back to them.

All four battalions were hit by machine gun fire from the Zwischen Stellung and the Canadian soldiers looked for the tanks to help them. They were to be disappointed because they had all become bogged down as Burstall had expected. It would be down to the support battalions to continue the advance alone.

In 5 Canadian Brigade's sector, 25th Battalion crossed the Lens road only to find two field guns and eight machine guns defending Turko Graben; 22nd Battalion mopped up, capturing nearly 400 prisoners. In 4 Canadian Brigade's sector, 21st Battalion silenced two machine guns in Les Tilleuls. It also discovered a large cave called the *Felsenkeller* and the staff of two battalion headquarters hiding inside.

On 2nd Division's left, 13 British Brigade (from the 5th Division) had moved up to cover the gap developing next to 3rd Canadian Division (the two divisions were moving away from each other). The 2nd KOSBs and the 1st Queen's Own crossed *Telegraph Weg* and moved towards the wire

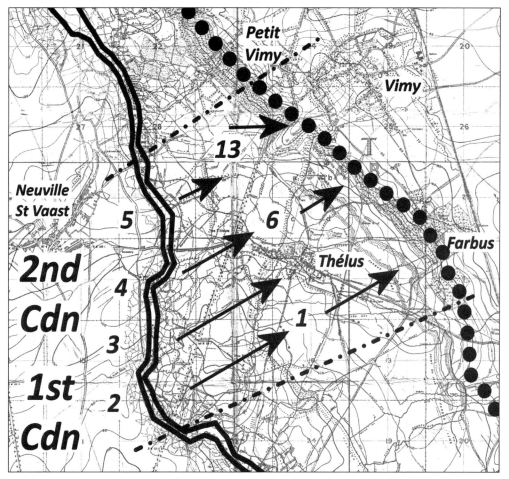

Both 2nd and 1st Canadian Divisions advanced to their objectives.

and concrete bunkers on the edge of Bois du Goulot. A machine gun team fired into the Queen's Own's left flank killing Lieutenant Hyde and wounding Second Lieutenant Lewis-Barned, but a volley of rifle grenades and a charge by the KOSBs silenced them. Lieutenant Colonel Sladen's KOSBs advanced down the slope towards Vimy village and Captain Pringle's company followed a gap in the trees. They captured over 150 men, two 210mm howitzers and four machine guns in the quarries at the foot of the slope. They also outflanked the Germans in Bois de Goulot and forced them to withdraw.

The Queen's Own found another seven abandoned artillery pieces and a huge stack of ammunition in the woods. The two battalions moved beyond the wood but found it was dangerous in the open, so Brigadier General Jones allowed them to pull back into the trees to avoid the German barrage.

The 6 Canadian Brigade took over the advance on 2nd Division's right and while 28th Battalion advanced along the north side of Thélus, 31st Battalion moved into the ruins. Bombers followed the trenches either side of the village and Lewis guns covered the infantry as they worked their way along the main street.

Brigadier General Ketchen's troops then wheeled left, to face Bois de la Ville, overlooking Farbus. Both 29th and 27th Battalions were met by machine guns and field guns firing at point-blank range from the trees. There was a cheer when a barrage of rifle grenades silenced the machine guns and then there was a bayonet charge down the hillside. The Canadians captured 250 men including a regimental staff and many gunners. The men of 27th Battalion painted their number on their prisoners' jackets so they got credit for capturing them. The east edge of the Bois de la Ville was secured and patrols were pushed through Farbus to the railway line beyond.

1st Canadian Division, Farbus

Major General Arthur Currie's men faced the longest advance across Vimy Ridge. They had to cross 4,000 yards of muddy wasteland cut by trenches and pockmarked with shell holes. On the left, the 16th (Canadian Scottish), 14th (Royal Montreal) and 15th (48th Highlanders) Battalions led 3 Canadian Brigade's advance across no man's land to the skirl of the bagpipes. Private William Milne crawled forward to silence the machine gun crew targeting 16th Battalion with bombs. He then did the same at the support trench. Milne was killed soon after but he was posthumously awarded the Victoria Cross.

On the right, the 10th, 7th and 5th Canadian Battalions rushed the first trench in 2 Canadian Brigade's sector. They overpowered the sentries and left guards at the dugout and tunnel exits before moving on. Some of the garrison in the second trench were caught underground but snipers and machine gun teams fought on until they were killed. The two brigades met the most resistance at the *Zwölfer Stellung* (the Twelve Position) just beyond the Arras–Lens road.

South-west of Thélus, 14th Canadian Battalion came under fire from four machine guns in a strongpoint in the Zwischen Stellung. Grenades silenced two teams, snipers killed the crew of the third and the fourth team died at the point of the bayonet. On the right flank, 7th, and 5th Canadian Battalions were delayed by machine guns firing from a sunken track but they captured their first objective, the Zwölfer Stellung, in forty-five minutes.

It was light when the rear companies took over the lead at 6.45 am. They advanced across the muddy ridge through the snow and smoke towards Zwischen Stellung. The Germans ran when they saw the Canadians coming and hundreds could be seen retreating over the edge of the ridge into Farbus Wood. On the left, Brigadier General Tuxford's 3 Canadian Brigade tackled Zwischen Stellung but 1 Canadian Brigade took over from Brigadier General Loomis's 2 Canadian Brigade because the trench turned back to the south-east. Brigadier General Griesbach reported his men had taken it by 8 am. The 4th and 3rd Canadian Battalions were 'advancing as if on parade' and they generally 'met remarkably little opposition'. Only 1st Canadian Battalion had a fierce fight with 125 Germans before they surrendered.

There was a brief break in the weather as 1st Canadian Division approached the edge of the ridge and 'for a fleeting moment was revealed the final issue of the day: the Germans saw that the ridge was lost, the Canadians knew that it was won.' But the snow flurries returned as General Griesbach's men wheeled left to attack their final objective, knowing that half of the field artillery was too far away to help. The men of 4th and 3rd Canadian Battalions used their ample supplies of wire cutters and rifle-mounted wire breakers to cut through the wire. Once at the edge of the ridge, they could see over Bois de la Ville and across the Douai plain far into the German rear areas.

The Canadians did not stop long to enjoy the view, they moved down the wooded slope to capture abandoned batteries. It brought the number of artillery pieces taken by 1st and 2nd Canadian Divisions to thirty-one. The machine gun teams also took the opportunity to fire overhead at the transport moving between Vimy and Willerval. Patrols eventually established observation posts along the lower edge of the wood. During the afternoon, Griesbach had to pull back his right flank into Farbus Wood to maintain contact with 51st Division because it had not advanced as far as expected.

Early in the afternoon, a squadron of the Canadian Light Horse left Neuville Saint Vaast and moved through 1st Canadian Division's lines. Around 4.20 pm two mounted patrols left Farbus Wood and headed towards Willerval. The first patrol charged into the north-west side of village and captured ten Germans before returning under machine gun fire, losing half their number. The second patrol came under fire as they cantered around the south side of the village and only two returned on foot. Meanwhile, the rest of the squadron had lost half its horses to artillery fire as it sheltered in Farbus Wood.

First Army Summary

As soon as the divisional commanders heard about the success on their respective fronts, they took steps to make sure their men consolidated their positions. Engineers supervised the building of strongpoints, entrenching battalions improved the trenches and built bridges over them, and labour companies repaired and built tracks. Stretcher bearers were busy collecting the wounded from the battlefield and prisoners were employed carrying them back to the aid posts.

There were no signs of any counter-attacks for some time but observers spotted German troops approaching during the late afternoon. Some marched towards Vimy while others headed for Farbus. A combination of machine gun fire from the outposts and artillery fire from the ridge stopped them getting close to the Canadian line.

Chapter 9

A Procession and Happily So
Third Army – 9 April

General Allenby had an anxious night before the battle. Ten divisions (around 350,000 troops) had to cram into a zone only two miles deep during the hours of darkness. The RFC pilots had successfully kept the enemy reconnaissance planes at a safe distance while the artillery had silenced many batteries and their observers. It also helped that the German high command was convinced an attack was not imminent.

As the men trudged along the roads and trenches they shivered in the cold night air, because Allenby had instructed everyone to leave their greatcoats behind. He thought they would become a heavy burden if they became covered in mud. They already had enough to carry with their rifle and bayonet, 170 rounds of ammunition, two Mills bombs, and a signalling flare. Every man had an entrenching tool but many also had to carry a tool such as a pick, a shovel or wire cutters. Every man carried three empty sandbags and parties had been detailed to carry barbed wire and pickets forward. But many men would have gladly risked adding greatcoats to the list to keep warm.

They then had to wait under a cold, dark sky as the artillery battered the German trenches on the other side of no man's land.

XVII Corps, North-East of Arras

Lieutenant General Sir Charles Fergusson was responsible for the three-mile front between Roclincourt and St Laurent. On the left flank, 51st Division had to advance towards Farbus Wood and Bailleul and 34th Division had to move east towards Gavrelle in the centre. On the right, 9th Division would move along the north bank of the Scarpe. The three divisions had to cross the German first line, code-named the Black Line, and the second line, code-named the Blue Line. The left and centre would stop on the Point du Jour position, code-named the Brown Line, but 4th Division would continue to the Méricourt–Oppy position, code-named the Green Line.

The corps heavy artillery was divided into twelve groups; while some targeted the front trenches, others hit more distant targets and the rest were dedicated to counter-battery fire. Fergusson only had eight tanks from C Battalion's No 7 Company. Four would support 34th Division's advance to the Blue Line and then head south-east to help 9th Division's attack on Athies. The four with 9th Division would clear St Laurent and two would then crawl north along the Blue Line while the other two would join the attack on Athies.

51st Division, Advance to Farbus Wood and Bailleul

On 5 April Sergeant Gosling's mortar had fired a shell with a faulty charge and it landed only a few feet away. Gosling jumped out of the emplacement and unscrewed the fuse, disarming the shell; he was awarded the Victoria Cross. A shell hit the emplacement the following day while Gosling was away; it killed all his comrades.

Major General George Harper's infantry either had to huddle in shallow trenches or lie in the open before zero hour. His plan was for two brigades to advance through the Blue Line to the Brown Line, each with a battalion from the third brigade attached. It left only two battalions to advance on the Point du Jour Line. Harper's scheme included two tanks but neither of them reached the front line on time.

Captain Hay-Will led the first wave of 4th Seaforths to success but Second Lieutenant MacGregor and Captain Harris drifted to the right during 154 Brigade's advance. MacGregor was injured reorganising his men so Hay-Will moved forward to capture the second objective. The right flank was stopped by machine gun fire so Sergeant Campbell's group stalked the crew. Five men were hit but Campbell killed twelve with his bombs and bayonet, allowing the rest to advance.

Captain Fraser's Seaforth company and a company of the 6th Gordons emerged from an old mine shaft to face a tough fight with fifty Germans holding Labyrinth Redoubt. Lieutenant Leslie was killed trying to make contact with the Canadians, so Fraser organised another successful attack covered by rifle grenades. Lance Corporal Palmer's bombers silenced a machine gun post, allowing the 9th Royal Scots to advance, and Lieutenant Colonel Green was able to report Poser Trench had been taken. Major Rowbotham and Captain Lindsay organised the 9th Royal Scots as they rounded up groups of prisoners.

The 4th Gordons stayed in touch with the Canadians but the 7th Argylls had swerved to the right, leaving their flank exposed. The Gordons reached Tommy Trench after suffering heavy casualties in Zwischen Stellung but Lieutenant MacNaughton led two machine gun teams to the Point du Jour

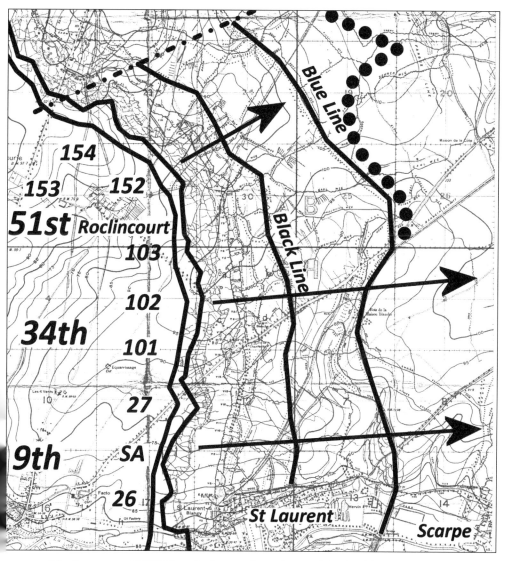

154

153   152

51st Roclincourt
103

102

34th   101

27

9th   SA

26

St Laurent

Scarpe

Blue Line

Black Line

The first stage of XVII Corps' advance along the north bank of the River Scarpe.

Line where they set up their weapons. He contacted Canadian patrols in Farbus Wood and then walked several hundred yards south, finding no one where the Argylls should have been. But MacNaughton had to withdraw his machine guns to the front trench when the British artillery shelled his position. The Germans would return during the night and they forced MacNaughton's small group to withdraw at dawn.

Meanwhile, the Argylls had accidently stopped in a trench in front of the objective, forcing the 7th Black Watch to consolidate Allgouer Trench behind them. It was an unfortunate mistake because the Germans had abandoned the objective, as MacNaughton had discovered. The Germans had returned by the time the Argylls realised their error and they advanced with two 7th Black Watch companies in support. Most of the experienced officers had been hit and their men had little idea where they were going. The Argylls veered ninety degrees to the right and advanced across 152 Brigade's front (which was pinned down). They crossed two communication trenches, assuming they were the Brown Line, and consolidated the third one, believing they had reached their objective. In fact they were 200 yards short of it and facing south rather than east.

The Germans had withdrawn from the front line north-east of Roclincourt where it faced 152 Brigade so their artillery could shell the advancing infantry. The 6th Seaforths and 6th Gordons missed several machine guns and they continued firing into the Scots' backs as they advanced past. One prisoner said there were few troops behind the Blue Line but those holding the Black Line had done their job. The Seaforths suffered over 325 casualties and only one officer was still standing by the time they reached the Blue Line.

A huge explosion killed or buried many of the 5th Seaforths and 8th Argylls as they crossed the Black Line. One German soldier had waited at a safe distance to detonate a store of shells under the advancing troops. He and five others intended to surrender but were shot and killed as soon as they emerged from their dugout. The German machine guns were still chattering as the Seaforths and the Argylls lost the barrage en route to the Blue Line. The leader of the first Argylls wave pulled his men back in error, adding to the delay. Both battalions eventually reached Regiment Trench but they could not capture Elect Trench. Brigadier General Burn had to report his men had failed to reach the Brown Line. However 51st Division had taken over 700 prisoners, 2 field guns and 29 machine guns.

34th Division, The Advance on Bailleul

Major General Lothian Nicholson's headquarters had received the word 'complete' three times by 4.30 am, meaning all three of his brigades were ready to advance east of Roclincourt. The messages would keep coming back after zero hour and most of them reported the objectives were being reached and plenty of prisoners were being taken. A contact plane flew overhead to check on progress around 9 am and flares reported troops had reached the Blue Line on the centre and right; the left hand brigade was in trouble.

Lieutenant Colonel Hermon of 24th Northumberland Fusiliers was killed crossing no man's land on 103 Brigade's front but Lieutenant Colonel Moulton Barrett made it across with the 25th Northumberland Fusiliers.

The two battalions easily cleared the first objective despite Scottish troops from 51st Division veering across their front. They then came under heavy fire in front of the second objective and Captain Beattie Brown and Lieutenant McLachlan were killed clearing the Black Line. The officers were hit one by one until only Second Lieutenants Kirkup and Snee were left to lead the survivors towards the Blue Line. The arrival of the 26th Northumberland Fusiliers, which again had few officers, resulted in chaos in Mettel Trench.

Moulton Barrett needed to silence the machine guns in Zehner Trench and Gaul Trench so he sent patrols forward to locate them. Captain Huntley was killed as he closed in on one weapon but a wounded Lance Corporal Bryan outflanked the two-man crew and killed them with his bayonet. His bravery allowed 51st and 34th Divisions to clear the Blue Line around Maison de la Côte. Bryan was rewarded with the Victoria Cross.

Brigadier General Trevor had told Lieutenant Colonel Richardson to move the 26th Northumberland Fusiliers forward to the Brown Line but they had been stopped by machine gun fire from the left flank. It was the same on the right where 27th Battalion was pinned down. Private Ernest Sykes carried four wounded men back and then remained out in no man's land until he had bandaged those too badly injured to be moved. He would be awarded the Victoria Cross for saving many lives.

The artillery and machine gun barrages had demoralised the Germans in the Black Line and the Blue Line opposite 102 Brigade to such a level that many surrendered to the 22nd and 21st Northumberland Fusiliers. The 20th Northumberland Fusiliers came under fire from the left flank, where 103 Brigade should have been, and they lost the barrage as they cut through the wire. They then suffered many casualties clearing the Brown Line in front of Bailleul. Captain Herm was wounded as the 23rd Northumberland Fusiliers cut through the wire but the rest of Lieutenant Colonel Porch's men cleared the Brown Line with bayonet and bomb. Brigadier General Ternan was able to report that 102 Brigade had advanced nearly two miles but 103 Brigade was not covering his left flank.

The 11th Suffolks passed the Black Line in 101 Brigade's sector without recognising the battered trench and kept moving up the slope to the Blue Line, the Lille to Arras railway cutting. The 10th Lincolns passed through the Suffolks only to be delayed by wire, so they lost the barrage. But they still kept pushing forward, finding the Germans had fled, leaving burning braziers, uneaten breakfasts and unopened parcels in their dugouts.

The 16th Royal Scots also reached the Black Line but Lieutenant Colonel Lodge lost control of the 15th Royal Scots and the two battalions became mixed up. They came under machine gun fire from the railway cutting and Second Lieutenants Flete and Thurburn were killed trying to silence the weapons. Captain Harrison and three other officers wanted to lead the 15th Royal Scots towards the Brown Line but they could only get one hundred men to join them as they advanced in a single line towards a battery of field guns firing over opened sights. The Lincolns and Royal Scots had to cut and crawl through the wire until a white flag appeared above the Brown Line and fifty Germans stood up with their hands over their heads. The Royal Scots sent patrols forward to what the aerial observers thought was a track. It turned out to be a trench covered with corrugated iron and Brigadier General Gore decided to consolidate the position after a large group of Germans were spotted assembling between Oppy and Gavrelle.

By nightfall Major General Nicholson knew his right and centre were almost on the final objective but his left was pinned down beyond the Blue Line. So he sent the 21st Northumberland Fusiliers to help Brigadier General Trevor to capture the Brown Line.

<u>9th Division, North Bank of the Scarpe</u>
The left brigade had to climb up the Point du Jour ridge, the centre brigade had to cross the spurs overlooking the River Scarpe and the right brigade had to move along the valley floor. It would be difficult to keep the waves of infantry in formation as they moved over the undulating terrain. The divisional artillery officer, Brigadier General Tudor, thought his gunners would find it difficult to fire at a low trajectory over the undulating terrain so he instructed them to fire high explosive shells at a high trajectory instead. He thought the bigger explosions would give the infantry more confidence than shrapnel while smoke shells would be used to screen the advance.

On 27 Brigade's front, the 6th KOSBs were hit by smoke shells falling short but Major Hay led his disorganised men through the British barrage. They missed the first objective because the trench had been obliterated but they took the Germans in the sunken road beyond by surprise. Lieutenant Colonel Smyth's men then turned their fire on a machine gun holding up the 12th Royal Scots on their right. Lieutenant Colonel Thorne was killed leading the Royal Scots towards Obermeyer Trench and there was confusion when the moppers-up missed some of the German dugouts in the thick clouds of smoke and dust. It delayed the 11th Royal Scots and 9th Scottish Rifles so Major Hay kept leading his men forward until they caught up. Lieutenant Colonel Croft and Captain Loftus of the Royal Scots were killed while Captain Murray was hit three times. One bullet had smashed his hand so he shot the mangled flesh and bone off so the stump could be bandaged up. He still made sure the stretcher bearers had taken everyone else to the aid post before he was carried to the rear.

The Royal Scots and Scottish Rifles came under fire from the railway and Maison Blanche Wood as they climbed up the slope to the Blue Line. They silenced two machine guns and made sure no Germans escaped from the cutting. They also pinned down another two machine gun teams shooting at 34th Division's flank. The Scots could see the Germans running in the distance and Brigadier General Maxwell reported the advance was 'a procession, and happily so; for the heavy wire protecting the Brown Line was untouched'. Some of the KOSBs rushed the solitary machine gun team still firing from Point du Jour and then sat down to eat their breakfast.

Brigadier General Dawson's men assembled in craters close to the German trenches before zero hour and then the engineers blew mines on the South African Brigade's front. The 4th and 3rd South African Regiments suffered from machine gun fire as they tackled the wire but the Germans fled as soon as they had cut through. Snipers were waiting at the railway cutting but the machine gun teams were slow and did not get their weapons into action. The 2nd and 1st South African Regiments then took over the advance beyond the Blue Line and passed through the gaps the Germans had left in the wire. They entered the Point du Jour trenches as the garrison surrendered or ran.

On 26 Brigade's front, the 8th Black Watch met little resistance north of St Laurent and Captain Shepherd and Lieutenant Austin led the advance to the Black Line. Two 10th Argyll companies joined the Black Watch en route to the Blue Line but Second Lieutenants Gawne, Tyser and Ross were killed approaching the railway. The Scots bombed their way into the cutting, taking one hundred prisoners. Even the regimental commander and his adjutant were captured because they had not realised they were under attack. The 5th Camerons then reinforced the 10th Argylls as they advanced across the spurs and valleys towards the Brown Line north of Athies.

Two of the four tanks assigned to join 26 Brigade's advance along the river bank were damaged by shellfire before zero hour. The 7th Seaforths advanced on a narrow front through St Laurent and cleared an island on the river. They then followed the valley floor and 'the spectacle of lines of men moving steadily forward with their rifles at the slope seemed more like a Salisbury Plain ceremonial manoeuvre than an attack in grim earnest.' But the Seaforths soon came under fire from the railway triangle across the river where 15th Division had been delayed. One tank broke down before it reached the railway while the other lost its way after its officer was killed.

Brigadier General Kennedy organised for smoke shells to screen the 7th Seaforths as they cut through the wire covering Athies. The moppers up had missed some dugouts and a few Germans emerged to fire into their backs until a working party of the 9th Seaforths dropped their shovels and killed or captured them all.

Major General Henry Lukin was able to report 9th Division had taken all its objectives on time and it had around 2,100 prisoners; the Méricourt–Oppy Line and Fampoux were there for the taking. Lieutenant General Fergusson had organised a barrage in front of 9th Division while 4th Division moved up but Brigadier Generals Kennedy and Maxwell thought an opportunity was being missed. They even asked permission to push their men through the exploding shells but their request was denied.

4th Division, Hyderabad Redoubt and Fampoux

Major General the Hon. William Lambton's men had spent the morning waiting around Saint Nicholas and Saint Catherine, north of Arras. They were cold and wet but the sight of many prisoners being escorted along the north bank of the Scarpe was cheering them up. They crossed the Blue Line around noon and deployed north of Athies as a barrage of high explosive shells crept across the Méricourt–Oppy Line. The gunners then turned their attention onto selected points as the infantry moved forward.

The 1st East Lancashires captured a battery and reached the Green Line as they formed a flank on 11 Brigade's left. The 1st Hampshire and 1st Somersets seized their section of the Méricourt–Oppy Line. The 1st Rifle Brigade then passed through the Somersets to attack the triangular work known as Hyderabad Redoubt. Corporal Bancroft drop-kicked a football into the strongpoint and the Germans surrendered as the Rifle Brigade passed through the gaps left in the wire.

Around 140 prisoners ran back – 'no escort was necessary, none was sent and no man showed any desire to go back with them.' There was such a rush to get to the cages (built to hold prisoners) that there was a crush to get through the gaps in the wire, 'which was 40 yards thick in places'. The rest had abandoned the machine guns which could have stopped the advance.

It was the longest advance, at 3½ miles, since the start of trench warfare. Brigadier General Berners even reported that a general officer had been captured on the Fampoux–Gavrelle road. His car was close by but his chauffeur had run away.

Brigadier General Carton de Wiart's men were delayed moving through 9th Division but the Germans in the Méricourt–Oppy Line only fired a few shots at 12 Brigade and then surrendered or ran. It was around 4 pm when the 2nd Essex and the 2nd Lancashire Fusiliers reached the sunken Fampoux–Gavrelle road where Captain Fanner walked up and down the line to make sure his men dug in correctly.

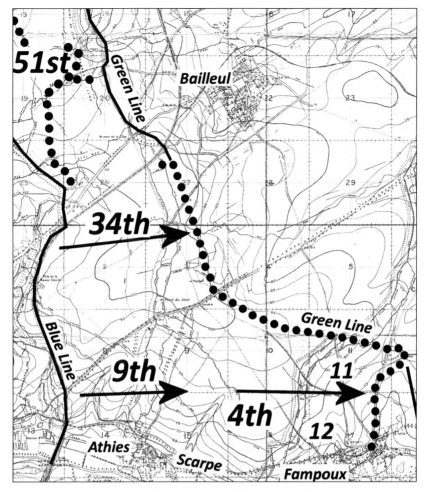

The second stage of XVII Corps' advance to the Green Line.

The 1st King's Own had stopped on the right flank to allow the 2nd Duke's to attack Fampoux. The howitzer barrage crept towards the ruins and the final 15-inch howitzer shell detonated a large ammunition dump in the village, scattering the garrison. But the Duke's suffered over eighty casualties from the machine guns entrenched along the railway embankment in just a couple of minutes. They dug in along the edge of Fampoux and had to watch as the Germans counter-attacked across the river.

Altogether, 12 Brigade had taken 230 prisoners but many were hit by the German bombardment as they headed to the rear. Captains Bowen and Howarth of the 2nd Lancashire Fusiliers had captured 9 guns but the brigade had taken 24 guns altogether and 10 of them were heavy howitzers.

Chapter 10

Guns Galloping into Action
Third Army's Centre – 9 April

VI Corps, South of the Scarpe
Lieutenant General Aylmer Haldane had three divisions to attack between the River Scarpe and Tilloy-lèz-Mofflaines. The three divisions had to clear the front line trenches, known as the Black Line, and then cross Observation Ridge, known as the Blue Line, and head to the Feuchy–Wancourt Line, or the Brown Line, an advance of around 3,500 yards. The Green Line was another 3,500 yards further on, beyond Monchy and Guémappe.

The corps had 160 howitzers and guns ranging from 6-inch howitzers up to a 15-inch howitzer, divided into nine artillery groups. A narrow gauge railway delivered around 100 tons of shells a day to the heavy artillery batteries.

Eight tanks belonging to C Battalion would help VI Corps. Two would attack the railway triangle in 15th Division's sector, while two tanks would silence the redoubts on 12th Division's front. One pair would crawl around the north end of Tilly while a second pair would drive past the south end and advance with 3rd Division. The survivors would accompany the infantry to the Feuchy–Wancourt Line. The plan was for one pair to move parallel to it, ripping up the wire entanglements. Another pair would drive straight towards Feuchy Chapel redoubt on the Cambrai road.

15th Division, South of the Scarpe
In 45 Brigade's sector, along the river bank, two 13th Royal Scots companies were hit by falling debris when the British tunnellers detonated two mines under the German bunkers protecting Blangy. One mine had missed its target and Sergeant McMillan had to run forward and use bombs to silence the machine gun team inside. Stokes mortars ceased fire when the rest of the Germans in Blangy waved a white flag. They then opened fire when the Scots began moving forward and Captain Turner's men showed no mercy as they cleared the ruins. A machine gun barrage covered the 11th Argylls and 6/7th Scots Fusiliers as they advanced to the Black

Line but Brigadier General Allgood reported his men could not clear the railway triangle until the tanks caught up.

The 9th Black Watch and the 8/10th Gordon Highlanders also advanced to the Black Line on 44 Brigade's front but Captain Story-Wilson was hit as he organised the consolidation of the Feuchy Switch south of the railway triangle. A tank helped the 7th Camerons advance to the Blue Line on Observation Ridge but the advance was stalled everywhere else.

Major General Frederick McCracken ordered the field artillery batteries to reduce their range to the embankment on the east side of the triangle at 11.30 am and then creep the barrage east along the railway. The infantry advanced once again as a tank crawled along the south side of the triangle and Brigadier General Marshall reported that the Blue Line had been reached just after midday.

Originally, 46 Brigade was supposed to advance along the south bank of the River Scarpe towards the Blue Line at 12.50 pm. News that the move had been postponed to 2 pm was late reaching Brigadier General Fagan and

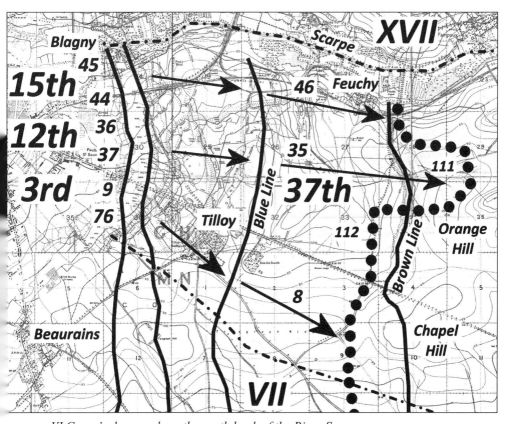

VI Corps' advance along the south bank of the River Scarpe.

two 12th HLI companies did not hear about the delay. They advanced at the original time only to see the creeping barrage fall behind them. All they could do was take cover in shell holes and wait for it to pass over before they continued east.

The 7/8th KOSBs, the 10th Scottish Rifles and the 12th HLI advanced over Observation Ridge and came under fire from half a dozen field gun batteries in Battery Valley. The Scots advanced in small parties, taking it in turns to fire or run forward, until they captured all thirty-six guns.

Up ahead, the river bank was covered in dust and smoke as 6-inch shells exploded in Feuchy. The shelling stopped when the KOSBs and 10th Scottish Rifles began clearing the ruins. Lieutenant General Haldane had sent his corps cavalry unit, the Northamptonshire Yeomanry, forward during the late afternoon and they captured another six field guns. They also secured all the bridges over the Scarpe before sending patrols into Fampoux where they met troops of 4th Division. The Scots followed the cavalry beyond Feuchy and a tank crushed the wire so they could enter the Brown Line. The position was taken by late afternoon, an advance of 5,000 yards and over 500 prisoners captured.

12th Division, East of Arras

Major General Arthur Scott had the luxury of using a network of cellars, caves and tunnels to get his men from the centre of Arras to the front line. Some troops spent up to a week living underground and they became used to the comparative quiet. The noise of the bombardment sounded like 'cannons loaded with double cracks' when they eventually came above ground.

One man who had spent time above ground was the press officer, Major Fauthorpe, as he looked for a good place to film the advance. He set his camera equipment up before zero hour only to be incapacitated when British gas shells exploded nearby.

Scott had been promised two tanks but one did not reach the rendezvous and the other failed to cross the British trenches. On the left, 36 Brigade's advance started well as the 7th Sussex and 11th Middlesex took many prisoners in the Black Line. The 8th Royal Fusiliers had difficulty clearing Feuchy Switch and were then pinned down in front of Hart Redoubt. Corporal Moakes captured a prisoner who was interrogated about the layout of the redoubt, allowing Second Lieutenant Beames to outflank it and take 200 prisoners. The 8th and 9th Royal Fusiliers were delayed clearing Hart, Hamel and Heron Redoubts but Lieutenant Colonels Elliott-Cooper and Overton were able to report that they had all been captured with the help of 35 Brigade.

In 37 Brigade's sector, the 7th East Surreys came under fire from machine gun fire in the Black Line. Sergeant Harry Cator crept forward, picking up an abandoned Lewis gun on the way, to silence the crew. He held his position until Sergeant Jarrott's bombers arrived and they captured 100 prisoners and another five machine guns between them. The 6th Queen's had less trouble and the 6th Queen's Own and 6th Buffs were able to cross Scott's Valley. The Queen's were pinned down in front of a redoubt until 36 Brigade outflanked it. The Buffs cleared a second redoubt north of Tilloy with rifle grenades but Captain Gordon was wounded clearing Estaminet Corner. The two battalions then crossed Observation Ridge and took the Blue Line at the bayonet but it was some time before Lieutenant Colonels Dawson and Cope could report Holt and Houlette Redoubts had been taken.

Brigadier General Vincent's 35 Brigade moved along the St Sauveur cave system, which ran under the Cambrai road, and used tunnels to appear in the British front line trenches. They then advanced in artillery formation across the Black Line and Observation Ridge. They had hoped to be joined by four tanks en route to the Blue Line, but they were either stuck in the mud or on fire.

Lieutenant Colonel Sansom's 9th Essex took time to clear Heron Redoubt, delaying the advance. It meant the 5th Berkshires lost the barrage as they approached the Brown Line. So one company outflanked Holt Redoubt, taking thirty-five prisoners and a machine gun. On the right, the 7th Norfolks were hit by British shells exploding short of their target, but they kept going and cleared Haucourt Trench. Lieutenant Colonel Walter then ordered the Norfolks to fire on the Germans opposing the Essex and Berkshires; nearly one hundred surrendered.

The Blue Line had held on three hours longer than expected and Vincent had been forced to deploy the rest of his brigade west of Observation Ridge but the Norfolks had not finished. Captain Gethin's men were rounding up dozens of Germans around Maison Rouge on the Cambrai road and 'only wanted to know where they ought to go'.

Lieutenant Colonel Willan had the 5th Berkshires advance in short rushes covered by bursts of Lewis gun fire as they moved beyond Observation Ridge and Battery Valley. Ahead of them were four batteries of German field guns. Some were firing, some had been abandoned and horse teams were pulling the rest to safety. Lieutenants Ramsay and Debeno and Company Sergeant Major Blake led the Berkshires through the battery lines claiming twenty-two guns, while the Essex chalked their name on another nine. An artillery officer helped the Berkshires repair two guns and they turned them on Germans on Orange Hill beyond the Brown Line.

Both the 9th Essex and 7th Suffolk had been unable to advance beyond Maison Rouge until forty minutes after the barrage had moved on. Both Lieutenant Colonels Trevor and Cooper found the artillery had done little to the wire and German machine gun teams were waiting in the Feuchy–Wancourt Line. All the tanks had either broken down or had been knocked out and it was impossible to cut through the wire, so the men sought cover where they could. One company of the Essex captured Chapel Work in front of Feuchy Chapel but Captain Nicholls of the Suffolks was killed as they tried to take Church Redoubt to the south-east. To the west, Brigadier General Vincent could see the artillery moving up and 'the sight of the guns galloping into action was not one of the least thrills of the day.' But he could also see the Germans returning to the Feuchy–Wancourt Line as his men struggled to cut through the wire.

3rd Division, Tilloy-lèz-Mofflaines
Many of Major General Cyril Deverell's men had spent nearly a week in the Ronville cave system. Others waited in the cellars beneath Arras and they began filing forward as the attack unfolded. The Germans still held their original trenches astride the Cambrai road but almost all had withdrawn around 500 yards to the Hindenburg Line opposite 3rd Division's right. The old front trench had been abandoned but outposts had been left in the second and third trenches.

The ten tanks allocated to 3rd Division had left their assembly area in the Citadel moat on the south-west side of Arras during the night. Six became bogged down on the north side while the lorries taking railway sleepers to help get them out were delayed in the traffic. They were released from the mud too late to take part in the attack. Another tank bogged down near the starting point, leaving only three to help 3rd Division clear Tilloy-lèz-Mofflaines.

On 9 Brigade's front, the 13th King's pushed quickly through Devil's Wood but were pinned down by machine gun fire in front of Tilloy. Major Campbell's men then faced sniper fire as they cut through the wire protecting Tilloy chateau and a third sticking point was the quarry east of the village. Lieutenant Greener of the 1st Northumberland Fusiliers fired rifle grenades into it while the 12th West Yorkshires poured enfilade fire into the position. The loss of the quarry triggered a general retreat and Lewis gunners stationed on the chateau roof shot at the Germans as they ran; over 470 of their comrades were heading to the cages.

The 12th West Yorkshire had far less problems as they advanced through the centre of Devil's Wood and Tilloy. The 1st Northumberland Fusiliers gave assistance when required, dealing with snipers hidden in the woods and houses. On the right flank, the 4th Royal Fusiliers cleared the String, the trench running across the centre of the Harp position, and seized the sunken road beyond it. The 2nd Suffolks cleared the east side of the Harp but only one tank was still running by the time the redoubt had fallen.

The combination of Stokes mortar shells and machine gun bullets overwhelmed the Germans facing 76 Brigade while the infantry followed the 'magnificent barrage'. The 1st Gordon Highlanders advanced to the fourth trench and then Lieutenant Colonel Compton Smith's 10th Welsh Fusiliers took the Black Line and Devil's Wood. Captain Watcyn Williams captured over eighty men hiding in the cellar of one house on the edge of the wood.

Brigadier General Holmes's 8 Brigade took over the advance beyond the Blue Line around noon. The 7th Shropshires and 2nd Royal Scots had seen one hundred Germans surrender around Tilloy. They were then sniped at as they moved past Bois des Boeufs until Captain Thursfield's company of Shropshires cleared it, taking ninety prisoners. The rest of the battalion would become pinned down beyond Maison Rouge because they needed a tank to cut the wire in front of Feuchy Chapel redoubt.

Captain Wilson and Sergeant Fullerton of the Royal Scots silenced two machine gun teams on the right flank and then captured a large number of prisoners in a dugout. They then veered to the south to avoid the machine gun from Feuchy Chapel but they were unable to reach the Feuchy–Wancourt Line.

Major General Deverell wanted to renew the attack at 6.45 pm but Brigadier General Porter received his orders late. The 1st Gordons advanced on time, only to find the bombardment had failed to cut the wire and they could not clear Feuchy Chapel redoubt. The 8th King's Own received their orders ten minutes before zero hour so they advanced late and could only reach the Neuville-Vitasse road.

37th Division, Orange Hill and Feuchy Chapel

Lieutenant General Haldane's plan was for 37th Division to advance towards Monchy once 12th Division had captured the Brown Line south-east of Feuchy. Major General Hugh Bruce-Williams had been moving his troops forward since mid-morning and 112 Brigade moved over Observation Ridge into Battery Valley early in the afternoon. The brigade waited there for four hours while the field artillery and the rest of the division moved forward.

Brigadier General Maclachlan was instructed to advance towards Monchy-le-Preux and the Green Line. Brigadier General Vincent told him that the western redoubt at Feuchy Chapel had been taken but neither of them knew the condition of the wire covering the Brown Line. Around 6.30 pm, 111 Brigade moved through 15th Division's position east of Feuchy. The 8th Lincolns and 8th Somersets advanced onto Orange Hill but the 8th East Lancashires and the 6th Bedfords were stopped by crossfire from the Brown Line and Feuchy Chapel redoubt. Haldane could report an advance of 5,000 yards but it was only on a narrow front, the rest of his corps was held up by the Brown Line.

Chapter 11

A Neat Little Success in their Usual Style
Third Army's Right – 9 April

VII Corps, Neuville-Vitasse and the Hindenburg Line

Lieutenant General Sir Thomas Snow's plan was to attack between Beaurains and Croisilles in echelon from the left. On the left, 14th Division would advance south-west across Telegraph Hill heading towards Wancourt, followed by 56th Division which would move through Neuville-Vitasse. General Snow hoped success on his left flank would outflank and demoralise the Germans holding the Hindenburg Line, allowing 30th Division to advance towards Héninel. There were concerns about the wire in front of 21st Division and Major General David Campbell had instructions to call off the advance east of Hénin if it was struggling.

<u>14th Division, Telegraph Hill</u>

Major General Victor Couper's men had dug eight assembly trenches east of Beaurains. The creeping barrage stopped moving at 7.34 am, when it was still 250 yards from the enemy front trench, and waited until the infantry had deployed. The topography of Telegraph Hill meant that the shells were whistling close overhead as the first wave moved forward.

On the left, 42 Brigade faced the south end of the Harp Redoubt, a large strongpoint around 1,000 yards wide. The 9th KRRC reached the north end of the String, in the centre of the Harp, and then bombed along it, capturing nearly 200 men. The 5th Ox & Bucks lost many men silencing three machine guns in the String. The tanks had struggled crossing the crater field created by the British artillery. Seven out of ten had bogged down on the Harp while the remaining three were damaged. Major Delmé-Murray's 5th Shropshires passed through and while Captain Burke was mortally wounded, his men took 300 prisoners at the Blue Line.

Captain Bradley had been shot rushing a machine gun post in front of 9th Rifle Brigade during the final stage of the advance. But he stalked it and then silenced the crew before capturing sixty men and two machine guns; some of over 200 taken. Lieutenant Colonel Pickering heard of the success by 'the safest method of communication' and gave 'a pat on the back to the carrier pigeons, who did well'. By mid-morning Brigadier General Dudgeon was pleased to report that Captain Benbow-Rowe was consolidating the captured trenches.

Meanwhile, 43 Brigade attacked the end of the Hindenburg Line where it met the original support trenches. The 10th Durhams suffered heavy casualties capturing the summit of Telegraph Hill but the 6th KOYLIs followed three tanks through the wire. Both battalions found most of the Germans hiding in their dugouts waiting to surrender. However, the few machine gun teams that fought on in the Hindenburg Line caused even more casualties. The 6th Somersets had to advance alone at 12.30 pm because all the tanks had been damaged or bogged down. Although the advance was successful, Brigadier General Wood's right flank was exposed because the first wave had fallen back after coming under heavy fire. Also the single company of the 1/14th London Regiment seen crossing Pine Lane had disappeared over the horizon.

56th Division, Neuville-Vitasse

Major General Charles Hull's 56th Division began moving forward at 7.45 am and the creeping barrage slowed down as the two brigades cleared the fortified village of Neuville-Vitasse. The German barrage missed 168 Brigade as it advanced north of Neuville-Vitasse accompanied by two tanks. The 12th London Regiment suffered heavy casualties approaching the wire. Some men on the left forced their way through the entanglement, silenced a machine gun and cleared a section of the trench. One tank had broken down but the second crushed the wire and let the right company through; the tank was soon on fire. The 13th London Regiment overran Pine Lane and Moss Lane and then helped the 8th Middlesex as they fought around the church. It was several hours before Brigadier General Loch was able to report that the north half of Neuville-Vitasse had been cleared.

The second phase of the advance began at 12.10 pm but the 14th London Regiment had an unusual experience. The left company drifted north into 14th Division's zone and advanced through a weakly held spot in the Hindenburg Line. They captured 150 prisoners and then advanced another 600 yards towards the Feuchy–Wancourt Line before they realised they were on their own. So they fell back to the first Hindenburg trench where they met the 1st London Regiment who were pinned down by machine gun fire from the Egg Redoubt. The 14th London Regiment bombers then helped clear the trench.

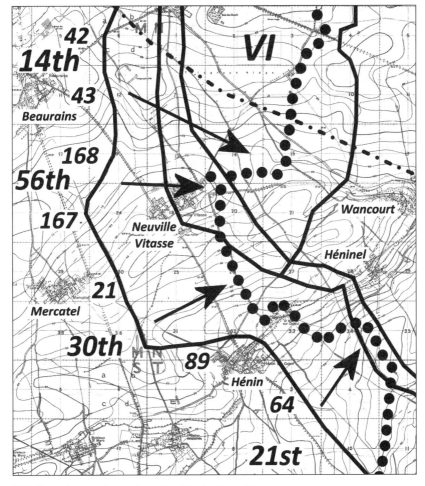

VII Corps' struggle to clear the Hindenburg Line.

The 8th Middlesex approached the south half of Neuville-Vitasse, in 167 Brigade's sector, only to find that wire had been erected across the street, where the artillery could not hit it. The Londoners were pinned down by the machine gun teams hidden around the church, so the bombers worked through the south edge of the village with the 1/3rd London Regiment and two tanks. Eventually nearly seventy men surrendered in Neuville-Vitasse, but it had taken the Middlesex over eight hours to reach the Blue Line, on the far side of the village.

The 3rd London Regiment suffered casualties as it approached Neuville-Vitasse Trench, east of the village, but two platoons captured Neuville Mill with the help of a fifth tank. The 1st London Regiment helped clear the first Hindenburg Line trench but the 7th Middlesex could not capture the support trench. Brigadier General Freeth had to report that the machine guns on his right flank, where 30th Division should have been, had the area covered. The Londoners spent the night trying to bomb their way forward.

Major General Hull had to report that 56th Division had cleared Neuville-Vitasse but had been unable to clear the Hindenburg Line and the location of his front line was still a mystery. The Londoners had captured over 600 prisoners but for the loss of nearly 900 casualties.

30th Division, Hénin and St Martin

Major General Jimmy Shea had organised several preliminary operations to clear enemy outposts between Hénin and Croisilles before zero hour. Lieutenant Parson was killed leading a company of the 2nd Wiltshire to capture the mill on the Neuville-Vitasse road. It failed and Lieutenant Frisby was injured as they withdrew.

On the right, 89 Brigade cleared Saint Martin hamlet, 'a neat little success carried out by the 2nd Bedfords in their usual style'. Captain Wynne reported that trench mortars had been unable to cut the Hindenburg Line wire and all Brigadier General the Hon. Stanley could do was ask the field artillery to have a go. The 18-pounders could do little because they were too far away to aim accurately at such a narrow target.

The advance was due to start late in the morning and the 18th King's and 2nd Wiltshires, on 21 Brigade's front, moved off at 11.38 am. They cleared a number of machine gun posts before they deployed along the sunken Neuville–Hénin road, code-named the Blue Line. One of D Battalion's tanks had broken down and another was bogged down south of Neuville-Vitasse. The infantry were hit by artillery and machine gun fire as they advanced slowly behind the barrage towards Neuville-Vitasse Trench. Again, the trench mortars had not cut gaps in the wire and the two remaining tanks ditched before they could crush it. Brigadier General Goodman's men were left sheltering in shell holes and had to wait until it was dark before they could to withdraw to the Neuville–St Martin road.

The 19th Manchesters reinforced the road position and their bombers were sent towards the Feuchy–Wancourt Line when Goodman heard that men were holding out in the Hindenburg Line. The report was not correct and the Manchester bombers could not to make any progress. Meanwhile, the German artillery knew the range of the sunken road and the exploding shells caused havoc amongst the troops sheltering there; Colonel Gillson's Wiltshires were reduced to less than 100 men. Snow fell at dusk and the temperature plummeted, freezing many wounded to death before the stretcher bearers could find them.

On the right, 89 Brigade headed towards the Hindenburg Line south of Héninel at 4.15 pm. But Lieutenant Colonel Douglas's 20th King's and

Lieutenant Colonel Rollo's 19th King's could not get through the Hindenburg Line wire. Each battalion suffered around 200 casualties from machine gun fire and the survivors sheltered in shell holes until darkness fell. It would need another, more powerful, bombardment to smash the wire.

21st Division, Hindenburg Line

Major General David Campbell's division held the line from the Cojeul stream at Hénin to the Sensée stream at Croisilles. Only 64 Brigade was due to advance on the left in the afternoon, alongside 30th Division; 100 Brigade would remain in its sector next to Croisilles. The troops spent a miserable day in the muddy trenches and they welcomed the sight of the smoke shells exploding in front of the German trenches just before zero hour.

The 18-pounders began shelling the area in front of the German wire at 3.54 pm as the 9th KOYLIs, 15th Durhams and 1st East Yorkshires advanced in section columns towards the narrow gaps in the wire. A machine gun section emplaced near St Martin kept the Germans pinned down on the left but the KOYLIs could not pass through the second belt of wire covering the front trench. The Stokes mortars gave covering fire as the Durham and East Yorkshire men threaded their way through the two wire entanglements and they captured the first trench.

The support waves could not get through the wire protecting the second trench and they fell back to the first and stopped all the counter-attacks. The Durhams failed to bomb north in front of the KOYLIs and they could not go any further. Brigadier General Headlam had to report that only part of the first objective had been taken and it was impossible to get any closer to Héninel.

An Evening Attack, Feuchy–Wancourt Line

Major Generals Deverell and Couper arranged a coordinated attack by the 3rd and 14th Divisions against the Feuchy–Wancourt Line on VII Corps' left. They wanted to attack before nightfall but the arrangements were rushed and brigade headquarters did not receive their telephone orders until eighty minutes before zero. In 14th Division's zone, Brigadier General Wood told Lieutenant Colonel Bellew of the 6th Somersets to take the 6th DCLI forward from his reserve. The temporary battalion commander, Captain Scott, only heard he was going to attack at 6.25 pm and his company commanders heard the news five minutes before the creeping barrage moved forward. It had passed beyond the German trench before the DCLI were moving and they were soon pinned down.

Lieutenant General Snow thought 30th and 21st Divisions stood little chance of breaking the Hindenburg Line so he discussed reorganising VII Corps front line after dusk. He wanted 14th and 56th Divisions to capture the Feuchy–Wancourt Line and outflank the Hindenburg Line, supported by all of VII Corps' artillery. So the two divisions shifted south and prepared to attack at 8 am.

Third Army Summary

Allenby's headquarters had received favourable reports of progress throughout the day. Early reports showed that thirty-six artillery pieces had been captured while 5,600 men had been taken prisoner and more were heading for the cages. Casualties had been high but reports suggested the Germans had lost many more.

North of the Scarpe, XVII Corps had advanced 1 mile on its left and 2½ miles on its right. South of the river, VI Corps had advanced over 2 miles in places but had only captured a small section of the Feuchy–Wancourt Line. Meanwhile, VII Corps had faced major difficulties breaking through the Hindenburg Line astride the Cojeul stream.

Haig met Allenby during the afternoon to discuss progress. A break-in had been achieved and two reserve divisions had been engaged either side of the Scarpe. The 3rd and 2nd Cavalry Divisions had also been moved past Tilloy-lez-Mofflaines but the question was what to do with them? Officers in the 4th and 9th Divisions believed the cavalry could advance into open country and the infantry could occupy it during the night. Lieutenant Colonel Croft, 11th Royal Scots (9th Division), even called Brigadier General Maxwell to ask him to send the cavalry forward. Haig and Allenby agreed to send one brigade forward to pass through 4th Division at Fampoux so it could advance towards Plouvain. They chose 1 Cavalry Brigade but gave it no instructions. Lieutenant General Charles Kavanagh was eventually told to stand his Cavalry Corps down and withdraw the two divisions behind Arras during the night.

Even if the cavalry had been ordered forward, it would have struggled to find a route across the battlefield. The engineers and pioneers worked all day and night to open the roads, filling craters and trenches for wheeled traffic, but the roads were jammed with horse-drawn wagons taking ammunition forward and bringing the wounded back.

Chapter 12

A Wondrous, Squelching Fight
First Army – 10 to 13 April

Canadian Corps, 10 April
4th Canadian Division, Hill 145

Major General David Watson wanted 10 Canadian Brigade to capture Hill
145 and Brigadier General Hilliam had deployed two battalions on the
south-west slopes by early afternoon. They faced four trenches on the
forward slope, all of them battered beyond recognition by the bombardment.
The barrage against the *Hang Stellung* on the reverse slope was repeated
and then both battalions advanced.

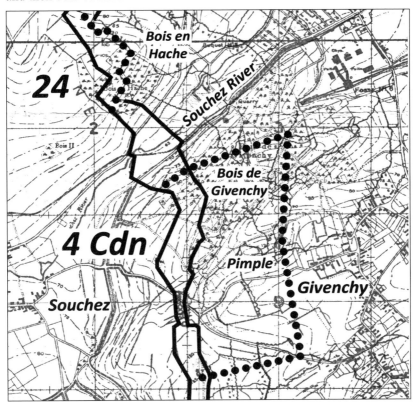

The capture of Hill 145 by 4th Canadian Division on 10 April.

On the left 50th Battalion was pinned down while Private John Pattison dodged from shell hole to shell hole towards the machine gun. He threw bombs at the post, killing and wounding some of the crew, before jumping in and bayoneting the rest of the crew. Pattison was awarded the Victoria Cross. The battalion swept over Hill 145 to the objective but it had suffered 250 casualties. On the right, 44th Battalion went through the north end of Bois de la Folie. The two battalions captured 150 prisoners and they handed over to 47th Battalion during the evening.

I Corps, 12 April
<u>24th Division, Bois en Hache</u>
The capture of Bois en Hache and Hill 120 would push the Germans off the ends of the Lorette and Vimy Ridges. Major General John Capper had 73 Brigade ready to attack on 10 April but Major General Watson had already used 10 Canadian Brigade to capture Hill 145 so the attack was postponed for forty-eight hours.

At 5 am on 12 April the 9th Sussex and 2nd Leinsters advanced across the crater fields in blinding snow. The thick mud meant the Lewis gunners could

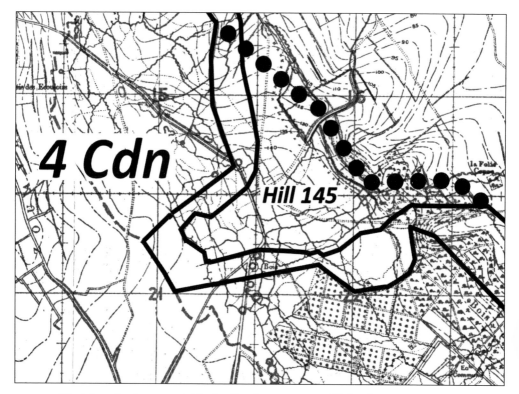

First Army's advance astride the Souchez stream on 12 April.

not go prone so they fired from the shoulder while the infantry trudged forward. Captains Liston and Kelly were killed as they followed a compass bearing but the Sussex negotiated the smashed wire and moved through the north corner of Bois en Hache. They established footholds in the second trench but were soon forced to withdraw to the first trench. It was 'a wondrous, squelching fight, man-to-man and fought out to a finish in muddy water-sodden surroundings in the grey dawn of a bleak and snowy April morning.'

The Leinsters moved through the rest of the wood and a wounded Corporal John Cunningham kept his Lewis gun firing after his comrades had been hit during a counter-attack. He continued to throw bombs when his ammunition ran out until he was injured a second time. Cunningham later died in hospital; he was posthumously awarded the Victoria Cross. Lieutenant Colonel Murphy's men went down the wooded slope as the skies cleared, coming under fire from across the Souchez stream. Lieutenant Mathias silenced one machine gun and Lieutenant Magner and around forty men held on in the second trench until their ammunition ran low.

The divisional pioneers, the 12th Sherwoods, dug a trench across no man's land, securing the position which overlooked the German trenches. All Brigadier General Duggan had to do was wait for them to withdraw.

Canadian Corps, 12 April
4th Canadian Division, The Pimple

The 10 Canadian Brigade had practised the attack many times by the time it climbed up the slopes of the Pimple (also known as Hill 120). Aerial photographs had allowed the map makers to plot the labyrinth of trenches but they could not show the warren of dugouts and tunnels under the hill. Brigadier General Hilliam's men were in position between the Souchez stream and Kennedy Crater before dawn but the Germans opened fire when they spotted 46th Battalion, on the left.

Two siege artillery groups began shooting blindly into a blizzard at 4.50 am and ten minutes later the Canadians advanced as the 18-pounder guns opened fire. They could barely see the exploding shells of the creeping barrage but the Germans could see less because the snow was blowing into their faces. Artillery fire had flattened many trenches and they were often found sheltering in dugouts or shell holes. Some sections of trench were unoccupied, because they were so deep in mud, and the Canadians passed through these gaps in the defence.

No man's land was still under fire when 46th Battalion advanced and half the leading company fell. The rest became disorientated in the blizzard and they veered into the path of 50th Battalion as it moved through the smashed tree stumps of Bois de Givenchy. But 46th Battalion's second company went in the right direction and along the slope overlooking the Souchez stream.

On the right, 44th Battalion took nearly eighty prisoners sheltering in the dugouts around the quarry on the Pimple's summit. Others ran down the slope and the Canadians followed, going 300 yards beyond their objective in the darkness.

As the dawn sky lightened, the snow slowed and then stopped, bringing a dreadful night to an end. The sun came out and the Canadians could see across the Douai plain to Lens and Avion, four miles to the north-east. They could also see columns of soldiers and horse-drawn transport heading towards them.

First Army, Exploitation
General Horne had moved XIII Corps forward to strengthen the boundary between the Canadian Corps and Third Army. Late on 10 April his headquarters had ordered the Canadian Corps to advance to the Vimy–Bailleul railway. General Byng was later told to wait until XIII Corps was ready. Major General Cecil Pereira's 2nd Division had taken over 51st Division's sector in the Point du Jour Line by dawn of 12 April. Lieutenant General Fergusson had also moved up 63rd and 31st Divisions ready to take over the line facing Bailleul.

Early on 13 April, First Army headquarters started to hear there had been a German withdrawal. Following the loss of Vimy Ridge, Crown Prince Rupprecht wrote, 'No one could have foreseen that the expected offensive would gain ground so quickly.' On 11 April he ordered a withdrawal to the German Third Position, known as the Avion Switch, and the Méricourt-Oppy Line. On average it involved a withdrawal of around 5,000 yards, moving the front line away from Vimy Ridge escarpment.

The early morning patrols reported empty trenches east of Souchez, but machine gun fire stopped 12 Canadian Brigade moving towards Givenchy for a while. Soon afterwards, 72nd and 73rd Canadian Battalions entered the village and discovered an abandoned 21-cm howitzer. Byng ordered all the Canadian divisions to send patrols forward mid-morning and they discovered abandoned trenches either side of Vimy. In the distance smoke could be seen rising from dugouts and explosions as excess ammunition was blown up.

By nightfall, 24th Division had occupied Angres on I Corps' front. Givenchy was occupied by 4th Canadian Division, while 3rd Canadian Division had moved through La Chaudière and Vimy. The 2nd Canadian Division had advanced to the Vimy–Bailleul railway while the 1st Canadian Division had occupied Willerval.

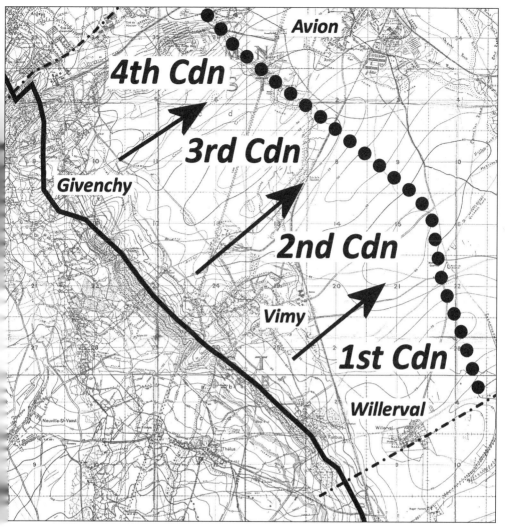

The German withdrawal on First Army's front on 13 April.

Late that evening, Horne issued orders to move forward without getting engaged with the Germans. Prisoners had been saying they had been heading back to the Méricourt–Oppy Line so they would be able to face the Canadians on favourable terrain (the Canadians overlooked them if they stayed close to the ridge; pulling back placed them in a better defensive situation). The new trenches were shallow but were protected by new entanglements and fresh reserves were waiting to repel any attacks. It left First Army with a serious problem: wheeled traffic could not get forward across the maze of trenches, shell holes and wire entanglements. Over 5,000 men were working around the clock to repair the road network but it would be some time before the artillery batteries could move forward.

First Army advanced another 1,000 yards the following day, meeting nothing more than rear guards. They came across many abandoned field guns and stacks of ammunition and they were put to good use. The Canadian gunners had been trained how to operate German guns and turn them against their former owners until their own guns could be brought forward.

The Canadian Corps had advanced around 7,000 yards in six days, capturing an important tactical position. General Horne declared the success was down to 'soundness of plan, thoroughness of preparation, dash and determination in execution, and devotion to duty'. The Canadians had captured over 50 artillery pieces, over 100 trench mortars and over 120 machine guns; it had also captured more than 4,000 prisoners. The Canadian Corps had suffered over 10,600 casualties.

At 8 pm on 13 April, Horne issued instructions to attack the German position between Acheville, Oppy and Gavrelle. The problem was the infantry had to dig assembly trenches, the engineers had to repair the roads, and the artillery had to cut the wire. All the work had to be carried out under the watchful eye of an alert enemy as the rain and the snow turned the ground into a quagmire.

Chapter 13

Risks Must Be Freely Taken
Third Army – 10 and 11 April

Haig had heard Horne's and Allenby's initial reports at Saint Pol on the morning of 9 April. Horne gave positive reports about First Army's situation but Allenby had mixed news about Third Army's situation. The generals had planned the next day's action but the weather took a turn for the worse when it started to rain during the evening. It turned to snow during the night, chilling the men to the bone, sapping the strength of the fit and the wounded alike. The unpredictable weather made flying difficult but the RFC pilots continued to fly missions; four of them crashed their planes.

XVIII Corps, 10 April
51st Division, Point du Jour Line
Major General Harper had to improve his position on his right where 152 Brigade had been stopped short of the Pont du Jour Line. The 1/5th Gordons advanced at the same time as 34th Division's left without a creeping barrage and they caught the Germans by surprise. Lieutenant Colonel McTaggart was unable to see 154 Brigade on his left but he could see the Germans were falling back so he ordered his support companies forward. The Gordons cut the wire, cleared the Point du Jour trenches, and captured fifty Germans around Maison de la Côte. They then established a position in the sunken road beyond.

Harper had been led to understand that 154 Brigade was already holding the Point du Jour Line. However, its right flank was holding Tommy Trench and communication trenches which faced south rather than east. Harper had also heard that his Scots were firing on each other, undermining the Gordons' position in the Point du Jour Line, so he ordered Brigadier General Hamilton to clear up the situation. The bombers made some progress along the communication trenches during the afternoon but the Point du Jour Line remained in German hands.

By nightfall Hamilton's men had dug a line of outposts in contact with the Canadians to the north. But the Gordons had been unable to advance

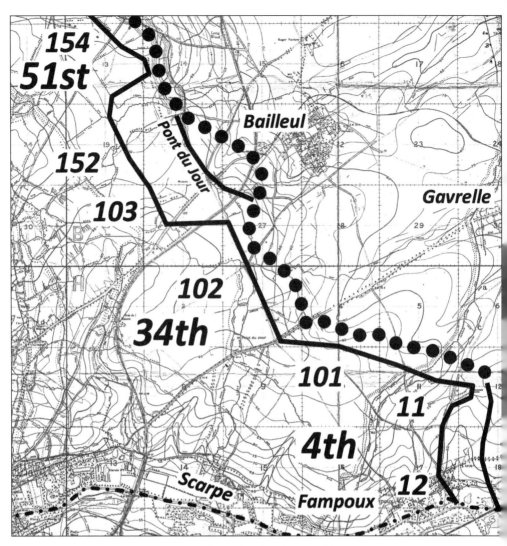

XVII Corps' advance towards Bailleul and Gavrelle on 10 April.

any further because the falling snow silhouetted all movement in the open. Brigadier General Burn had to send the 1/7th Gordons forward because the 1/5th Gordons had lost all its officers, either to enemy action or the appalling weather.

34th Division, Point du Jour Line
At 5 am a second attempt was made to reach the Point du Jour Line in front of Bailleul. The Northumberland Fusiliers of 103 Brigade reached the Brown Line. Captain Neeve worked along Gaul Trench and a sunken road to position his Lewis guns on the flank of Maison de la Côte observation

point. The Germans ran but the Northumberland Fusiliers were too exhausted to catch them so they stood up and fired instead, cheering every time they hit someone. Brigadier General Trevor ordered a withdrawal when the Germans advanced from the sunken Fampoux–Bailleul road during the evening. He called down artillery fire to disperse the counter-attack and then ordered his men to return to their positions.

On the division's right, 101 Brigade's patrols advanced down the slope towards Gavrelle, passing many German artillery pieces stuck in the mud. The village appeared to be abandoned but Major General Nicholson had no reserves to check it out because his men were exhausted. They could do no more but they had captured nearly 800 prisoners, fourteen artillery pieces and many mortars and machine guns. It had cost 34th Division over 2,765 casualties.

4th Division, Fampoux

Lieutenant General Fergusson briefed Allenby on XVII Corps' situation during the morning. He doubted he could seize Roeux because his artillery was moving forward, but he believed the 1st Cavalry Division could seize Greenland Hill and Plouvain ready for 4th Division to occupy it. Lieutenant General Kavanagh issued a move order to Major General Richard Mullens before midday and 1 Cavalry Brigade began its difficult journey along the north bank of the Scarpe.

Major General Lambton was preparing 4th Division's attack when he received new orders to support the cavalry, so he changed his instructions and arranged for patrols to reconnoitre the ground instead. They all found out the Germans were ready and waiting. On 12 Brigade's front, Second Lieutenant Gilbert was killed as the 1st Hampshires crossed the Roeux–Gavrelle road but Lieutenant de Gaury captured a trench west of Greenland Hill. Brigadier General Berners had to report two platoons of the 1st Somerset had been shot down as they left Hyderabad Redoubt.

Brigadier General Carton de Wiart had already taken steps to advance east of Fampoux but again there were problems. The 1st King's Own had secured the embankment and the railway bridge over the Scarpe but the rest of the battalion was pinned down by machine gun fire from Roeux chemical works.

The 5th Dragoon Guards reached Fampoux around 4.30 pm and Captain Winterbottom spoke to Brigadier General Makins. He contacted his battalion commanders and concluded that a mounted advance could be a disaster. A heavy fall of snow and a counter-attack proved that they had made the right decision, so the cavalry withdrew.

VI Corps, 10 April

Neither Allenby nor Haldane were aware that a small part of the Feuchy–Wancourt Line, on Orange Hill, had been taken. Allenby wanted VI Corps to clear the Brown Line and to advance to the Green Line east of Monchy-le-Preux and Guémappe. He planned to start at 8 am on 10 April and the cavalry were alerted so they could take advantage of any breakthrough. But not everyone was as convinced about the merits of combined warfare, as the infantry, artillery tanks and cavalry jostled for position on the battlefield.

> *With the tactical handling of tanks reduced to an equitable distribution between four corps, and with the last completely organised enemy line beyond effective range of our field guns, congestion behind the battle front was made infernal by the prancing about of the cavalry in readiness to be sent forward should our infantry succeed in widening the breach.*

Haldane decided to postpone his attack until noon, the time VII Corps advanced to the south. He heard about 37th Division's capture of Orange Hill during the morning and was able to include the information in his 10.30 am orders. Major General Scott had to capture the Feuchy Chapel redoubt first and then clear the Feuchy–Wancourt Line. Then 12th Division could advance across Chapel Hill while 37th Division moved towards Monchy-le-Preux. It would allow 15th Division to advance along the Scarpe and 3rd Division to reach Guémappe.

<u>12th Division, Orange Hill</u>

Another 600 yards of the Feuchy–Wancourt Line was cleared next to the Scarpe by 15th Division during the morning. Brigadier General Vincent instructed Lieutenant Colonel Haig to lead the 5th Berkshires and three companies each from the 11th Middlesex and 7th Sussex through the Scottish position. They then wheeled right behind the German trenches as the rest of 35 Brigade cleared Orange Hill. Vincent deployed his single tank on the Cambrai road to help clear Feuchy Chapel redoubt.

<u>37th Division, Advance towards Monchy</u>

Major General Bruce-Williams' advance would start with 63 Brigade advancing east while 111 Brigade approached Monchy from the north-west. After 12th Division cleared Chapel Hill, 112 Brigade would advance on 111 Brigade's right.

Observers on Orange Hill watched as the 8th Somersets, 8th Lincolns and 4th Middlesex crossed Lone Copse valley under crossfire from Pelves

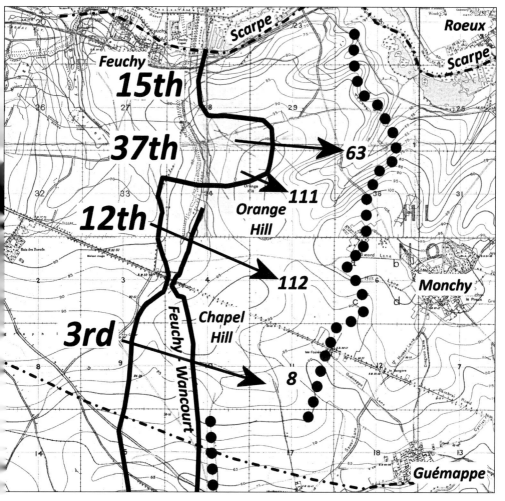

VI Corps advance towards Monchy and Guémappe on 10 April.

Mill ridge and Roeux across the river. The 10th York and Lancasters were pinned down as they neared Monchy on the right. The 10th and 13th Royal Fusiliers were also pinned down west of the village because 111 Brigade had no artillery support.

On the Cambrai road 12th Division had cleared Feuchy Chapel redoubt, allowing the 8th East Lancashires and 6th Bedfords to lead 112 Brigade over Chapel Hill. They deployed as soon as they crossed the summit as the machine guns in Monchy and Guémappe found their range. The two battalions dug in either side the Cambrai road, near Les Fosses Farm, where they were reinforced by the 11th Warwicks and 10th Loyals. A plan to advance after dusk had to be cancelled because the orders reached the front line around the same time the creeping barrage started moving forward.

3rd Division, Guémappe

Brigadier General Holmes had reorganised 8 Brigade so all four of his battalions were in line south of the Cambrai road. Most of the Germans had been withdrawn from the Feuchy–Wancourt Line and the rest surrendered as the 1st Gordons and 7th Shropshires advanced over Chapel Hill. Meanwhile, the 2nd Royal Scots and 8th East Yorkshires found the 6th KOYLIs and 10th Durhams moving across their front as they tried to escape the machine gun fire coming from Wancourt. Holmes was able to report an advance of 3,000 yards but his men were pinned down on the slope in front of Guémappe.

The Cavalry

Contact planes circled over the Monchy area all morning, noting where the infantry were lighting flares. They flew back to the corps report centres and dropped their marked up maps onto the ground. It was a fast way of getting information back; unfortunately getting messages and reinforcements forward took a lot longer.

The cavalry had been out in the open all night and the snow showers had affected man and horse alike. It was 11.45 am before Lieutenant General Kavanagh was instructed to send 2nd and 3rd Cavalry Divisions forward. On VI Corps' front 3rd Cavalry Division's 8 Cavalry Brigade was already moving down the Cambrai road by the time 37th Division was closing in on Monchy. But the road was full of traffic and the horses were suffering in the bad weather.

Major General Walter Greenly moved 2nd Cavalry Division forward into VII Corps' sector during the afternoon. The Germans on Hill 90 spotted 3 Cavalry Brigade during the breaks in the snow showers and long-range fire brought it to a standstill. The 5 Cavalry Brigade also halted because it was clear the infantry had not broken through. There was no water around Neuville-Vitasse so 3 Cavalry Brigade returned to their bivouacs, but 5 Cavalry Brigade stayed out on the battlefield. The troopers spent a miserable night huddled in shell holes, holding the reins of their poor horses as they stood around the edges.

Kavanagh instructed Major General John Vaughan to advance north of Monchy during the afternoon and he sent 8 Brigade forward. A squadron of 10th Hussars moved towards Lone Copse at around 5 pm under machine gun fire from Roeux. The Hussars and the Essex Yeomanry then galloped onto Pelves Mill spur north-east of Monchy, drawing fire from all directions. It was a dangerous move and they withdrew when a blast of heavy snow blinded the Germans. It was the same story south of Monchy, where 6 Cavalry Brigade drew fire from the village. Both

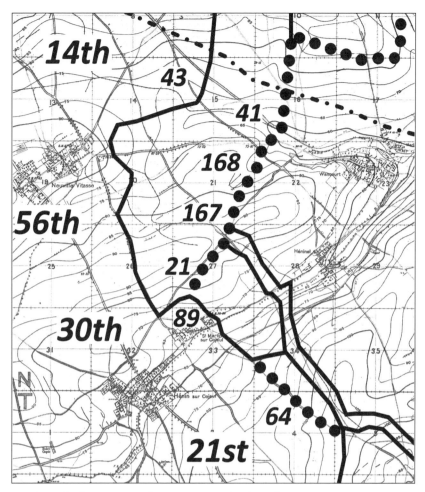

VII Corps' advance towards Wancourt and Héninel on 10 April.

brigades withdrew behind Orange Hill and bivouacked in the open for the night.

VII Corps, 10 April
14th Division, Wancourt
The plan was for 43 Brigade to advance at 11.45 am but a message from 56th Division said it was going to starting firing, not start advancing, at that time. So Brigadier General Wood's timings had to be postponed by thirty-five minutes. The 6th KOYLIs and 10th Durhams overran a few outposts as they advanced down the valley towards Wancourt, only to come under fire from Hill 90 on their right, where 56th Division should have been. It pushed the two battalions north, right into the path of 3rd Division.

Major General Couper ordered Brigadier General Skinner to move his

41 Brigade forward through the blizzard, ready to advance towards Wancourt at 2.15 pm. Three battalions moved in artillery formation as the snow blinded the British and Germans alike. Lieutenant Colonel de Calry's 7th Rifle Brigade were stopped by a wire entanglement but two companies of the 7th KRRC entered the Feuchy–Wancourt Line. On the right, 8th Rifle Brigade failed to capture Hill 90 so it had to form a defensive flank.

56th Division, Hindenburg Line

Major General Hull's advance was delayed until midday to give his men time to break free from the Hindenburg Line trenches east of Neuville-Vitasse. Lieutenant General Snow had heard about a withdrawal from the Feuchy–Wancourt Line; he wanted to follow it up and be across the Cojeul stream before nightfall.

The 1/14th London Regiment had cleared 168 Brigade's section of trenches before dawn. The bombers had squelched their way through trenches filled with mud and water. No wonder the Germans were withdrawing, they were looking for drier ground. There were problems on the right, in 167 Brigade's sector. Neither the 1/8th Middlesex nor the 1/3rd London Regiment could reach the Feuchy–Wancourt Line because the Germans were determined to hold Hill 90 for a little longer.

30th Division, Hill 90

The Hindenburg Line trenches were in a better state on the west end of Wancourt Ridge. The 19th Manchesters cleared enough trenches to contact 56th Division but Major General Shea had to report that his men were unable to progress towards Héninel.

21st Division, Hindenburg Line

The Germans tried all day to push 64 Brigade out of the Hindenburg Line south of the Cojeul stream. At dusk they drove the 1st East Yorkshires back on the right flank and the rest of the brigade followed. Brigadier General Headlam wanted two companies of the 10th KOYLIs to counter-attack, but the British artillery was firing short so Lieutenant Colonel Postlethwaite had to wait until the guns extended their range before they advanced. The delay allowed the German machine gun teams to deploy their weapons so Major General Campbell banned an advance over the top. But the bombing contest continued and an injured Private Horace Waller threw many grenades as he defended one of the KOYLI's trench blocks. He continued fighting on alone, long after all his comrades had been hit, saving the situation. Waller was eventually killed; he was posthumously awarded the Victoria Cross.

Third Army, 11 April

Thoughts of using cavalry to break through had to be abandoned because the horses could not cope with the bad weather. They had spent the winter under cover; some horses died from the shock of having to stand out in the open on short rations, others had to be destroyed.

But Allenby was still optimistic. He stated: 'Third Army is now pursuing a defeated enemy and … risks must be freely taken. Isolated enemy detachments in farms and villages must not be allowed to delay the general progress. Such points must be masked and passed by. They can be dealt with by troops in rear.' The bad weather had prevented the Royal Flying Corps from spotting German divisions moving opposite Third Army; the first time Allenby heard about them was when prisoners were interrogated.

Haig also wanted Allenby to keep pushing. On the left, XVII Corps would take Plouvain and Greenland Hill; VI Corps would capture the Green Line east of Monchy and Guémappe in the centre; VII Corps would cross the Cojeul at Wancourt and Héninel. Fifth Army was about to attack the Hindenburg Line at Bullecourt and Haig was hoping the two armies could push cavalry through the gaps opened by the infantry.

XVIII Corps, 11 April

51st Division, Point du Jour Line

Major General Harper intended to postpone the attack on the Point du Jour Line south of Farbus Wood until 6.30 pm to give the artillery time to cut the wire. That was until Corporal Mitchell, a divisional observer, went exploring and discovered that the Brown Line had been abandoned. He returned to report he had seen stacked packs, unopened parcels and half-eaten meals in the dugouts. Patrols crossed no man's land and discovered the same; the Germans had gone. Brigadier General Hamilton sent 154 Brigade forward to occupy the Brown Line, instructing the 7th Gordons and 9th Royal Scots to move towards the railway.

34th Division, South of Bailleul

Major General Nicholson sent patrols towards the Fampoux–Bailleul road early in the afternoon. Those on 101 Brigade's front discovered the Germans had withdrawn and were digging a new trench beyond the road. Outposts were established close to the new trench while contact was established with 4th Division on the right.

4th Division, Fampoux

Major General Lambton planned to advance towards Roeux at midday but Lieutenant General Fergusson wanted him to move earlier. Mist meant the observers could not adjust their guns during the six-hour bombardment, so few targets were hit.

A flank was formed by 11 Brigade east of Hyderabad Redoubt but Brigadier General Gosling's men were shelled as they assembled north of Fampoux. Machine guns on the railway embankment around the station and around the chemical works and chateau opened fire when the 2nd Seaforths and 1st Irish Fusiliers advanced. A seriously wounded Lieutenant Donald Mackintosh led some Seaforths to a trench close to the Roeux–Gavrelle road. He was wounded a second time but stopped a counter-attack with the help of a few Irish Fusiliers. Mackintosh crawled out of a trench to shout 'Carry on!' as the final group of fifteen men set off for the final objective. His third wound was fatal; he was posthumously awarded the Victoria Cross. A few men got close to the station but the 1st Warwicks and Household Battalion could not reach them and they suffered more casualties as they withdrew. Lambton wanted to try again but Gosling had no time to organise anything; it had cost his brigade over 1,000 casualties.

Brigadier General Carton de Wiart's men deployed on the river bank east of Fampoux and fanned out as they advanced towards their objective. The creeping barrage was inadequate as well as moving too fast as 12 Brigade trudged across the marshy ground. Machine guns in Roeux wood pinned down the 2nd Duke's on the railway embankment while the 1st King's Own and two 2nd Lancashire Fusiliers companies lost the barrage as they skirted the marsh. Another attack at 2 pm failed for the same reasons and Carton de Wiart's men had to fight off counter-attacks in a blizzard.

Fergusson had planned to send cavalry through the gap created by 4th Division but 1 Cavalry Brigade only sent Lieutenant Kingstone's squadron of the 2nd Dragoon Guards forward. Second Lieutenant Quested and six troopers galloped towards Fampoux station to find out 'what, if anything, was happening'. Machine gun fire brought down the horses but the men made it back to report there had been no breakthrough. Major General Mullens withdrew the brigade at dusk.

VI Corps, 11 April

Lieutenant General Haldane planned to attack around Monchy-le-Preux at 5 am but the late postponement of the zero hour had created problems. The infantry battalions had not heard of the change and set off at the original zero hour in the miserable weather; they advanced behind a ragged creeping barrage because the gun teams had not had enough time to register their guns. Only four of C Battalion's tanks joined the advance into Monchy.

15th Division, North of Monchy

Major General McCracken's infantry advanced out of Lone Copse valley without any artillery support. Machine gun fire from Roeux pushed 45 Brigade up the slope and the 6/7th Scots Fusiliers and 6th Camerons soon withdrew to the sunken road on the crest on the west side of valley. Meanwhile, Lieutenant McIndoe collected around one hundred men who had made it into Monchy and they dug in on the north-east side of the village.

In 46 Brigade's sector, the leading companies of the 10/11th Highland Light Infantry advanced through the wood north of Monchy, only to be pinned north-east of the village. The support companies entered the village and began clearing houses until their officers made them join the rest of the battalion. One company of the 12th HLI then took over clearing the village.

McCracken wanted to capture Pelves Mill ridge so he could report he had made progress on his left. But the 8th Gordons could not cross Lone Copse and they withdrew as soon as it was dark.

37th Division, The Capture of Monchy

Major General Bruce-Williams' plan was for 111 Brigade to advance east of Monchy while 112 Brigade covered its right flank. Lieutenant Colonel Preton-Prinney's 13th Rifle Brigade came under heavy fire, suffering ten officer casualties alone, but it captured a trench on the north-west side of Monchy. The tanks accompanied the 13th KRRC through the village until they were knocked out. Around 150 prisoners were taken. Then the rest of the Germans fell back so that their artillery could bombard the village. 'The enemy shelling increased to absolute drum fire and casualties increased … by Jove their gunners warmed us up a bit!'

The 11th Loyals advanced past the south side of Monchy but the 11th Warwicks were pinned down in front of Guémappe. So the Warwicks redeployed and moved across the Cambrai road, accompanied by a tank, to reinforce the Loyals. They cleared a trench south-west of La Bergère.

At 8 am Brigadier General Challenor was instructed to move 63 Brigade across Lone Copse valley onto Infantry Hill east of Monchy. The 10th York and Lancasters moved at 10.30 am only to be pinned down on the Pelves Mill ridge by the machine guns from Roeux. So Bruce-Williams ordered Challenor to reinforce the attack on Monchy instead. The 8th Lincolns and 4th Middlesex moved forward in short rushes until they filled the gap between the York and Lancasters and Monchy.

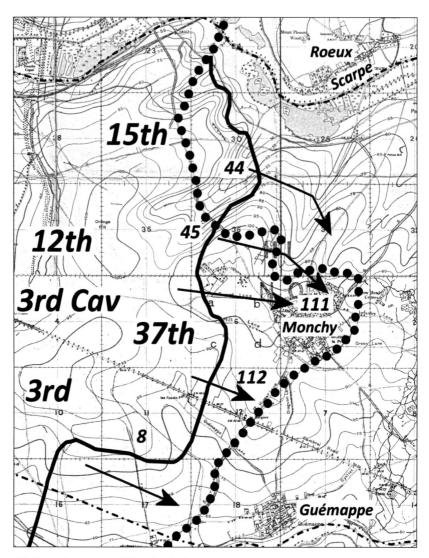

VI Corps' capture of Monchy-le-Preux on 11 April.

3rd Cavalry Division, The Counter-Attack against Monchy

Lieutenant General Haldane had 3rd Cavalry Division in reserve and both 6 and 8 Cavalry Brigades had spent the night waiting north-west of Feuchy Chapel. Brigadier Generals Harman and Bulkeley-Johnson were told the Germans were retiring in front of 37th Division and they had to move quickly to take advantage of the situation. But while Monchy and La Bergère had been taken, 'the story of the cavalry was a tragedy. A rumour spread that the Boche had retired to Boiry-Notre-Dame.' The truth was the

German line had been dented but it had not been broken; they were regrouping ready to counter-attack.

Three squadrons of the 3rd Dragoon Guards galloped along the Cambrai road at 8.30 am, followed by the rest of 6 Cavalry Brigade. But the cavalry troopers had to deploy into attack formation along the Monchy–Wancourt road, under machine gun fire from Guémappe. Bulkeley-Johnson then instructed Lieutenant Colonels Whitmore and Hardwick to each send a squadron forward.

Lieutenant Colonel Whitmore ordered Lieutenant Chaplin to reinforce the north-west corner of Monchy and his squadron of the Essex Yeomanry galloped forward under fire. Lieutenant Colonel Hardwick also sent Captain Canning's squadron of the 10th Hussars forward to join the Yeomanry in the village square. The plan had been for the Yeomanry squadron to head north along the Pelves road while the Hussars followed on the Roeux road, but they were both under fire.

The infantry welcomed the arrival of the rest of the two regiments but the German observers were also watching the cavalry; 'they appeared galloping up in squadrons – cheers! But the enemy saw them and shelled them so terribly that 50 per cent were down in ten minutes.' The cavalry's machine gun teams set up around the edge of Monchy while Lieutenant Colonel Hardwick led a squadron of the 10th Hussars around the north side of the village. It was under heavy fire so Hardwick and his adjutant, Captain Greenwood, took their squadron back into the ruins.

Lieutenant Colonel Lord Tweedmouth moved a squadron of the Royal Horse Guards into Monchy but casualties were mounting, particularly amongst the officers who were easy to spot, moving amongst their men. Tweedmouth arrived just after Bulkeley-Johnson was killed and he took command of 6 Cavalry Brigade while Lieutenant Colonel Whitmore tried to make sense of what was happening. He discovered that 15th Division's infantry had fallen back to the north while most of the infantry in Monchy were either wounded or taking cover around the chateau, having lost all their officers. The only good news was that there was a tank crawling around the ruins.

The shelling increased in intensity around midday until 'it had the appearance, to those who were outside, of being a veritable furnace, and it was a wonder to them that anyone could be alive in this heap of ruins.' The bombardment indicated a counter-attack was imminent and the troopers searched the ruins looking for abandoned Lewis guns to replace their damaged Hotchkiss guns. Others led the horses to the rear but German artillery observers spotted them leaving the west side of Monchy. Many horses cantered off in a panic during the bombardment that followed and 'only sixty out of 400 horses escaped'. The village streets were left strewn with dead, injured and starving horses; a pitiful sight. There was no counter-attack but Germans could be seen assembling in the distance.

Lance Corporal Harold Mugford had deployed his machine gun with a commanding view of the ground east of Monchy. He was waiting for the counter-attack when an exploding shell wounded him and killed his assistant. Mugford refused to go to the dressing station and carried on firing his weapon even after another explosion broke both his legs. He was later wounded a third time at the dressing station but survived to receive his Victoria Cross.

As the cavalry held on in Monchy, G Battery of IV Brigade, Royal Horse Artillery, deployed in an exposed position on the south-west outskirts. One gun team had been knocked out by an exploding shell by the time Lieutenant Colonel Lord Tweedmouth ordered the rest to withdraw. Two sections redeployed alongside the Cambrai road but were again ordered to withdraw early in the afternoon; they joined K Battery on Orange Hill. The gun teams had given valuable support to the troops around Monchy and each battery had fired around 450 rounds.

Around 2.30 pm there were signs that the Germans were ready to counter-attack at La Bergère crossroads, south-east of the village. Brigadier General Harman sent a North Somerset Yeomanry squadron forward on foot but all they found were thirty men of the 6th Bedfords in a trench beyond the Cambrai road. They were led by Private Batchellor who had been making them collect all the rifles and bombs they could find in between the counter-attacks.

12th Division, Holding Monchy

Lieutenant General Haldane instructed Major General Scott to take over Monchy before it was lost. He ordered 36 and 37 Brigades to take over the village but they faced a difficult approach march through a blizzard. Lieutenant Colonel Dawson of the 6th Queen's Own eventually reached the cavalry's headquarters in the square and Lieutenant Colonel Whitmore handed over command. The Queen's Own immediately attacked, allowing the exhausted men to withdraw. But the 10th York and Lancasters, the 8th Lincolns and a few cavalry detachments remained until the following night.

By nightfall snow began to cover the bodies scattered about Monchy's rubble-strewn streets. Stretcher bearers had been busy collecting the wounded men but there was still one ghastly task left to carry out. Lieutenant Swire of the Essex Yeomanry had to search the ruins for injured horses so he could put them out of their misery.

3rd Division, Guémappe

Brigadier General Porter received his orders to attack late and it was a rush to organise an advance between the Cambrai road and the Cojeul stream. The gunners had also had insufficient time to register their targets and the artillery barrage was negligible. No shells hit Guémappe, where the machine gun fire was coming from, and enfilade fire from Wancourt pushed the troops across the slope. The battalions became mixed up as they picked their way across the broken ground and the junior officers found it impossible to reorganise their platoons. Melting snow had turned the slope leading down to the Cojeul into a bog and men found cover in the water-filled shell holes:

> *All day anyone moving from shell hole to shell hole was sniped and machine-gunned and movement, except singly, was folly. The conduct of the men, who early on must have realised the hopelessness of their task, was beyond praise.*

VII Corps, 11 April

Lieutenant General Snow's orders instructed the same four divisions to capture Wancourt and advance astride the Cojeul stream. But this time there were only four tanks to help them.

14th Division, Wancourt

Major General Couper had to capture Hill 90 on his right flank before his left could move down the valley towards Wancourt. Brigadier General Skinner was assured the village was being attacked and he in turn promised Lieutenant Colonel Bury that the 7th KRRC would not be subjected to enfilade fire. Both the 7th Rifle Brigade and 7th KRRC withdrew 200 yards so the gunners could target the hilltop opposite 41 Brigade but the 'artillery barrage entirely failed' because they did not have enough time to prepare. It meant the 'advance was checked from the very beginning by heavy machine gun fire from the front and enfilade from the right and rear'.

56th Division, Hill 90

Major General Hull was happy with the assistance given by the four tanks but he was unimpressed with the artillery's contribution:

> *Not satisfied that the infantry are receiving sufficient support from the artillery. The situation demands that as many batteries as possible be pushed forward so that the enemy machine guns are dealt with at a decisive range.*

The 1/7th Middlesex bombed north along the Feuchy–Wancourt Line while the 1/9th London Regiment worked east along the Hindenburg Line to the Cojeul stream. They captured over 300 prisoners between them in a fierce fight lasting 48 hours.

30th Division, Cojeul Stream

The infantry headed for gaps in the wire next to the Cojeul stream east of Saint Martin. Shells were whistling overhead, only they were exploding too far in front of them. Two 20th King's companies passed through the northern gap and bombed along the Hindenburg Line while two tanks approached from the front.

> *And now comes the thrilling part. We got a message to say that a tank was coming over the hill, followed immediately by another. Then we heard the Boche were running like hares… After the tanks had played about a bit, our gallant lads made another effort, but with the same result. As a matter of fact the 20th King's made six efforts, but each time a tank approached the machine gunners got down in their dugouts and when it had passed they immediately reappeared.*

Brigadier General Mayne eventually signalled the tank and told the officer to drive up and down the wire while he directed the artillery onto the trench. The bursting shells kept the machine gun teams underground allowing the 1/9th London Regiment to enter the trench from the opposite end. They bombed along it in front of Captain Lancaster's company and 'after that it was plain sailing'.

Meanwhile, two companies of the 2nd Bedford had passed through the gap on the south side of the stream and bombed up the slope. The rest of the battalion took the opportunity to advance along the Cojeul towards Héninel.

21st Division, Hindenburg Line

On VII Corps' right, the artillery had struggled to cut the wire protecting the Hindenburg Line in front of 21st Division. On 62 Brigade's front, the 10th Green Howards and 1st Lincolns headed for the handful of gaps in the wire. But the barrage had not silenced the machine guns hidden in ground-level concrete casemates. They were soon all back on their start line.

A sentry keeps watch across a snow covered no man's land.

Straining to move an 18-pounder field gun through the mud en route to the Hindenburg Line.

Men of the 1st Australian Division rest near Bapaume during Fifth Army's advance.

The crew of a 15-inch howitzer prepare to fire in support of Third Army's attack.

Aiming an 18-pounder during 9th (Scottish) Division's advance east of Arras.

The Canadian advance across Vimy Ridge begins.

Canadian troops pass a bogged down tank on Vimy Ridge.

Canadian reserves move forward to the summit of Vimy Ridge.

Canadian machine gun teams dig in, ready for the counter-attacks against Vimy Ridge.

Canadian soldiers exchange war stories over a mug of coffee.

Putting up ladders so the troops could climb out of the trench.

A wiring party carry their tools and materials towards the front line at Feuchy.

The cavalry wait for the breakthrough that never came.

Canadian soldiers escort prisoners to the rear.

Prisoners help carry Canadian wounded to the first aid post.

Sorting out the wounded at Tilloy-lèz-Mofflaines dressing station.

A Vickers gun team of the Machine Gun Corps keep a look out for German planes.

Canadians use head straps, called tump lines, to carry wiring equipment to the Avion sector.

Carrying hot food and drink up to 12th Division's line, east of Arras.

Chapter 14

Substitute Shells for Infantry
Third Army – 12 and 13 April

Third Army had to keep pushing east, astride the Scarpe, while First Army covered its left flank. The plan for 12 April was to clear the resistance on its flanks, so VI Corps could advance in the centre. North of the Scarpe, XVII Corps had to capture Roeux while VII Corps had to reach the Sensée stream. Only then could VI Corps advance east of Monchy.

But Allenby's divisions were exhausted after being in action for three days in miserable weather. They had suffered many casualties and Allenby wanted a slow, deliberate advance which would 'substitute shells for infantry'. Eight fresh divisions were heading for Third Army but they could not be used without GHQ's permission. Meanwhile, fresh German reserves were arriving and they were looking to regain the Feuchy–Wancourt Line. They were also preparing their next line of defence, the Drocourt–Quéant Line.

XVII Corps, 12 April

Lieutenant General Fergusson wanted time to survey the area around Roeux before he advanced but Allenby told him to attack as soon he was sure he had 'a reasonable chance of success'. Late on 11 April, Major General Lukin was told his 9th Division had to move through 4th Division's line at Fampoux the following afternoon. It left little time to prepare.

9th Division, Fampoux

The plan was for 27 Brigade to capture the Roeux area, while a smoke barrage covered the north flank along the railway. But there were problems. Lukin decided against deploying troops east of Fampoux because the area was being watched from the chemical works. So Brigadier General Maxwell's Scots had to assemble north of the village and then move a mile across open ground to reach its first objective. There was no time to arrange additional smoke to cover the flank, leaving the Scottish troops exposed to artillery fire during the thirty-minute advance. The men waited in trenches

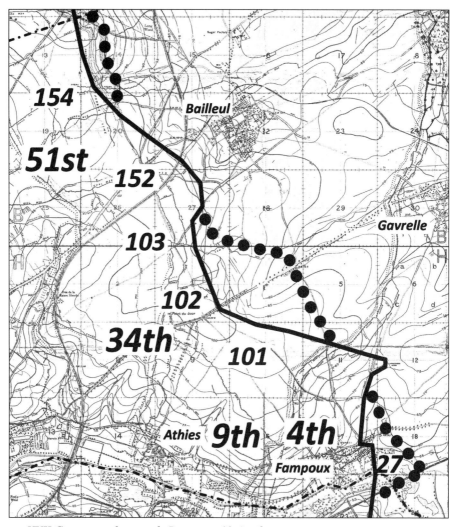

XVII Corps attack towards Roeux on 12 April.

knee-deep in sticky mud, watching as their trenches collapsed every time a shell exploded nearby. The snow showers became heavier as the day wore on and they shivered as they waited in vain for hot food and drinks to arrive.

The corps artillery had been instructed not to increase its fire so as not to alert the Germans, so few heavy shells hit the objective. A few batteries had been given incorrect instructions and the gunners targeted Roeux village rather the chemical works and the station which overlooked the Scots' route. To make matters worse, the Germans had dug a new trench north of the railway and the aerial observers spotted it too late to tell the artillery.

Major Campbell's 12th Royal Scots and Major MacPherson's 11th Royal Scots came under fire as soon as they moved off:

At zero B company and the first wave of A company climbed out of the trenches but progress was impossible in the face of such fire and two officers and fifty-one men were casualties in less than two minutes. Patterson and Spencer died gallant deaths standing up on the parapet helping the men out of the deep and muddy trenches.

The artillery and machine gun fire increased as the Royal Scots passed through 4th Division's line and they lost contact with the creeping barrage before they reached the railway. Captain Turner, Lieutenant Smith and Tredgold were killed at the head of the 11th Scots while Majors MacPherson and Hay and Captains Armit and Noble were wounded. There were over 400 casualties and the survivors withdrew from what was 'a sacrifice rather than an attack'.

VI Corps, 12 April
17th Division, Pelves Mill
On the south bank of the Scarpe, 17th Division had taken over the line and Major General Philip Robertson had been instructed to clear Pelves Mill ridge north of Monchy. The 6th Dorsets advanced an hour after the attack north of the river but it soon came under fire from Roeux, where 9th Division had failed. There was no point going any further and Brigadier General Yatman recalled the battalion.

VII Corps, 12 April
14th and 56th Divisions, Cojeul Stream
Lieutenant General Snow wanted a bridgehead across the Cojeul but it took until after dusk before 41 Brigade crossed between Wancourt and Héninel. The new position was handed over to 50th Division during the night and the Germans were also making moves while it was dark. They abandoned Wancourt to take up positions on the high ground overlooking the Cojeul so they could cover the withdrawal from Hill 90 and Héninel. Bombers from 50th and 56th Divisions were kept busy making sure all the dugouts were empty and the password 'Rum Jar' was chosen so they did not shoot each other. Shouting the code word up and down the trenches caused a lot of amusement.

30th and 21st Divisions, Cojeul Stream
The 18th Manchesters used rifle grenades and Lewis gun fire to cover a

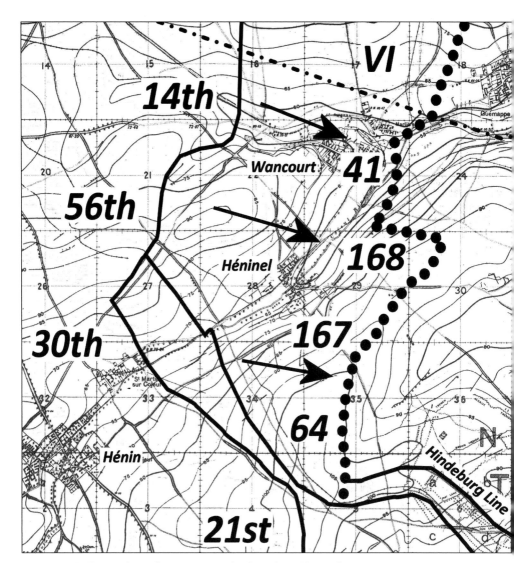

VII Corps cleared Wancourt and Héninel on 12 April.

bombing attack across the Cojeul near Héninel. They later handed over the captured trench, the last part of the line held by 30th Division. On 21st Division's front, the 12th Northumberland Fusiliers discovered the Germans were withdrawing from the Hindenburg Line. They only intended to evacuate the trenches south of Héninel but the Northumberland Fusiliers forced them out of another 250 yards. The Germans eventually established a new line on the ridge called the Hump.

Third Army, 13 April
General Allenby's orders for 13 April had XVII Corps holding its position

around Fampoux while VI Corps advanced astride the Cambrai road. The improved weather meant the RFC could do a full day's flying and there was plenty of work to do.

XVII Corps, 13 April

Although the situation north of the Scarpe had been quiet, Lieutenant General Fergusson received news about a withdrawal opposite First Army during the afternoon. The Germans had pulled back over 3,000 yards, abandoning all the ground overlooked by Vimy Ridge. On Third Army's left flank, 2nd Division had occupied Willerval and Bailleul before establishing a line facing Arleux on their left flank and Oppy on their right.

Opposite XVII Corps' left, 34th Division discovered the Germans had abandoned the area south of Bailleul. General Nicholson's troops moved forward but they found the Germans waiting for them on the Méricourt–Oppy Line where it crossed the Douai road west of Gavrelle.

VI Corps, 13 April

General Haldane had set zero hour for 5.30 am and his plan was for 50th Division to move along the spur across the Cojeul from Wancourt. This would allow 3rd Division to advance through Guémappe and astride the stream. Meanwhile, 56th Division would advance towards Chérisy as 21st Division moved closer to Fontaine-les-Croisilles.

50th Division, East of Wancourt

Major General Percival Wilkinson's men had found it difficult to take over 14th Division's sector astride the Cojeul. The 9th Durhams' left was pinned down by machine gun fire from Guémappe but the right advanced up the slope beyond the stream. Lieutenant Colonel Bradford's men got close to the mill on the summit but his men could not hold the exposed position. Machine gun fire drove a second Durham battalion (either the 6th or 8th) into the path of the Londoners on their right.

56th Division, Hill 90

The 1/16th London Regiment was also hit by the machine guns in Guémappe as they climbed the slope and then from the trench on the next spur when they crossed the summit of Hill 90. Captain Newham reported his men had only reached some abandoned practice trenches before they started falling back, having suffering 300 casualties. The 1/9th London Regiment went further because they were protected by a dip in the ground but they soon found there was no one on their flanks. They too fell back after suffering 400 casualties.

21st Division, Fontaine

The two tanks allocated to 62 Brigade broke down and Brigadier General Rawling had to report that it was impossible to advance over the top under fire from machine guns dug in across the Sensée. But the 12th Northumberland Fusiliers' bombers made some progress towards the stream. General Snow cancelled further attempts because VI Corps had called off its attack.

3rd Division, Evening Attack on Guémappe

General Wilkinson had been injured in the leg so he invited General Deverell to visit him to discuss progress beyond the Cojeul stream. The previous plan to let 50th Division advance ahead of 3rd Division was flawed because the machine guns in Guémappe could fire into the flank of the Northumbrian men as they climbed out of the valley. Meanwhile, the Germans on Wancourt Tower spur could enfilade an advance on Guémappe. General Wilkinson offered to clear the spur if 3rd Division attacked the village that evening. General Deverell agreed and General Snow approved of the plan.

The idea was sound but the plans did not match the situation on the ground. General Wilkinson incorrectly believed that Wancourt tower had been captured. Brigadier General Cameron also did not send two companies to reinforce the tower position. It meant there were no British troops around Wancourt Tower and 50th Division's artillery was instructed to shell the wrong spur.

An attack against Guémappe looked straightforward on the map but Brigadier General Potter faced a difficult situation. The 12th West Yorkshires only had 1,000 yards go along the Cambrai road to reach Guémappe but the late cancellation of 29th Division's attack left them exposed to fire from Infantry Hill on their left flank. The 1st Northumberland Fusiliers had a staggered front and Lieutenant Allan's men had to advance thirty minutes early so they would be in line with Captain Hogshaw's company by 6.40 pm. It was a bad time to be moving because the setting sun lit up the western sky, silhouetting Lieutenant Colonel Herbert's men against the horizon.

A weak barrage failed to suppress the garrison in Guémappe while the guns overshot Wancourt tower ridge. The Northumbrians were soon pinned down and they had to withdraw from their exposed position as soon as it was dark. General Potter had to report over 300 casualties and VI Corps' front had not advanced a yard.

Third Army, 14 April

General Allenby still needed VI and VII Corps to move towards the Sensée stream and Generals Snow and Haldane arranged to attack at 5.30 am.

VI Corps, 14 April

General Haldane wanted to capture the ridge which ran from Pelves, through Bois du Sart, to the Saint Rohart Factory on the Cambrai road. The plan was for 29th Division to relieve 12th Division but the withdrawing cavalry were blocking the Cambrai road. They agreed to postpone the attack until the following day after General de Lisle reported he would not be ready before dusk.

17th Division, Pelves Mill

Outposts north-east of Monchy stopped an attack from Bois du Sart and Bois du Vert around 4.30 pm.

29th Division, Monchy

The 1st Essex and 1st Royal Newfoundland advanced towards Hill 100 only to find the Germans had withdrawn from Shrapnel Trench opposite 88 Brigade. So they kept going. Captain Foster's company of the Essex were overwhelmed as they moved through Bois du Sart and then the Germans overran the companies of Captains Carolin and Brown. Burning huts

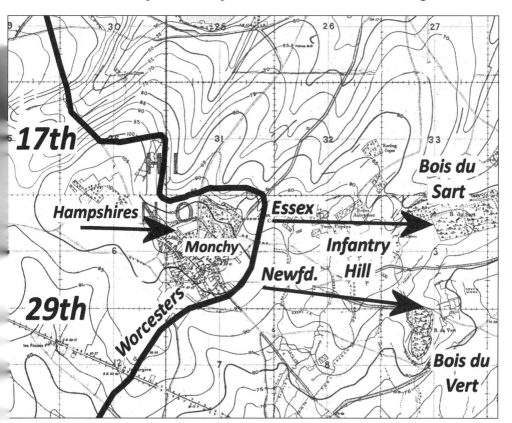

VI Corps' advance across Infantry Hill, east of Monchy, on 14 April.

illuminated the advancing Newfoundlanders as they disappeared over the crest, heading for Bois du Vert; they were never seen again.

A wounded Captain Carolin tried to contact Brigadier General Cayley to ask for artillery support but the telephone wire had been cut and his runners were killed. It would take an hour to get a message back to the artillery, by which time it was too late. Wounded men were streaming back through Monchy with news of a disaster, so Lieutenant Colonel Forbes-Robertson sent his signal officer forward to check. He returned with bad news: every man in the village had been wounded and the Germans were approaching. So Forbes-Robertson sent his adjutant back to find what reserves he could while he led his headquarters staff into the village. The few dozen men ran through the bombardment but only ten reached a shallow trench on the far side.

Forbes-Robertson, Lieutenant Keegan and Sergeant Waterfield kept the Germans at bay while the 2nd Hampshires approached Monchy. Lieutenant Colonel Beckwith noticed the German shells were bursting in overlapping, parallel lines so he led his men through the gap in the explosions and entered the ruins. Captain Cuddon took over the defence of the village and welcomed the assistance of the 4th Worcesters which threw back its left flank to enfilade the advancing Germans. They stopped attack after attack and Monchy remained in British hands.

But few men from the two battalions which had advanced across Infantry Hill returned; the Essex suffered over 650 casualties and the Newfoundlanders nearly 490. Forbes-Robertson and his handful of men were relieved at dusk, having helped stop the attack of an entire division. Those who took over Monchy endured a miserable night in a shallow trench because they had no greatcoats, no blankets and no one dared brew up any tea in case they were spotted.

VII Corps
50th Division, Wancourt Tower
There had been no coordination between Lieutenant Generals Haldane and Snow over the situation on the corps' boundary. The bombardment of Guémappe corresponded to 29th Division's attack east of Monchy, but it had not been coordinated with 50th Division's advance beyond the Cojeul. It meant the Germans would be free to enfilade 150 Brigade's attack on Wancourt tower spur.

Brigadier General Cameron had to instruct the 9th Durhams to stand fast so that the Germans in Guémappe could not hit them in the flank. The 6th and 8th Durhams and 5th Borders had deployed along the Cojeul but a last-minute change in time meant the messengers had to run between the

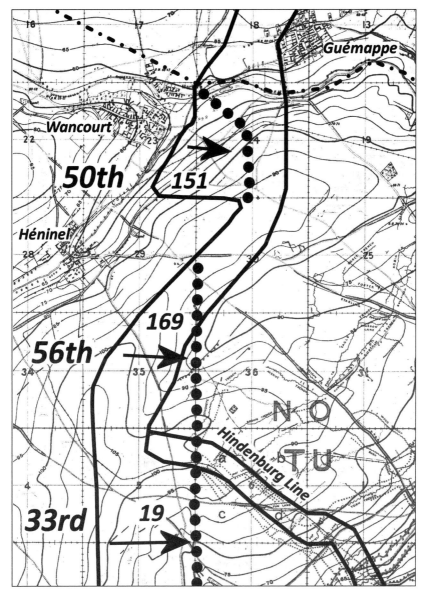

VII Corps' struggle on the high ground east of the Cojeul stream.

companies to pass on the instructions. The Durhams became disorganised as they crossed the spur and they dug in under fire, some of them in 56th Division's area. Some of the 6th Durhams advanced 600 yards east of Wancourt tower but no one returned. A company of the 8th Durhams were around Wancourt tower when it collapsed during the night but Captain Williams had to withdraw his men from the isolated position before dawn.

The 6th Northumberland Fusiliers would secure Wancourt tower late on 15 April but the Germans rushed the position as the 7th Northumberland Fusiliers were taking it over late the following night. The Germans then evacuated the position and an attempt to capture it again on the afternoon of 18 April was betrayed by a wounded prisoner. Artillery fire dispersed the troops before they could assemble.

56th Division
Some progress was made south of Wancourt tower but the 1/9th London Regiment was hit by machine gun fire before it was hit by a counter-attack.

33rd Division, The Hump
The 1st Scottish Rifles bombers could only clear a short length of the Hindenburg Line while the 5/6th Scottish Rifles had to pull and push each other out of the trenches which had been dug deep and wide enough to stop tanks. Captains Brown and Company Sergeant Major John Erskine VC (awarded during the Somme) were killed, leaving Captain Malloch and Lieutenant Downie to lead 19 Brigade's advance to the top of the Hump. They found themselves in an isolated position but they had captured nearly 700 prisoners.

Siegfried Sassoon along the Cojeul Stream
On 16 April the 2nd Welch Fusiliers were east of the Cojeul and Second Lieutenant Siegfried Sassoon recalled the occasion:

There must have been some hazy moonlight, for I can remember the figures of men propping themselves against the walls of the communication trench. Seeing them in some sort of ghastly half-light, I wondered whether they were dead or asleep, for the attitudes of some were like death, uncouth and distorted.

During a raid, Sassoon recalled what it was like to be found alone in a trench in the middle of a battle:

I had caught an occasional glimpse of a retreating German but the whole thing had been so absurdly easy I felt like going on still farther... What I expected to find there I can't say. Finding nothing, I paused for a moment to listen – there seemed to be a lull in the proceedings of the attack; spasmodic machine guns rattled; high overhead there was an aeroplane. I thought what a queer business it all was and then decided to take a peep at the surrounding countryside. No sooner had I popped my head out of the sap than I received what seemed like a tremendous blow in the back, between the shoulders. My first notion was that I had been hit by a bomb from behind. What had really happened was that I had been sniped from the front. Anyhow, my attitude towards life and the war had been instantaneously and completely altered for the worse. I leaned against the wall and shut my eyes... After about a quarter of an hour I began to feel active and heroic again, but in a different way – I was now not only a hero but a wounded hero!

Chapter 15

Come on Men, Bugger the Tanks
Bullecourt – 10 and 11 April

Haig wanted Fifth Army to attack between Bullecourt and Quéant. However, General Gough had been made to hand over several divisions and a lot of his heavy artillery for the main attack. It only left him with enough resources to attack a small sector of the Hindenburg Line. He also had to bring all his reserves, guns and ammunition forward over roads which had been damaged by the Germans during their withdrawal to the Hindenburg Line.

Fifth Army had captured all the outpost villages between Croisilles and Doignies on 2 April. Three days later Gough issued orders for an attack against Bullecourt. The plan was for V Corps and I Anzac Corps to advance side-by-side through Bullecourt to Hendecourt and Riencourt. The 4th Cavalry Division could then pass through the gap and meet the Cavalry Corps as it advanced south-east from the Arras front. Fifth Army had been given D Company's tanks for the attack and five were allocated to each corps.

General Gough had planned to attack on 9 April, simultaneously with the main advance. However, General William Birdwood asked for a postponement because the field artillery were short of horses and it had taken too long to haul the guns forward. The corps' heavy artillery had been shelling the wire, a task they were unsuited for because they were firing from a long range.

Major General Braithwaite's 62nd Division took over V Corps' sector west of Bullecourt on 5 April. It was a second line Territorial division and Bullecourt was going to be its first offensive battle. The 2/5th, 2/8th and 2/7th West Yorkshires pushed north of Ecoust to establish a jumping off line close to the Hindenburg Line. They sent out patrols before dawn on 9 April and all tried to cut gaps in the first belt of wire while under fire.

The original plan was to deploy the tanks in pairs but Lieutenant Colonel Hardress Lloyd was concerned they would be picked off if they were dispersed along the two-mile front. They would also struggle to make gaps in the thick belts of wire. The company commander, Major Watson, suggested concentrating all the tanks on a 1,000-yard front so they could create one huge gap in the Hindenburg Line. He also suggested dispensing with the preliminary artillery bombardment so the attack would be a surprise.

Gough agreed to let the tanks advance together against the Hindenburg Line east of Bullecourt, in front of the 4th Australian Division. After crushing the wire, four tanks would lead one battalion into Bullecourt while the others led the rest of the division towards Riencourt. Once Bullecourt had been taken, 62nd Division would advance west of Bullecourt, heading for Hendecourt.

Gough's late change in plan created a problem for Major General William Holmes. Neither the tank crews nor the infantry had time to practise the advance or check out the ground. The tanks also had to make a night approach across the battlefield so that the Germans would not see them until zero hour. But most of all, while the Australians had seen tanks, they had never attacked with them before. Evening patrols reported considerable damage to the wire but that the Germans were alert. General Holmes then issued his final orders for the morning.

4th Australian Division, 10 April

Major General Holmes' Australians waited anxiously in no man's land in the dark, straining to hear the tanks' engines, as the snow fell. Brigadier General Brand asked to delay zero hour by thirty minutes when they failed to appear but it was dawn when an exhausted tank officer finally arrived. He reported the drivers had been struggling to drive through the blizzard and they were still ninety minutes away. It would be suicidal to wait any longer and General Holmes said, 'we must postpone the show. I think there is just time to get the boys back.' He was right. A fall of snow hid the cold, tired troops as they fell back.

62nd Division, West of Bullecourt, 10 April

Lieutenant General Sir Edward Fanshawe, commanding V Corps, sent a message to 62nd Division's headquarters before midnight stating that 'zero hour will be 4.30 am'. Major General Braithwaite took it to be a definite order to attack, rather than a conditional instruction which was dependent on the Australians capturing Bullecourt. For a second time, the West Yorkshire patrols were fired on as they approached the wire.

Lieutenant Colonel James reported that his men could see no sign of the tanks nor the Australian infantry on the 2/7th West Yorkshires' right flank. He then reported a rumour that the Australian attack had been cancelled and said, 'this fully explained the strong opposition we were met with. It is, however, hard to understand how the information re the cancelling of this operation was not sent earlier by the [12 Australian] brigade on our right.'

As dawn approached it was clear that the Australians were not going to attack, so the patrols withdrew with difficulty and the 2/7th West Yorkshire suffered the most, losing over 100 casualties from the machine guns in Bullecourt. Braithwaite eventually heard the attack had been called off at 4.55 am, confirming that he had made the right decision not to commit any more of his men.

4th Australian Division, East of Bullecourt, 11 April

A gap had been left between Major General William Holmes' brigades to allow the tanks to advance. The plan was for 12 Australian Brigade to advance across the Hindenburg Line on the left as two tanks turned along the trenches, tearing up the wire. On the right, two tanks would do the same in front of 4 Australian Brigade, allowing it to advance to Riencourt. The infantry would start their advance 600 yards from the German trenches at 4.30 am, an hour and a half before sunrise. They would not wait for a signal from the tanks, they would just advance fifteen minutes after they had crawled past.

The artillery bombardment started with a barrage of gas shells on Bullecourt. The guns then continued to fire at a normal rate, so as not to alert the Germans, while a machine gun barrage was used to drown out the sound of the tank engines. The Australians moved out into no man's land for a second time and either lay there or huddled in assembly trenches as snow blew across the battlefield. They waited as zero hour came and went, but again the tanks had been delayed.

The five tanks destined to support 12 Australian Brigade were struggling to negotiate the railway embankment and the first tank did not reach 4 Australian Brigade until 3.20 am. The commander took one look at the boggy ground and told Captain Jacka VC (awarded during the Somme campaign) that the infantry would move faster than the tanks. Both Colonels Drake-Brockman and Peck asked if the tanks could advance fifteen minutes early but General Holmes said they 'must stick to the programme'. Two of the tanks broke down, another got stuck in a sunken road. Flares in the sky above Bullecourt meant that the Germans had seen the tanks and the machine gun teams in the Hindenburg Line began firing. Two tanks were hit before they reached the start line while a third drove along the brigade front and fired on 48th Australian Battalion:

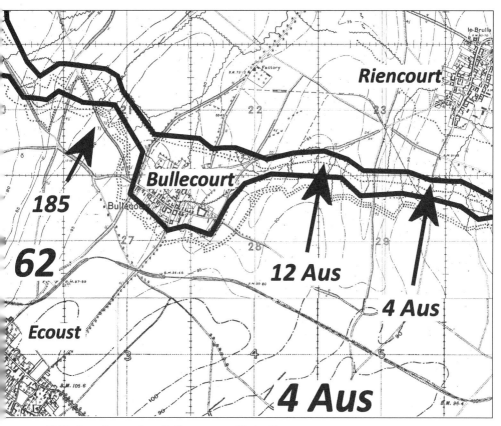

Fifth Army's attack at Bullecourt on 11 April.

> *A chorus of shouts went up from the Victorians. The fire ceased, and the tank stopped; at one of its openings appeared the head of an officer who asked what troops these were. On learning that they were friends, he came out of the tank, apologised for having fired on them, and, after inquiring as to the direction of the German line, re-entered the tank, which then made off in the dark…*

The tank was destroyed soon afterwards. Another tank crawled past only to break down in front of the waiting infantry.

The orders issued to 12 Australian Brigade were unclear. Lieutenant Colonel Denham had been told his 46th Australian Battalion could 'not advance until fifteen minutes after the tanks pass the jumping off line, and will move right forward into their objective following behind the tanks.' When a company commander asked what to do if the tanks did not turn up, Denham said they would have to advance without them but, crucially, he did not give the latest time to move. It was an unfortunate oversight. It left

46th Australian Battalion lying in the snow for twenty-five minutes longer than necessary. The sky was getting light and the creeping barrage had long since moved on when Captain Davis rang battalion headquarters at 5.10 am to tell him that only one tank had passed his men. Denham gave the order to advance immediately. A request by Lieutenant Colonel Leane, of 48th Australian Battalion, to bring the creeping barrage back had already been refused in case the tanks were already in the German lines. They were not.

The late start left the Germans free to shoot at 46th Australian Battalion as they advanced almost at the run. The left flank were mown down as they followed the tank through the wire and the right veered away from the swarm of bullets into uncut wire. But the centre cleared OG1 trench as the Germans fled. Another tank was hit by a shell as 48th Australian Battalion continued the advance and many of Lieutenant Colonel Leane's men were hit getting through the wire, including Captain Mott. Captain Leane (the colonel's nephew) cleared part of OG2 and Brigadier General Robertson knew that most of his objectives had been taken by 7 am.

Flares lit up the snow-covered ground, silhouetting the four waves of infantry on 4 Australian Brigade's front. Lieutenant Colonel Peck and Major Black were worried that their men were overtaking the tanks in no man's land but they could not wait for them. Up ahead, bullets hit the wire and it 'seemed to swarm with fireflies' when the German machine gun teams opened fire. Major Black shouted 'come on men, bugger the tanks' and his men ran up and down the wire looking for gaps to enter OG1. Both battalions pushed on, followed by the 15th and 13th Australian Battalions, and they used saps and communication trenches to get under the wire protecting OG2.

Casualties were heavy but Captain Dunworth and Lieutenant Thompson led the bombers along the trench on the left while Captain Murray's men secured the right flank. The Australians sniped and fired their Lewis guns at the fleeing Germans and Brigadier General Brand reported his objective had been taken. The tanks had done little to help: one had got lost and been knocked out some 500 yards outside the brigade's area; a second struggled to get through the wire and was then knocked out near OG1 trench; the third returned with engine trouble.

But as the sky lightened, the surviving Australians could look back at the hulks of the burnt-out and abandoned tanks silhouetted against the snow; they could also see the bodies of their comrades. Captain North's company of the 47th Australian Battalion was the only one to reach 12 Australian Brigade; no man's land was swept with fire and there were still too few men to close the gap between the brigades.

Just after 8 am General Brand asked for a protective barrage but the artillery group commander questioned the request because he had been told tanks and infantry had been spotted moving through Riencourt. The messages reaching Brand reported a different story but the artillery commander referred the issue to Birdwood and he would not allow the barrage.

Gough thought the operation was going according to plan and he instructed Major General Alfred Kennedy to move 4th Cavalry Division forward at 9.35 am. The troopers soon discovered the truth. A dismounted party from the Lucknow Brigade was pinned down by machine gun fire as it waited for gaps to be cut in the wire. A squadron of the 17th Lancers then came under artillery fire and had to withdraw. It was clear there had been no breakthrough and neither Bullecourt nor Riencourt had been captured.

Around 10 am the Germans counter-attacked from several directions. Robertson and Brand had been unable to reinforce their position and did not have any artillery support. The 46th Australian Battalion was driven out of OG1 trench on 12 Brigade's left. Colonel Leane's isolated 48th Australian Battalion then fought its way back from OG1 trench. Meanwhile, Brand had ordered 4 Australian Brigade to withdraw because it had run out of bombs:

> *A full hour after every other battalion had left the trenches, the 48th came out under heavy rifle and machine-gun fire, but with proud deliberation, and studied nonchalance, at a walking pace, picking their way through the broken wire, carrying a proportion of their Lewis guns, carefully helping the walking wounded and with their officers bringing up the rear.*

The 4 Australian Brigade suffered over 2,250 casualties out of around 3,000 men who had gone into action; 12 Australian Brigade suffered over 900 casualties. The Germans claimed to have captured over 1,150 officers and men. The Australians would blame the failure and the high number of casualties on the late tanks and the lack of artillery support.

Lagnicourt, 1st Australian Division, 15 April

Major General Harold Walker had a problem. His sector was double the length of the average quiet sector, measuring in at more than 7½ miles. Both 3 and 1 Australian Brigades only had two battalions in line, leaving each battalion responsible for nearly two miles of front. Even so, General Gough instructed Walker to establish outposts close to the Hindenburg Line to make the Germans believe an attack was imminent.

The four battalions pushed parties forward on the night of 13/14 March but found themselves in exposed positions because the Germans had chosen their line well. Each sentry post only had five men while the pickets, 150 yards behind, only had around eighteen men and a Lewis gun each. It was then another 600 yards back to the support platoon and each one had to cover 1,000 yards. The Germans could watch them all, making it impossible to erect wire entanglements. The Australians had to hide during daylight hours and camouflage their trenches with grass as best they could when it was dark. It made it virtually impossible for units to keep in touch with each other and they resorted to waving their rifles above ground at set times to communicate.

The artillery had been placed on the flanks so it could support the Bullecourt area; it was spread equally thin, at an average of one gun every 175 yards. It had also been noticed that the German howitzers had starting using 5.9-inch shells armed with instantaneous fuses. They burst as soon as they hit the ground, causing many casualties amongst the gunners.

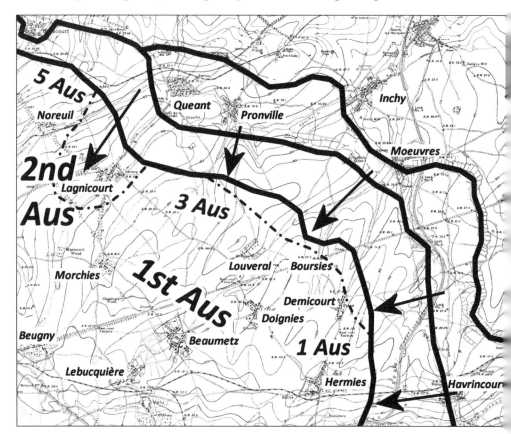

The German counter-attack against I Anzac Corps on 15 April.

Around 3.30 am on 15 April the Germans started shelling and outposts soon noticed movement. The Germans were on the move against 1st Australian Division's whole front. Lieutenant Leslie spotted the first party of men moving towards 3rd Australian Battalion's front near the Canal du Nord just after 4 am. The outposts saw exactly what they faced when the Germans on the Spoil Heap fired white flares, lighting up no man's land. The Australian outposts did not have rockets to warn their artillery and there were too few guns to make a difference when they did get the message to open fire. Even so, 3rd Australian Battalion held its line.

Astride the Cambrai road, 4th Australian Battalion stopped the first attack but the next one infiltrated Major Sasse's line in several places. Lieutenant Agnew was wounded holding Boursies chapel and a flamethrower silenced another outpost, east of Demicourt. The Australians were unable to leave their foxholes as the Germans pushed east because snipers shot anyone who showed themselves. Captain Woodman was wounded organising the defence of Boursies, so Lieutenant Macalpine took over. He held on until Major Woodforde arrived with three 1st Australian Battalion companies.

Brigadier General Bennett's 3 Australian Brigade was stretched along a 6,000-yard line north and east of Lagnicourt. A short bombardment hit the outposts around 4 am and then the outposts spotted Germans moving in front of 11th Australian Battalion. Captain O'Neill's men kept them at bay while the headquarters staff crawled forward, carrying bandoliers of ammunition around their shoulders. Lieutenant Pope made sure his men held their fire when the Germans went prone, saving their ammunition for when they had a clear view of their target. They used a gully to infiltrate Captain Hemingway's line and 11th Australian Battalion's outposts were overrun one-by-one. Their sacrifice gave the reserve company and two 10th Australian Battalion companies time to form another line. Pope was one of the many killed; he was posthumously awarded the Victoria Cross.

Another attack infiltrated between 17th and 12th Australian Battalion and they both blamed each other. In 2nd Australian Division's sector, Lieutenant Shield had told 17th Australian Battalion's outposts to fall back through Captain Sheppard's position to Captain Ronald's line. Lieutenant Colonel Pye's men then fought together to make sure the Germans did not enter Noreuil. Lieutenant Harrison was mortally wounded trying to organise 12th Australian Battalion's retirement and Captain Vowles was woken up to be told the Germans were already in Lagnicourt. His four Lewis guns had been overrun and he had no flares to call for artillery support so he had to withdraw from the village.

The Germans were amongst Major Dodd's and Lieutenant Colonel

Riggall's batteries but the gunners continued firing their guns with their fuses set to zero. Around 4.30 am Lieutenant Colonel Stevenson telephoned his four batteries to find out what was going on. The news was bad: 'Dropping the telephone for a moment, Stevenson looked down the valley and saw signs of fighting in bewildering diversity, all round the position of the batteries. He immediately gave the order to retire.' The gunners removed the breech blocks and dial sights from their guns and fell back. Altogether seven batteries west of Lagnicourt were abandoned and the gunners ran back towards Vaulx-Vraucourt, where they were stopped.

Captain Newland was holding on in a sunken lane south-east of Lagnicourt and Lieutenant Colonel Elliott had sent his headquarters staff, cooks and signallers to help. But Lieutenant Webster led them into Lagnicourt by mistake and they were driven back. The Germans emerged from the village behind Newland's position forcing him to line both sides of the cutting. Sergeant Whittle then ran forward and silenced a machine gun team before they could fire down the road into their flank. Newland would be awarded the Victoria Cross for his actions at Boursies and Lagnicourt over the past few days.

A straggler told Captain Boylan that 'the Germans have broken through in their thousands' so he took his company of the 9th Australian Battalion forward and joined Lieutenant Colonel Elliott south-west of Lagnicourt. They stopped the Germans advancing any further.

As the first streaks of grey appeared in the sky, it was possible to see the Germans milling around. Observers directed the gunners against targets and the combination of artillery and machine gun fire trapped many in Lagnicourt.

Brigadier General Smith had heard about the breakthrough and had been busy deploying the rest of 5 Australian Brigade to contain it. He had ordered 19th Australian Battalion to cover the north side of the breakthrough and Captain Taylor deployed south-east of Noreuil. He saw around 200 men approaching from the direction of Lagnicourt but told his men to hold their fire until he was sure whether they were friend or foe. Many Germans were hit when the order to fire was given. General Smith had told Lieutenant Colonel Ralston to move his 20th Australian Battalion east of Vaulx-Vraucourt and Captain MacDonald found Lieutenant Colonel Elliott.

Lieutenant Colonel Elliott was the first to counter-attack from the south, with 9th Australian Battalion. The 20th Australian Battalion joined in from the west while 19th Battalion advanced from the north-west. Many surrendered and the field artillery cooperated with the advancing Australian infantry while the heavy artillery targeted those running towards the Hindenburg Line.

Some lay out in the open until it was dark and then returned to the Hindenburg Line, reporting many 'destroyed' guns in a great success. But the Germans had only held the disabled Australian guns for two hours; they were back in action as soon as the Australian gunners had refixed the breeches and sights. Only four 18-pounders and a howitzer had been put out of action. Explosive charges had been fitted to other guns but they had not been detonated.

The Australians had suffered over 1,000 casualties, including over 350 missing; the Germans had suffered similar losses. Alert outposts and a stout defence had averted a disaster but two problems had to be addressed: divisional sectors had to be stronger and the batteries had to be better protected.

Chapter 16

The Nivelle Offensive
16 and 21 April

The withdrawal to the Hindenburg Line had seriously disrupted General Nivelle's plans for his spring offensive. The shortening of the line had increased the German reserve by fourteen divisions but it had also released a similar number of French ones. The withdrawal meant the French could now attack the flank of the German position north of the River Aisne while their artillery could enfilade the Chemin des Dames ridge. Nivelle knew the Germans were fortifying the ridge but he stuck to his original plan:

8 April, the British would attack east of Arras
10 April, the Group of Armies of the North would attack on the
    Somme
12 April, the Group of Armies of the Reserve would attack the
    Chemin des Dames
13 April, the Group of Armies of the Centre would attack east of
    Rheims

Alexandre Ribot had replaced Aristide Briand as Prime Minister of France on 20 March and his Minister of War, Paul Painlevé, disapproved of Nivelle and his plans. He liked it even less when he heard that the three Army Group commanders, Generals d'Espèrey, Micheler and Pétain, doubted Nivelle's optimism.

World events were also increasing Ribot and Painlevé's concerns. A recent revolution in Petrograd, Russia (now Saint Petersburg), meant the offensive on the Eastern Front would either be delayed or cancelled. The United States' imminent entry into the war meant the Allies could look forward to receiving American aid in the near future, making it less important to defeat the Germans in 1917.

Nivelle still believed he had everyone's support when he issued his final instructions on 4 April. He was wrong. A letter criticising Nivelle's plan landed on President Ribot's desk the following day. It had been written by the ex-Minister of War Adolphe Messimy who was serving as a brigade commander at the front. Ribot took the letter seriously because he thought had been dictated by General Micheler.

The attack was only days away so the Prime Minister summoned Nivelle and his four army group commanders to a Council of War in Compiègne the next day. They were interviewed by President Raymond Poincaré, Prime Minister Ribot, the Minister of War Painlevé, and the Minister of the Marine Lucien Lacaze. Poincaré rejected the idea of keeping the French armies on the defensive and was against launching an all-out offensive. Instead they agreed the reserves would only be deployed if the initial attack broke through. But Nivelle was offended that everyone doubted his plan and even offered to resign; Poincaré and Ribot refused to accept. Chief of the Imperial General Staff General Robertson went as far as saying Nivelle had 'a rope around his neck'. Ribot summed up the French predicament: 'our hand has been forced, it is too late to go back.'

On 6 April a company commander told his sergeant to take the 3rd Zouaves' plan of attack to the rear. He went missing, as did the paperwork. It was only a battalion level plan but it contained enough information to betray Fifth Army's plan of attack. General Olivier Mazel heard the news the following day but decided not to change anything.

The Germans had been watching the construction of roads, railways and dumps behind the front line, so the attack was no secret. The movement of fifty-three divisions behind the French lines was also impossible to hide. The Germans were busy preparing to meet the attack, erecting wire, digging trenches and building fortifications. Fresh divisions had been deployed in the threatened zone while the German infantry had been trained in the art of fighting a defensive battle or *Abwehrschlacht*. They knew they were supported by hidden artillery batteries well supplied with ammunition. Divisions were also moving into the area, bringing the total in line to 21 with 17 in reserve. If the Germans had a copy of the plans, they knew exactly when the attack was going to start.

The British attack was planned for 8 April with the French starting four days later. But weather interfered in the preparations and zero hour on the British front at Arras was postponed by twenty-four hours. Poor visibility repeatedly interfered with the French preliminary artillery bombardment and it was eventually decided that the Army Group Reserve (GAR) would attack the Chemin des Dames on 16 April while the Army Group Centre (GAC) would advance east of Rheims the following day.

First and Third Armies had advanced 5 miles in places on a 17-mile front around Arras when the Nivelle Offensive began at 6 am on 16 April. General Olivier Mazel's Fifth Army attacked with twelve divisions and while V

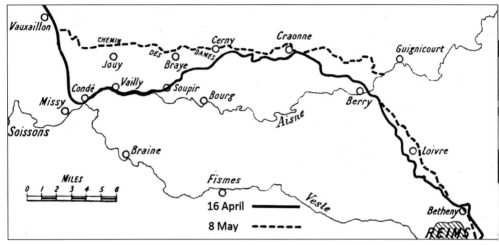

The Nivelle Offensive started on the Aisne on 16 April.

Corps advanced across the east end of the Chemin des Dames ridge, XXXII Corps advanced astride the Aisne. Over 120 tanks took part, three times as many as the British used on 9 April, but many were hit by artillery fire before they deployed. The German infantry had been trained to hide until they drove past so they could attack the French infantry who were following.

General Charles Mangin's Sixth Army attacked Chemin des Dames ridge capturing over 3,500 prisoners on the first day. But the advance had not been as successful as Nivelle had promised and counter-attacks had driven the French back in places. General Nivelle thought the Germans planned to hold the ridge, so he instructed General Mazel to continue pushing his Fifth Army astride the Aisne. The Germans responded by withdrawing several miles from the area north-east of Soissons, back to the Hindenburg Line. Fourth Army extended the attack east of Rheims on 17 April but, again, General François Anthoine reported no breakthrough.

By 20 April the French attacks had cleared the Aisne valley west of the Oise–Aisne Canal, part of the Chemin des Dames, and had made progress east of Rheims. They had taken 20,000 prisoners and 147 artillery pieces. French casualties soon topped over 95,000 but the German line had not collapsed.

Nivelle's attack had failed and Prime Minister Alexandre Ribot's politicians wanted a scapegoat. A depressed Nivelle used Tenth Army to attack on 21 April but the breakthrough never came. General Phillipe Pétain was appointed Chief of the General Staff on 29 April. The attacks continued and many more prisoners and guns were taken but still there was no breakthrough to report when the British and French met in Paris on 4 May.

The French were closing down their offensive and Ribot wanted to sack General Nivelle. Pétain was appointed commander-in-chief of the Armies of the North and North-East and General Ferdinand Foch was appointed Chief of the General Staff, leaving General Nivelle a mere army group commander by 15 May. He would resign on 29 June, on General Pétain's recommendation, and was appointed commander-in-chief in Northern Africa.

Nivelle's replacement, Pétain, faced a mutiny. The failure of the Nivelle offensive and the associated political fallout had lowered the army's morale. The first acts of insubordination took place on 29 April and an entire division refused to attack four days later. Incidents spread quickly and there were 119 cases of indiscipline, most at the end of May and the beginning of June. The mutineers wanted the military authorities to get a grip on the realities of warfare. They were against futile attacks, they were against poor medical facilities and they wanted more leave. They were also aware there had been a revolution in Russia.

Men were refusing to go to the front, some were returning from leave drunk and others were carrying out minor acts of sabotage. Altogether 49 divisions were affected by the mutiny, 24 of them seriously. Nearly 3,000 sentences of hard labour were issued while 629 death sentences were handed out; only 43 men were executed. President Poincaré and General Pétain worked hard together to restore order. Improved billets and facilities were introduced while wine sales were limited. The situation was soon in hand but offensive action was out of the question for the time being.

Chapter 17

The Most Savage Infantry Battle
23 and 24 April

General Allenby wasted no time in calling for a renewal of Third Army's offensive on the evening of 14 April. He wanted to continue the advance towards the Sensée stream between Vis-en-Artois and Fontaine-lès-Croisilles within forty-eight hours but his plan was overruled by GHQ. General Haig wanted First, Third and Fifth Armies to attack side-by-side.

General Haldane's divisional commanders suggested a preliminary attack around Monchy-le-Preux because it would make it easier to advance south of the Scarpe. Haig disagreed when he met Generals Horne, Allenby and Gough at Saint Pol on 16 April. The only preliminary attack would capture Guémappe on 18 April while the main attack was planned for 20 April. First Army was to capture the Oppy Line and Gavrelle; Third Army was to advance astride the Scarpe river and Fifth Army was to advance beyond Bullecourt.

Haig's plan fell apart the following day. Horne asked for a postponement because the bad weather was affecting First Army's artillery registration. Allenby then reported that Snow and Haldane wanted to take Guémappe in the main attack. Meanwhile, Gough wanted Third Army to reach the Sensée stream before he advanced beyond Bullecourt. Haig agreed to all three suggestions and he postponed the operation until 23 April.

The artillery began targeting the trenches and wire on 20 April. Tear gas was fired at the German batteries while many guns shelled the villages close to the front during the night. But plans for a coordinated attack were dashed when General Horne reported it would take until 21 April to cut the Oppy Line wire. He suggested only attacking Gavrelle and Haig reluctantly agreed.

Preparations behind Third Army's front progressed under difficult circumstances. The roads were full to capacity and the labour units worked around the clock to keep them open. The Scarpe had been dammed near Fampoux, allowing pontoons to bring ammunition forward and then take wounded to the rear, but the overworked ammunition columns were delivering their loads across temporary tracks to the new battery positions.

There were nineteen tanks running, three having been damaged on 20 April. Two tanks of C Battalion were allocated to 37th Division while 51st Division had five tanks to clear the Roeux area. Two each from the same battalion were allocated to 17th and 15th Divisions south of the river. A pair from D Battalion had been given to 30th and 50th Divisions and two pairs were given to 33rd Division, so they could work either side of the Hindenburg Line.

First Army, 23 and 24 April
I Corps, La Coulotte
General Horne had wanted to capture all the trenches between Avion and Gavrelle but a lack of troops and the poor weather reduced the objective to a small sector between Hill 65 and the Vimy–Lens railway. It meant I Corps and Canadian Corps would advance either side of the Souchez stream towards La Coulotte, which had been described as 'a veritable fortress'.

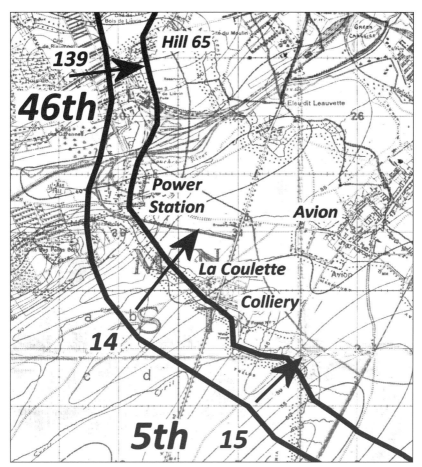

The Canadian Corps' attack at La Coulotte on 23 April.

There was a disagreement over what the Germans were planning to do opposite I Corps. The corps commander, Lieutenant General Arthur Holland, thought the Germans were preparing to abandon Lens but 46th Division's commander, Major General William Thwaites, believed they were digging in. Holland instructed Thwaites to attack at the same time as the rest of First Army but he was to use only two battalions and they would deploy only one company each.

The 8th Sherwood Foresters captured the trenches on the west side of Hill 65 but the Germans emerged from the cellars of the miners' cottages to drive them back. The 6th Sherwood Foresters were pinned down by machine gun fire from the buildings around Colliery Number 7. Brigadier General Shipley had to report that counter-attacks had driven 139 Brigade out of the German trenches and hardly any men had made it back across no man's land.

Canadian Corps, La Coulotte, 23 April

Major General Stephen's 5th British Division was still serving with the Canadian Corps and there were conflicting reports over the state of the German wire in front of it. Initially aerial observers and patrols said it had been badly damaged. But Brigadier General Turner heard that the entanglement was still an obstacle a few hours before zero and the artillery could do little in the darkness.

All four battalions were hit by machine gun fire as they tried to cut through the wire. Lieutenant Colonel Fergus's 5th DCLI advanced under cover of a railway embankment but Captain Langdon was one of the many hit by machine gun fire coming from the power station on 14 Brigade's left flank. Elsewhere the Germans were considering surrendering but they changed their minds when they saw Captain Wreford's men struggling to get through in the wire. The 1st Devons suffered nearly 250 casualties, including 13 subalterns.

Captains Wynne and Morris led a few 1st Bedfords into the German trench near Fosse 3 colliery but Captain Magnay was killed taking some of the 1st Norfolks through the wire. One observer noted 'for a short time the parties looked as if they were going to accomplish the impossible' but 15 Brigade faced another belt of wire some fifty yards deep. The German bombers moved in on the isolated parties while machine gun fire stopped reinforcements crossing no man's land. The survivors fell back during the afternoon; 5th Division had suffered 1,600 casualties.

Third Army, 23 and 24 April

The offensive on 23 April was going to be a shadow of the one launched on the 9th. This time there would be no surprise; there was only half the number of tanks available, and the barrage was shorter and less powerful. The Germans had also had time to move extra batteries into the area and many had been waiting silently below their camouflage netting for the next attack. Reinforcements had also moved into the area and Third Army would be facing many fresh units.

But everyone, British, Canadian and German alike, had to endure the wet weather which soaked the men, turned the soil into mud, and filled shell holes and trenches with water. Zero hour was 4.45 am on 23 April and the creeping barrage advanced 100 yards every four minutes. Mist was rising from the wet ground and the hundreds of smoke, shrapnel and high explosive shells created a thick fog which would last until three hours after zero hour. The rest of the day would be dry but the clear skies meant that the night would be cold, chilling the shivering men to the bone.

XIII Corps

Lieutenant General Sir Walter Congreve's XIII Corps had taken over the Point du Jour Line opposite Bailleul on 13 April. It reported to General Horne because the sector had been passed to First Army.

63rd Division, Gavrelle

Brigadier General Philips wanted to postpone the attack because his patrols reported the Oppy Line wire was uncut. Major General Charles Lawrie refused because an air patrol had reported gaps in front of 189 Brigade. Philips remained unconvinced and he told Commander Bennett of the Drake Battalion to head for gaps in the wire on a single company frontage, promising smoke and mortars would cover his flank.

The 7th Royal Fusiliers were pinned down at the wire by machine guns firing from the open left flank and few entered the German trench. The 4th Bedfords, Nelson and Drake Battalions all made it through the wire but they became mixed up as they advanced through Gavrelle. The problem was increased because Commander Asquith had moved the Hood Battalion forward ahead of the arranged time, to avoid the German bombardment.

The creeping barrage advanced again at 6.1 am but the Bedfords and the Nelson Battalion came under terrific fire from the railway east of the village. The Drake Battalion was unable to advance beyond the cemetery. It did not help that the infantry had advanced beyond the range of the field guns and the long wait in the choking dust in Gavrelle had made the men tired and lethargic.

The battalion commanders decided it would be madness to try again and they consolidated a position around the village before the Germans responded. Lieutenants Morrison and Tamplin were both killed as the Hood

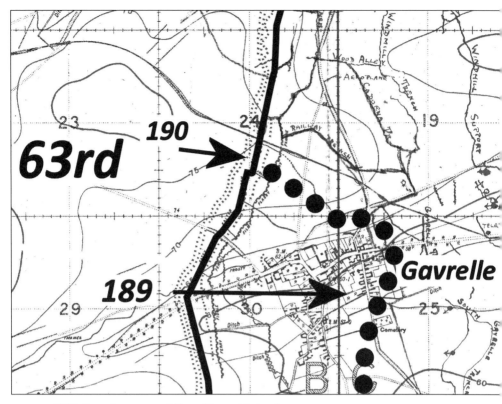

XIII Corps' capture of Gavrelle on 23 April.

Battalion fought off a counter-attack, Lieutenant Cooke was killed holding off the Germans with his Lewis gun, but Sub-Lieutenant Matcham held the support line. Lieutenant Colonel Collins Wells used some of the Bedfords to reinforce the Hood's left flank but Lieutenant Colonel Whiteman was killed as he organised the Hawke Battalion's defence.

Later that evening, Lieutenant Colonel Osmond sent a company of the Honourable Artillery Company (HAC) forward to help the struggling 7th Royal Fusiliers. They bombed north up the Oppy Line and almost reached the railway, securing the division's left flank.

Early counter-attacks on 24 April were stopped but the main attempt to retake Gavrelle was made at 3.30 pm. The British batteries were alerted when waves of German infantry were seen advancing astride the Fresnes road. High explosive and shrapnel disorganised wave after wave as they closed in on the village and machine gun fire finished them off.

XVII Corps
37th Division, South of Gavrelle

Major General Bruce-Williams' men had relieved 4th Division in front of Oppy on the night before the attack. They soon discovered that the incomplete assembly trenches were nothing more than shallow ditches so all they could do was sit in them, huddled together, and wait for zero hour. The German machine gun teams were waiting for the attack all along the front and the first wave was pinned down close to the enemy wire. But the second wave cut gaps and encouraged their comrades to join them as they entered the German trenches.

The three battalions of 111 Brigade cleared the first and second objectives south of Gavrelle, and the 13th KRRC reached the Plouvain road but its position was 'certainly unsatisfactory' and under enfilade fire from the left. Both the 13th and 10th Royal Fusiliers went beyond the Roeux road but they could not reach the summit of Greenland Hill. Brigadier General Compton instructed Lieutenant Colonel Pretor-Pinney to take the 13th Rifle Brigade forward to fill the gap in the centre of the brigade. Major Jackson took over the disorganised battalion when Pretor-Pinney was mortally wounded and he stopped a counter-attack during the afternoon before sending Captain Boyle's company forward in skirmish order to stop the Germans using a crossroads as a rally point.

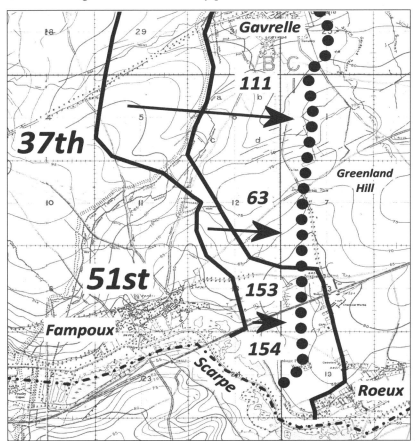

XVII Corps' advance towards Greenland Hill and Roeux on 23 April.

On the right, 63 Brigade had formed up in the old Oppy Line. The 10th York and Lancasters failed to capture the first objective because they had lost the creeping barrage but the 4th Middlesex advanced beyond the Roeux road. Brigadier General Challenor sent the 8th Lincolns forward to take the advance forward to the Plouvain road but it failed under enfilade fire. The 6th Bedfords made a third attempt to advance but a wounded Captain Blake was unable to reach the Middlesex.

Bruce-Williams was told the Germans were falling back from Greenland Hill during the afternoon so he instructed Brigadier General Maclachlan to push his 112 Brigade through 63 Brigade at dusk. The information was untrue and the advance made no headway. The front between Gavrelle and Roeux was at a stalemate.

51st Division, Greenland Hill and Roeux

There were arguments over what the final objective should be on 51st Division's front. General Harper wanted to advance as far as Delbar and Hausa Woods because they overlooked Roeux from the east. Lieutenant General Fergusson doubted the Scots could reach them and he was also worried that they would be approaching the field artillery's extreme range. But Harper persisted until he got his way. He had also wanted to use gas but the mule trains struggled to carry the cylinders forward.

On 153 Brigade's front, the 1/7th Gordons' left was pinned down and only a few continued towards the Blue Line; only five men returned. The right cleared the station buildings but Lieutenant Still, the only officer still standing, led two companies along the north side of the railway. They captured two trench mortars, a machine gun and fifty wounded Germans in an abandoned first aid post. The 1/7th Black Watch were pinned down in front of the chemical works (known as the 'comical works' by the Scots) and seven subalterns were hit one after another trying to cut through the wire.

Brigadier General Campbell had no idea how far his men had advanced, although some had been seen disappearing into the clouds of dust and smoke covering the chemical works. He soon found out the truth: the 1/6th Black Watch and the 1/6th Gordons had been shot to pieces as soon as they advanced. A wounded Lieutenant Colonel Dawson told Brigadier General Campbell that the Gordons had been forced off Greenland Hill and were digging in along the Roeux–Gavrelle road. Around 9 am a single tank from C Battalion crawled forward, drawing fire from every gun in range; it was soon riddled with holes.

Once again troops had to advance from the cramped trenches east of Fampoux towards the buildings between the Douai railway and Roeux. The barrage supporting 154 Brigade was weak because many of the gunners had been gassed and the 1/4th Gordons and the 1/7th Argylls were pinned down as soon as they clambered out of their trenches. The single tank allocated to Brigadier General Hamilton's attack had been delayed because an aid post had laid their wounded under the railway bridge, blocking the road. Second Lieutenant Smith persevered and his driver eventually caught up with the Argylls. The sight of the tank crawling past, firing 6-pounder shells into the ruins ahead, stirred the Scots to advance towards Roeux again.

Parties of Lieutenant Colonel McClintock's Gordons moved into the chemical works, pointing out German hideouts to the tank crew. McClintock was wounded as the 1/4th and 1/6th Gordons occupied a line of shell holes east of the complex but he became concerned when he saw the tank heading south towards Roeux. It skirted the north and east edges of the village as the Argylls fought 'perhaps the most savage infantry battle that the division took part in'. The tank then headed for home, low on ammunition and fuel.

With no tank to help them and no officers to lead them, the Argylls fell back through Roeux until the 1/9th Royal Scots helped them hold the western outskirts. The tank returned to help the Royal Scots and Private Fernie silenced a machine gun with his Lewis gun as they entered Roeux Wood. Second Lieutenant Campbell also used his Lewis gun to shoot down the retreating Germans, but the tank became bogged down in the soft ground. Major Rowbottom was wounded and only a few of his Royal Scots entered the wood, under sniper and artillery fire; they were never seen again.

There was a plan to renew the attack on the chateau and chemical works at 11.5 am and Lieutenant Colonel Unthank sent two 1/4th Seaforth companies forward to carry it out. They used a single plank bridge to cross the Scarpe because the railway bridge was under artillery fire. They then crossed the marshy ground south of the railway, as the German shells buried themselves deep in the mud before exploding. The Seaforths met Lieutenant Still's tank (now commanded by a sergeant) as it headed back and the crew reported that Roeux had been cleared. Sergeant Gray captured a machine gun on the railway embankment, allowing Captain Fraser's company to clear the chemical works, but the rest of the Seaforths were pinned down in front of the chateau.

General Fergusson wanted to move some his heavy guns forward to shell Roeux but artillery observers had the roads covered and one battery lost all its four 9.2-inch howitzers to enemy fire. The Germans were happy to keep their batteries deployed well back, where they were difficult to spot, and wait for the British to advance into range.

After dark there were counter-attacks over Greenland Hill and from Roeux, so SOS flares were fired to alert the gunners. Each time the British artillery scattered them because the observers were making the most of a new power buzzer. A simple one-way message code identified the target area and the gunners were able to respond immediately, time after time.

On one occasion the British heavy artillery hit the chemical works by mistake and the 1/4th Seaforths fell back after Captain Fraser was hit. The German infantry occupied the complex but their own bombardment stopped them going any further west. It seemed that everyone was having difficulty directing their guns.

Lieutenant Colonel MacDonald split the 1/6th Seaforths into two groups to try to help. The north group failed to get past the railway station and two officers found they had been cut off by a German counter-attack by the time they reached the forward troops. The second group found the Germans in the chemical works, so they dug in close to the railway, facing the ruined factory buildings. Virtually everything 51st Division had captured had been lost but the division's history proudly states:

> *From the most difficultly situated assembly trenches, an attack had been launched against a position of considerable strength. The men had advanced against stout opposition and had suffered heavy casualties, had then been systematically bombarded in shallow trenches and shell holes, and had then been repeatedly counter-attacked. They maintained a portion of their gains against all comers…*

Casualties had been so high that General Harper had to deploy 153 Brigade astride the railway. Early the following morning patrols and observers established exactly where the front line was. Greenland Hill, the chemical works, Roeux village and Mount Pleasant Wood were all still in German hands. The only ground taken was along the Gavrelle road on the left flank.

VI Corps
In the centre of Third Army's front, VI Corps held a salient around Monchy-le-Preux. Lieutenant General Haldane's artillery had a difficult task forming a creeping barrage along the irregular front. The infantry had an equally difficult task because the flanks had to advance 2,500 yards to the Blue Line while the centre only had 900 yards to go.

<u>17th Division, Pelves Mill</u>
The 6th Dorsets came under fire from Roeux as they advanced along the river bank in 50 Brigade's sector. Captain Allen was killed leading the 10th West Yorkshires towards Pelves Mill and Brigadier General Yatman reported it was impossible to reach Rifle Trench in the face of such heavy crossfire. Further up the slopes machine gun fire stopped the 8th South

Staffords and 7th Border Regiment advancing across Lone Tree Copse valley, in 51 Brigade's area. Brigadier General Trotter moved the 10th Sherwoods and 7th Lincolns forward but only a few men reached Bayonet Trench at the third attempt.

29th Division, Monchy
Brigadier General Lucas had deployed the 2nd SWBs and 1st KOSBs north of Monchy. The men of 87 Brigade sheltered in a trench full of water as the British shells exploded around them before zero hour. Captain Dickinson captured Snaffle Trench behind a ragged creeping barrage, while Second Lieutenant Woolveridge moved through Arrowhead Copse on the right. But

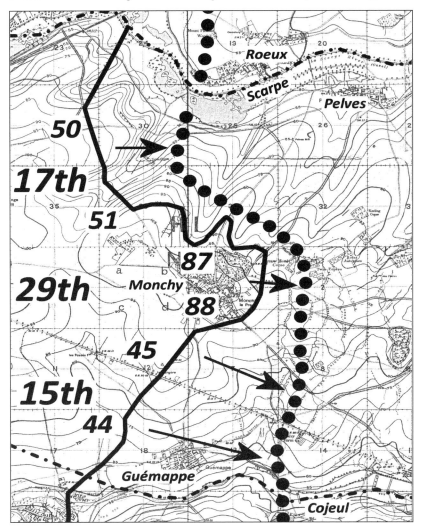

VI Corps' advance beyond Monchy and capture of Guémappe on 23 April.

1st KOSBs ran into the creeping barrage in the dark because some of the guns were firing short. Lieutenant Colonel Welch's men reached their objective, on the summit of Infantry Hill, and Second Lieutenant Wyatt stopped a counter-attack from the direction of Bois du Vert.

Casualties had been high during the advance and the snipers took their toll as the men dug in. Colonel Raikes only had 150 Borderers still standing to hold the Twin Copses area but the Lewis gunners stopped the midday counter-attacks from Cigar Copse and Bois de Aubépines. General Lucas deployed the 4th Worcesters on Raikes' left flank but Lieutenant Colonel Beckwith's men were unable to capture the trench facing Bois du Vert, leaving the left flank exposed. Lieutenant Colonel McCammon moved the 2nd Hampshires forward to cover it and Captain Cuddon's bombers captured fifty Germans who had infiltrated behind the Worcesters.

15th Division, Guémappe

Major General McCracken's men held the line between the Cambrai road and the Cojeul stream. Brigadier General Allgood had to deploy the 11th Argylls in a forward position, alongside 29th Division, but the 13th Royal Scots were in echelon behind, in line with the rest of 15th Division.

Machine gun fire drove the Argylls north but Stokes mortars and a shower of grenades convinced the Germans to abandon the sunken Dragon Lane so they could reach Bullet Trench. Second Lieutenant Henderson consolidated Dragon Lane with the few Argylls capable of fighting. The 13th Royal Scots' left made progress but the right flank was stopped by machine gun fire from Guémappe. A wounded Captain Farquharson staggered back to report 45 Brigade's situation while his men secured Bayonet Trench.

Guémappe blocked 44 Brigade's route along the Cojeul stream and Brigadier General Marshall wanted the 8th Seaforths to clear the ruins. They crept forward until they were close enough to charge Guémappe but it took them two hours to clear the ruins with the help of Captain Morrison's company of the 9th Black Watch. It meant General Marshall's plan had broken down at an early stage.

The barrage had long moved on by the time the 7th Camerons and 9th Black Watch were advancing towards the St Rohart factory. Lieutenant Anderson was killed just before zero so his trench mortar battery failed to neutralise the machine gun post in front of the Camerons, but Captain Stuart and Lieutenant McKay still captured the north end of Bullet Trench. Morrison was killed leading the Black Watch's attack on Hammer Trench north-east of Guémappe, but Sergeant Gibb silenced the machine gun holding up the advance. Lieutenant Carmen had led some of the Black

Watch down String Trench as far as the Cojeul stream south-west of the village.

<u>The Afternoon Counter-Attacks</u>
General McCracken intended to advance again east of Guémappe at noon but the Germans struck first. A counter-attack drove 50th Division's right back along the Cojeul, exposing 15th Division's position around Guémappe. Machine gun fire across the stream forced most of the 8th Seaforths to retire but one party held on near the cemetery, stopping the Germans re-entering the village. The 9th Black Watch were also driven from Hammer Trench.

A counter-attack from Bois du Vert late in the afternoon hit 88 Brigade on 29th Division's right. It overran part of the Hampshires; Lieutenant Colonel McCammon was mortally wounded and both Captains Cornish and Robertson were taken prisoner. The Worcesters' right company was also overwhelmed and some of Hampshires followed when they fell back to Shrapnel Trench.

The counter-attacks meant that 29th Division was unable to attack again until the following morning. They had also exposed 15th Division's flanks, forcing General McCracken to delay his attack until 6pm. He wanted the bombardment to concentrate on the trenches between Monchy windmill and the Cojeul for an hour before 46 Brigade advanced. Unfortunately, Brigadier General Fagan received the order too late to pass it on and the 10/11th Highland Light Infantry suffered casualties as they advanced though the British barrage. Machine gun fire from Cavalry Farm on the Cambrai road stopped the Highlanders and the 10th Scottish Rifles short of their objective, but Major Dennis's 6/7th KOSB company cleared String Trench along the Cojeul stream. A counter-attack eventually forced the Highlanders and the Scottish Rifles back towards Guémappe.

<u>Later Attacks</u>
As soon as General Allenby had the results of the morning's attack he issued orders to clear the rest of the Blue Line because he wanted to push on to the Red Line. The 29th Division had to secure Infantry Hill east of Monchy, and 86 Brigade was chosen to do it. The attack went well to begin with but Brigadier General Williams had to report that the 1st Dublin Fusiliers had been driven back to Shrapnel Trench. It would be left to 3rd Division to establish outposts close to the Blue Line.

Minor actions continued on 15th Division's front the following day. The 12th HLI and 10th Scottish Rifles cleared the Blue Line but they could not capture Cavalry Farm; a second attack by the 7th Camerons also failed. The 7th Camerons and the 9th Black Watch rushed the farm during the night of

26 April but they could not hold it because of vicious crossfire. The Camerons had to rush to bury their dead before dawn but they took the greatest care with their dead comrades:

> *In order to save space, the majority of the men were buried lying on their side. A touching feature was the fact someone had taken each man's arm and put it around the body lying next to him. From the top of the trench one could imagine that the men were sleeping, embraced in each other's arms.*

VII Corps, 23 April

General Snow wanted his three divisions to advance down the slope towards the Sensée stream. A detachment of 33rd Division was detailed to capture the Hindenburg Line on the east bank, to stop the Germans enfilading the advance.

50th Division, Wancourt

On VII Corps' left, 50th Division had to advance astride the Cojeul stream between Guémappe and Wancourt. Red star shells alerted the enemy artillery on 150 Brigade's front while Brigadier General Price's men were delayed by the slow-moving British barrage. The 1/4th Green Howards' left flank captured many prisoners with the help of a tank, but its right was pinned down near the wire. The second tank turned back with engine trouble but the 1/4th East Yorkshires still captured a battery of field guns near the Guémappe–Chérisy crossroads, despite losing many of their officers.

The two battalions cleared the first objective before 8 am but they then had to wait four hours before they could advance to the second objective. The Germans infiltrated between them while machine gun fire from across the Cojeul pinned the Green Howards down. A wounded Captain David Hirsch was soon the only officer left and he staggered up and down the parapet encouraging his men to hold on, until he was killed; he was posthumously awarded the Victoria Cross. Lieutenant Luckhurst of the Trench Mortar battery took control of around 150 men and he too was killed. But the Green Howards held on with the help of a company of 1/5th Durhams who had brought them ammunition.

The failure of 30th Division allowed the Germans to outflank the East Yorkshires and only 225 managed to fight their way back, leaving nearly 370 dead and wounded comrades behind. The Germans then turned on the Green Howards and it was down to the NCOs to lead them back; they suffered a similar number of casualties. Nearly 600 men were taken

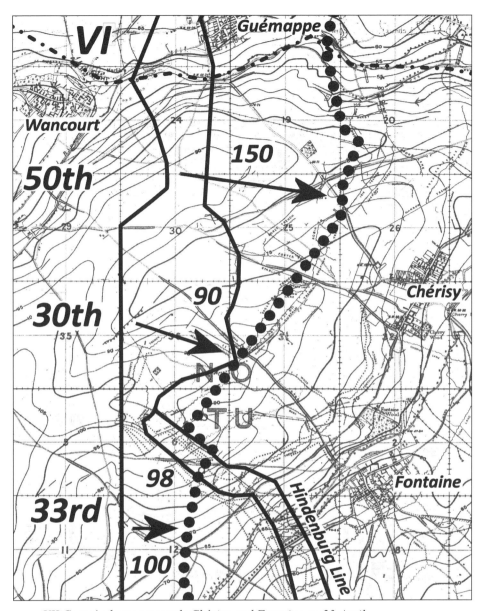

VII Corps' advance towards Chérisy and Fontaine on 23 April.

prisoner, but the 1/5th Durhams and 1/5th Green Howards had stopped the Germans breaking through.

Major General Percival Wilkinson noted that 'after so brilliant a success in the morning it was more disappointing that the ground captured was retaken by the enemy…' It was even more so because the battery of captured guns was lost. All four battered battalions were back on the start line before midday.

30th Division, Chérisy

In VII Corps' centre, 90 Brigade faced the ridge overlooking Chérisy. Machine gun fire hit the 17th Manchesters and 2nd Scots Fusiliers as they left their trench and Lieutenant Colonel McConaghy was one of the Fusiliers' early casualties. One tank bogged down while the other was destroyed by shellfire. German artillery then joined in and the two battalions lost many men as they approached the German trenches. Major Campbell had to report that the Scots Fusiliers had suffered 450 casualties, over 200 of them missing.

Brigadier General Lloyd had cancelled 16th Manchester's attack because 50th Division was back in its starting trench so the 2nd Green Howards advanced alone. Lieutenant Newbury occupied the German trenches while Lieutenant Camm cleared some quarries on the left flank. They eventually had to withdraw after being shot at by the British artillery and the RFC's planes.

33rd Division, Hindenburg Line

Brigadier General Heriot Maitland's 98 Brigade had to fight its way across the Hump and down the Hindenburg Line to the Sensée stream. The attack began with the engineers detonating explosives, destroying the barricades blocking the trench. Lieutenant Colonel Elgee's 1st Middlesex advanced astride the support trench while Lieutenant Colonel Browne's 2nd Argylls did the same astride the front trench. But machine gun fire pinned down the troops as they breasted the summit of the ridge, leaving the bombers to fend for themselves in the trenches. Attempts to reach them failed but the dwindling group of men continued firing on the Germans across the stream, allowing the 1st Queen's to advance towards the Sensée.

A tank gave covering fire as the 1/4th Suffolks worked their way along the south side of the Hindenburg Line. One man found seventy men hiding in a tunnel and he escorted them back, cheerfully telling his mates that 'he had surrounded them'. The rest of the battalion reached the Chérisy–Croisilles road, 2,000 yards from its starting line. Two companies of the 2nd Welsh Fusiliers pulled 650 prisoners out of their dugouts and then blocked the entrances to stop anyone reoccupying them. The Fusiliers stopped when Captain Owen was killed and the Suffolks halted when they ran out of bombs.

Around 11 am the Germans fired 'a colossal collection of every kind of aerial torpedo, pineapple, bomb and rifle grenade' as their bombers approached. The surrounded Argylls and Middlesex fought on and Company Sergeant Major Todd helped a wounded Captain Henderson lead the Argylls' last stand. Many died in the onslaught and Henderson would be awarded the Victoria Cross for making the final suicidal charge with only three men. Nearly 250 men, many of them wounded, were eventually taken prisoner.

The Suffolks were withdrawing from their position on the Croisilles–Chérisy road when a large group of Germans emerged from a tunnel and occupied their front trench. Second Lieutenant Woods was killed leading one group back and the Suffolks were lucky to escape. Lieutenant Rigby was mortally wounded as he counter-attacked and his two companies of the 5th Scottish Rifles fell back. Fortunately for Major General Reginald Pinney, the Germans had also lost a lot of men and they abandoned their trenches.

On 33rd Division's right, 100 Brigade had to ford the Sensée stream and secure a bridgehead on the far bank. Brigadier General Baird had arranged for machine gun positions to be constructed in no man's land and 100th Machine Gun Company transport delivered twelve guns and thousands of rounds of ammunition during the night. They remained hidden, ready to give covering fire at zero hour. But there was a disaster because both tanks broke their chains and slipped off their transports while they were being moved to the front and they arrived too late to take part.

Captain Godfrey led two companies of the 1st Queen's forward with Lieutenant Colonel Johnson's 16th KRRC following in support. They captured the first Hindenburg trench but wire and machine gun fire from pillboxes further up the Sensée valley stopped them reaching the second. Mist meant visual signals could not be used so an officer's groom repeatedly rode his horse back and forth with messages.

The German bombers closed in under cover of the mist and attacked at five separate points around noon. Captains Goner and Scott of the KRRC helped the Queen's hold on until the Germans rushed the trench barricades around 2 pm. The Queen's and KRRC scattered and were 'picked off like rabbits… scarcely a man returned unwounded, while many were shot down in their tracks.'

The Afternoon Attack
General Allenby told his divisional commanders they had to capture the Blue Line at 2.25 pm. They had less than four hours to prepare and each divisional commander had to decide how they would use their artillery because they each faced a different problem.

<u>50th Division, Wancourt</u>
All four battalions of 150 Brigade had lost many men in the morning attack so Major General Wilkinson gave Brigadier General Price two of 151

Brigade's battalions. This time the artillery provided excellent cover and the 1/9th Durhams and the 1/5th Border Regiment both 'repeatedly got in with the bayonet' to silence two machine gun teams. Many Germans surrendered or fled but while the centre of the attack advanced 1,600 yards, machine gun fire pinned the flanks down. The Durhams and Borders discovered many wounded comrades who had been taken prisoner during the morning attack and stretcher bearers went forward to take them back for treatment.

30th Division, Chérisy

Brigadier General Goodman had little time to get the message to the battalion commanders and the company commanders had to run along the trenches to tell their men to prepare to advance. One captain was killed en route and his company did not advance when the rest moved off. The 20th King's were supposed to mop up but they too had no time to organise anything.

> *The company commanders re-joined their companies at 5.45 pm and they immediately detailed the mopping up parties required. Zero being fixed for 6 pm, there was no time for them to report to the respective units they had been detailed to… Apart from this there were no guides and they only had a map reference to find the troops.*

The advance was hurried and the 18th Manchesters were unable to reach the first trench so they fell back. Some of the 19th Manchesters reached it but were soon driven out and the survivors took cover in some practice trenches in no man's land.

33rd Division, Hindenburg Line

The delay was even worse on 33rd Division's front, where the British guns fired short. The creeping barrage exploded around 98 Brigade's trenches before the battalions received their orders to advance. The 2nd Argyll's commander and adjutant were hit so their advance was a shambles. Some officers misunderstood their instructions and did not advance, while Second Lieutenants Hanmer and Phillips were hit leading the Argylls over the top. The 1st Middlesex and the 2nd Argylls could not reach their isolated comrades; the 2nd Welch Fusiliers could not make any progress either. The advancing troops had encountered a line of British dead on the crest, the result of the German machine gun teams judging the range perfectly. Each attempt to advance only added to the pile of bodies.

Meanwhile, Lieutenant Colonel Garnett was given the order to attack at 6.24 pm at 6 pm, leaving him no time to organise the 5th Scottish Rifles. They tried in vain to advance over the same ground the Suffolks had covered on the right. Instead 33rd Division found itself on the defensive an hour later when the 2nd Welch Fusiliers came under attack.

Summary

There were more counter-attacks against VII Corps during an uneasy night. At one point some of the gunners on 30th Division's front removed the breechblocks from their guns when groups of Australian infantry withdrew through their battery positions. But the attacks had been made to stop the British interfering with their withdrawal. The situation calmed down at dawn on 24 April and it was clear the Germans had abandoned the slopes overlooking the Sensée stream. They were now dug in along the Croisilles–Chérisy road where they were again waiting for the British to appear over the crest. General Snow ordered a cautious follow up and while 50th Division moved its right flank forward, 30th Division occupied the German trenches which had been the previous day's objective. On 33rd Division's front the exhausted men of the Middlesex and Argyll were found to be still holding on. Although VII Corps had advanced over 1,500 yards, most of the ground had been abandoned by the Germans. The only reassuring news was that VII Corps had taken 1,800 prisoners.

Sixth Army's new chief of staff, Colonel Fritz von Lossberg, and General Ludendorff wanted to fight a different defensive battle. They wanted to use an elastic defence that could absorb and break up the enemy attack, rather than holding the front in strength. Counter-attacks, supported by artillery bombardments, would drive the British back with heavy casualties.

Lossberg also wanted to hold an outpost zone so a new fortified line could be built to protect the battery positions. It could also be used to rally units to counter-attack. The Drocourt–Quéant Switch (or Wotan Stellung) would be improved along the same lines as the Hindenburg Line, making it the main line of defence. Work also started on another line, the *Wotan II Stellung* Line, in front of Douai.

The terrain north of the Scarpe was perfect for Lossberg's plan but it was a different story to the south. Near the river, VI Corps held the commanding position of Monchy, while VII Corps looked across the Sensée valley from the slopes above Guémappe and Wancourt.

Chapter 18

No Quarter was Asked For or Given
28 and 29 April

The French Minister of Munitions, Albert Thomas, had met British Prime Minister, David Lloyd George, to explain his government's thoughts about the current situation. Their lack of manpower ruled out a battle of attrition and the Allies would have to suspend operations if Nivelle's offensive did not achieve immediate success. The French were hoping Russia would recover from their recent revolution and continue the fight on the Eastern Front (they would not). They were also hoping the United States, which had declared war on Germany on 6 April, would deploy a large army in France (they would).

Lloyd George told the British War Cabinet about the French position on 16 April, the day the Nivelle Offensive began. The Director of Military Operations at the War Office, Major General Frederick Maurice, informed GHQ two days later. Haig argued he had to continue the Arras offensive while the German's were facing an attack on two fronts. In his opinion it would be costlier in the long run if they stopped and gave the Germans time to recover.

Lloyd George agreed a compromise with the French government on 20 April. The British would continue their offensive and review the Allied situation at the beginning of May. Haig met Nivelle at Amiens on 24 April and explained that he wanted to save some of his reserves for a summer attack in Flanders. Nivelle confirmed he would continue attacking, pinning German reserves on the Aisne.

But it would not be for the two commanders to decide Allied strategy. Haig was summoned to meet Paul Painlevé in Paris on 26 April. The Minister of War was not impressed with French progress on the Aisne and was considering removing General Nivelle. At the same time Haig's Chief of the General Staff, Lieutenant General Lancelot Kiggell, was telling Generals Allenby and Horne they would continue attacking as long as the French did.

Haig wanted the Chief of the Imperial General Staff, General William Robertson, to tell Painlevé to continue the French offensive. In the meantime, Haig's next despatch stated that the Arras offensive would be continued 'until such time as the results of the French offensive should have declared themselves'. While the future of the spring campaign was in the balance, all Haig could do was discuss the next attack with his army commanders.

The uncertainty caused GHQ a major headache. Divisions were being kept in the Flanders area, ready to attack if the French halted their offensive. This left First and Third Armies relying on the same tired divisions that started the campaign. First Army would try again to advance past Arleux and Oppy while Third Army would clear Roeux and Plouvain south of the river. Fifth Army would also make another attempt to capture Bullecourt.

Plans were circulated for a larger offensive on 3 May, followed by an attack against the Drocourt–Quéant Switch a couple of weeks later. It was also hoped that Fifth and Fourth Armies could attack the Hindenburg Line. The forward planning sounded very decisive and optimistic but each stage relied on the success of the previous one, and GHQ was relying on tired divisions, worn out guns and only a handful of operational tanks.

First Army

The Germans had dug an extra trench west of Arleux and General Horne wanted it cleared before he tackled the Rouvroy–Fresnes Line. Lieutenant General Byng issued orders to advance through Arleux toward Fresnoy while Lieutenant General Congreve had to take Oppy.

Zero hour was set for 4.25 am and while the troops welcomed the milder weather, an early morning mist reduced visibility. Unfortunately the preliminary bombardment concentrated on hitting the front trench while most of the German troops were in the support trench waiting for the opportunity to counter-attack. It did not help that the support trench was often on a reverse slope where it was difficult to hit.

Canadian Corps, The Arleux Loop
2nd Canadian Division, North of Arleux

The division only used 25th Battalion to attack and its leading companies were pinned down in front of the wire for a time. Unfortunately the Canadians mistook the first sunken road they crossed for their objective. It was some time before they discovered that 5 Canadian Brigade's objective, a second sunken road between Méricourt and Arleux, was 300 yards further to the east.

1st Canadian Division, Arleux

Brigadier General Loomis had three of 2 Canadian Brigade's battalions in line but patrols reported the wire was only partially damaged. They also

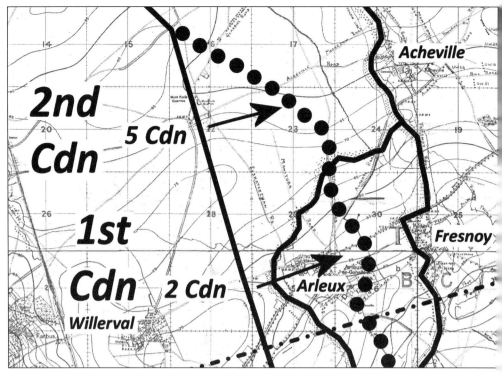

The Canadian Corps' capture of Arleux on 28 April.

noted that the enemy had an 'unusually large number of machine guns' in and around Arleux.

The centre and right of 5th Canadian Battalion reached the sunken Méricourt road north of Arleux. But the left was pinned down in front of the wire until the support company followed the centre and bombed along the trench. Even then the left company's problems were not over because 25th Canadian Battalion had stopped short, leaving its flank exposed to enfilade fire, and it was forced to fall back to the German trenches.

Two hidden machine guns pinned 10th Canadian Battalion down near the wire until the bombers silenced them. The Germans then fell back towards Fresnoy, abandoning Arleux, and the retirement was so organised that the Canadians initially thought they were British troops advancing through the gloom.

On the right, the 8th Canadian Battalion was hit by machine gun fire from Arleux and the wood to the south as they crossed a low rise. The left and right companies overran the trench but the centre company lost all its officers at the wire and the battalion reserves had to be deployed before it resumed the advance. The left was then pinned down by a strongpoint south of the village but the right crossed the Arleux–Oppy road and reached the objective. General Loomis sent a company of the 7th Canadian Battalion forward to silence the strongpoint, allowing 8th Canadian Battalion to advance through the south end of the village.

The Canadian artillery broke up the afternoon counter-attacks, so the Germans chose to consolidate the Méricourt–Oppy Line instead. It allowed 25th Canadian Battalion and 5th Canadian Battalion's left to reach the Méricourt road the following afternoon. General Horne considered 2 Canadian Brigade's capture of Arleux to be 'the only tangible success of the whole operation'.

XIII Corps
2nd Division, Oppy
General Pereira had to break through the Oppy Line and take the wood and village beyond. The problem was his division only had 8,500 fighting men and they were all tired. The artillery planned a double creeping barrage and it was hoped the Germans would man their parapet after the high explosive one had passed overhead only to be caught out by the shrapnel one.

The German artillery responded immediately as 5 Brigade advanced across no man's land. Captains Barnes and Giles led the 2nd Ox and Bucks through gaps in the wire but the 2nd Highland Light Infantry had to cut their way through and they lost the barrage. The two battalions reached the sunken Oppy–Arleux road but machine gun fire from the wood and the village stopped them going much further. The Highlanders' right flank came under attack when the 17th Middlesex were driven from Oppy Wood and they too fell back to the German second trench. The 17th Royal Fusiliers had been detailed to carry ammunition and equipment forward but Captain Taylor decided to help the Highlanders instead. He soon found that his flank and rear were under attack. General Bullen-Smith was able to report that both the Highlanders and the Royal Fusiliers were holding on; but only just.

In 6 Brigade's sector, the 17th Middlesex passed through the smashed wire and found a small number of Germans in the trench beyond. Captain Parfitt led his men through the shattered trees of Oppy Wood but the Germans were waiting for them in the village beyond. The 13th Essex's left reached some abandoned practice trenches south of the ruins but the right could not get through the wire. Colonel Martin had to deploy a third company to protect his right flank where 63rd Division should have been.

As the Middlesex cleared the village, the Germans infiltrated the wood, cutting off Parfitt's men. The 13th Essex's commanding officer, Lieutenant Colonel Martin, sent a 1st Berkshires company to help but they were unable to get far. Some of the Middlesex men made a run for it but only four men got back alive. More returned after dark, having spent the day hiding in the wood.

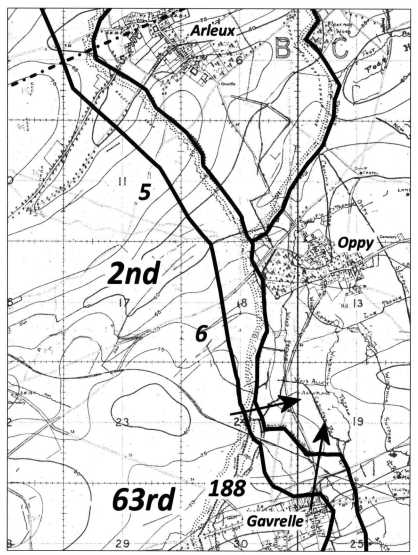

XIII Corps' attacks at Oppy and Gavrelle on 28 April.

General Walsh reported his men had made progress but the Germans had defended wisely. Their machine gun teams had broken up the attack, so their infantry could counter-attack. He had no reserves left because the 1st King's and 2nd South Staffords were busy mopping up and carrying ammunition. To make matters worse, the lack of information and the confused nature of the fighting meant the artillery did not know where to shell.

So General Pereira sent the 23rd Royal Fusiliers and the 1st KRRC of 99 Brigade forward to clear Oppy. Unfortunately heavy fire prevented the

KRRC reaching the Essex and everyone had fallen back to the German front trench by the time the Royal Fusiliers arrived. General Walsh later had to report it had been necessary to evacuate this trench at dusk. While the Germans had not been concerned about losing the Arleux Loop, they were not going to give up the Oppy Line.

63rd Division, Gavrelle

Major General Charles Lawrie had to form a flank for 2nd Division by clearing the area north of Gavrelle. His flank was a salient around the village so 188 Brigade had to make two converging attacks starting 1,000 yards apart and it was difficult to plan.

Lieutenant Colonel Hutching's 1st Royal Marines advanced east but were pinned down by enfilade machine gun fire coming from a strongpoint on the railway. Brigadier General Prentice sent Second Lieutenant Hawes and the Honourable Artillery Company bombers forward but it took them several hours to silence it. It took Second Lieutenant Reginald Haine six attempts to capture a second strongpoint. A counter-attack would eventually drive the Marines back.

The 2nd Royal Marines had advanced north from Gavrelle across the railway but artillery fire forced them to retire, leaving Lieutenant Newling's platoon holding Gavrelle windmill. The withdrawal also left Sub-Lieutenant Walker's company of the Anson Battalion isolated east of Gavrelle. Petty Officer Scott helped them fight their way back, bringing 250 prisoners with them.

First Army, 29 April

2nd Division, Oppy

Lieutenant General Congreve issued orders to Major General Pereira at 7 pm on 28 April. He wanted 2nd Division to capture the Oppy Line between Oppy Wood and Gavrelle. The artillery shelled the German positions throughout the night and the infantry advanced at 4 am.

Captain Hooke was wounded leading two 24th Royal Fusiliers companies forward on 5 Brigade's front. Second Lieutenant Kitmister took over but the machine guns in Oppy Wood stopped his men reaching their objective.

An understrength 99 Brigade had taken over from 6 Brigade and the 24th Royal Fusiliers and 1st Berkshires both captured the Oppy Line south-west of the village. Counter-attack after counter-attack was stopped but the Berkshires were reduced to around sixty men who were short of ammunition and grenades. A store of German bombs was used to stop the fifth attack but a wounded Captain Stokes eventually had to fall back. The Germans then turned on a group of men taking cover in a sunken road, forcing a wounded Captain Jerwood to abandon the position. Lance Corporal James Welch killed one man and then captured four more after chasing them with his empty revolver. He had kept his machine gun in action for five hours, using parts from abandoned weapons to repair it when it stopped firing. Welch's crusade only ended when he was wounded by a shell; he would be awarded the Victoria Cross.

Lieutenant Colonel Harris's 22nd Royal Fusiliers were delayed by the second belt of wire on the right flank and the barrage had moved on by the time two groups had cut their way through. Machine gun fire decimated the northern group and Sergeant Fred Palmer was one of the few survivors who took cover in shell holes close to the wire. Palmer had only recently been recommended for the Victoria Cross.

Major Gregg and all but one officer of the southern group were hit, leaving Second Lieutenant Jeffcoat and Company Sergeant Major Hogan to lead the survivors through the wire. Jeffcoat sent some of his men north along the trench and then led the rest south. His group bombed for 400 yards until they met men of 63rd Division near Gavrelle. It had been a desperate fight in which 'no quarter was asked for or given'.

Jeffcoat had cleared the Oppy Line but he was short of men and bombs. The German bombers went looking for Jeffcoat's party as soon as the Berkshires had been driven back so he sent a desperate message to Lieutenant Colonel Barnett-Barker asking for men to help him secure the Oppy Line. Captain Bowyer and one hundred men of the 23rd Royal Fusiliers helped him clear some of the trench but they dared not go too far in case they ran out of bombs. Lieutenant Jeffcoat was mortally wounded during the fighting and only fifteen of his men returned.

After two days of hard fighting, General Pereira had to report that the situation opposite the Oppy Line was unchanged. All his battalions had lost many men and 99 Brigade was down to around 850 tired men.

63rd Division, Gavrelle

General Lawrie also reported 63rd Division was well below strength and he was having to form composite battalions to hold the line around Gavrelle. He even had to use his pioneers, the 14th Worcesters, who normally did construction work, to hold the line south of the village.

The following day 190 Brigade made a new attack from the north side of Gavrelle with a composite battalion of the 4th Bedfords and 10th Dublin Fusiliers. They crossed the railway line with help from the 1st HAC, but a counter-attack later that night threatened to drive them back so Second Lieutenant Alfred Pollard took a bombing party forward to clear the trench; Pollard was awarded the Victoria Cross.

Third Army, 28 April

General Allenby's plans seemed to pay little attention to the lie of the land. Divisions were expected to advance from objective to objective as they had been drawn on the maps. The area east of Arras may have looked flat on the map but the Germans were taking full advantage of the low ridges and shallow valleys.

XVII Corps, 28 April

Lieutenant General Fergusson had two objectives on the north bank of the Scarpe. The 37th Division had to capture Greenland Hill while 34th Division had to clear Roeux on the river bank. Both divisions had been in action earlier in the campaign and they were well below strength due to enemy action and sickness. On average 34th Division's battalions had 500 fighting men, but nearly half were replacements for recent casualties. They typically only had three months of training and had never been in action before. The situation was worse for Major General Bruce-Williams because 37th Division had not received any replacements yet and some battalions only had 200 fighting men and few officers.

<u>37th Division, Greenland Hill</u>

Brigadier General Compton had deployed a company of the 9th North Staffords (Pioneers) east of Gavrelle and they provided covering fire for 111 Brigade. The 13th Rifle Brigade and 13th Royal Fusiliers advanced 800 yards beyond the south edge of the village. On 63 Brigade's front, the 8th Lincolns and 8th Somersets disappeared into the mist as they chased Germans across the north slope of Greenland Hill towards Fresnes-lès-Montauban. Brigadier General Challenor did not know they had passed through Railway Copse and crossed the trench defending Fresnoy. The 10th York and Lancasters took up a position south of Square Wood but two of the 4th Middlesex companies headed towards Fresnoy.

There had been a breakthrough but it was only a local one. The German artillery might have been withdrawing but their infantry was counter-attacking. General Challenor had no idea what was happening beyond the crest of the hill until his men fell back over Greenland Hill, taking the York and Lancasters with them.

In 112 Brigade's sector, the 6th Bedfords reached Cuthbert Trench but they had a problem. The 10th Loyals had come under enfilade fire from the chemical works and had taken cover in a trench 300 yards short of their objective. It allowed the Germans to enfilade the Bedfords and less than sixty able men fell back to the new trench after all their officers had been hit.

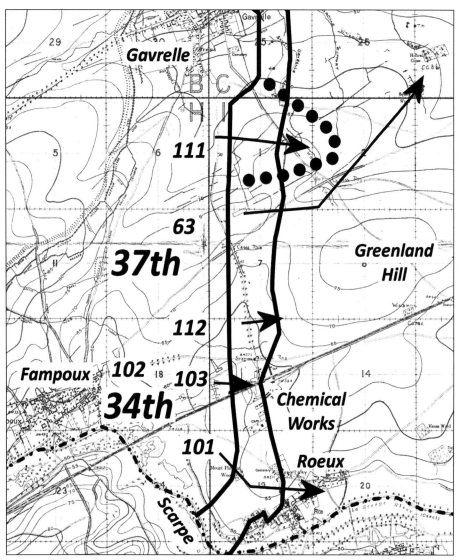

XVII Corps' struggle for Greenland Hill and Roeux on 28 April.

Brigadier General Maclachlan reported that Cuthbert Trench had been captured and Bruce-Williams told General Lukin the same when 9th Division took over the line two nights later. The Scots soon found out they were mistaken when they discovered forty exhausted Bedfords in Cuthbert Trench. They had spent the past forty-eight hours in no man's land without food or water. General Lukin decided against trying to hold the exposed position north of Greenland Hill and gave instructions to abandon all the ground 37th Division had taken on 28 April.

34th Division, Roeux

Major General Nicholson faced the problem of how to clear Roeux. The barrage had been carefully calculated to give the infantry enough time to move through the ruins: it would move at 25 yards a minute while they were in the open, 12 yards a minute in the west part of the village, and 14 yards a minute in the centre and east parts.

The 25th Northumberland Fusiliers advanced north of the railway but they could not clear the station buildings. Instead they took cover in shell holes near their objective, aware that 37th Division was not on their north flank. Brigadier General Griffin's report of the situation meant that 102 Brigade could not move along the railway to capture the chemical works after dusk. So the isolated Northumbrian men fell back during the night.

Brigadier General Gore had attached a company of the 16th Royal Scots to 101 Brigade's three assault battalions, so they could mop up Roeux. The 11th Suffolks advanced behind a barrage which was 'too ragged and inaccurate to disorganise the German resistance'. It missed the machine guns near the chateau and then jumped from one side of the chemical works to the other. The Suffolks were stopped by wire woven into the hedges surrounding the chateau gardens and Lieutenant Ritchie could only lead a few of the 10th Lincolns into Roeux.

The Germans let Second Lieutenant Walker's company of the 15th Royal Scots pass through Mount Pleasant Wood only to open fire on Captain Pagan's and Lieutenant Dixon's companies. The Scots cleared Roeux quicker than expected and reached the far side ahead of the barrage. But only 175 men made it through and the Lincolns were lagging behind on their left. Pagan was killed during a counter-attack leaving Lieutenant Robson no option but to withdraw. The area west of the village was still swept by machine gun fire so Robson and around thirty survivors, many of them wounded, made a desperate attempt to escape by swimming along the river. They did not get far before they were forced to surrender.

Captain Warr had sensed something had gone wrong and he stopped the rest of the 16th Royal Scots entering Roeux. A counter-attack around 8 am drove them back until the 20th Northumberland Fusiliers steadied the line. Around 300 out of the 400 Royal Scots that had gone into action had been killed or captured.

General Nicholson moved 102 Brigade forward to make another attack astride the railway, only this time it was going to be a night attack with no covering barrage. The problem was Brigadier General Thomson was told too late to organise it. The 22nd Northumberland Fusiliers arrived in time to advance at 3 am on 29 April but the 23rd Northumberland Fusiliers arrived an hour late. The German machine guns dealt with each of them in turn.

VI Corps, South of the Scarpe

General Haldane once again faced the problem of how to advance across the ridges and gullies on the south bank of the Scarpe. He also had to hope that XVII Corps had captured Roeux across the river.

12th Division, South of the Scarpe

An intense bombardment warned the infantry, British and German alike, that zero hour was imminent. Two minutes later General Scott's men started moving and the German guns opened fire on Lone Copse valley three minutes later. The 5th Berkshires captured Bayonet Trench and part of Rifle Trench on 35 Brigade's front before they were pinned down by a machine gun on the river bank. Corporal Hedgman eventually silenced the weapon and his men took twenty prisoners.

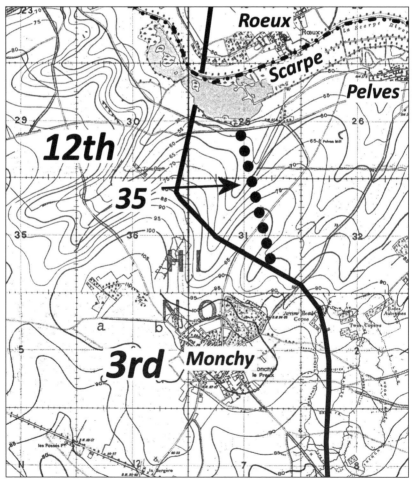

VI Corps' attack, south of the River Scarpe on 28 April.

The artillery had missed the middle of Rifle Trench and the 7th Norfolks' left was pinned down, but the right went beyond Rifle Trench, only to be pinned down on Pelves Mill ridge. The two halves of the battalion were unable to establish contact with each other so Brigadier General Vincent sent the 7th Suffolks forward to help. Machine gun fire from Roeux stopped two attempts to clear the rest of Pelves Mill ridge. All the Suffolks' officers were hit and only 190 men answered the battalion roll call when they came out of the line. The following morning the 9th Essex captured another part of Rifle Trench but a bombing counter-attack along New Street forced them to withdraw.

Summary
As April came to an end, GHQ would have calculated the casualty returns for the battle. First Army's casualties were around 24,000 while Third Army's were around 52,000. Fifth Army had suffered approximately 4,200. The combination of rain and snow had also taken its toll: the three armies reported over 50,000 sick for the month. On a positive note the number of German prisoners taken was nearly 18,000. First Army had also captured 69 artillery pieces while Third Army had taken a staggering 185 guns.

Chapter 19

Theirs was an Unenviable Task
3 May

By 25 April the Aisne offensive had achieved considerable success but it had not achieved the decisive result promised by Nivelle. It had also used up most of the French shell reserve and there had been close to 100,000 casualties, leading to a breakdown in the medical evacuation system. General Joseph Micheler, commander of the French Reserve Group, suggested reducing the scope of the offensive to the Chemin des Dames ridge and Rheims. Nivelle agreed, only to learn that Pétain had been appointed Chief of the General Staff on 29 April. While it undermined his authority, worse was to come.

Haig realised the French offensives would be called off when he heard about Nivelle's situation. All he could do was secure a good defensive line around Arras and try to stop the German reserves moving north to Flanders. Haig wanted to be holding a 'good defensive line' when he closed down the offensive and he believed a single big attack had more chance of success than lots of small ones.

Haig explained how he intended to close down the offensive to Generals Horne, Allenby and Gough on 30 April. First Army would renew its attacks on Arleux, Oppy and Gavrelle while Third Army would push beyond Roeux, Monchy and Guémappe. Fifth Army would, once more, try to advance beyond Bullecourt. The artillery would start their bombardment in a few hours and the first attack would start on 3 May; the final one would be against the Drocourt–Quéant Switch on 15 May. Haig also informed General Gough that his Fifth Army headquarters would soon be moving north to take control of the northern half of the Flanders operations. He would be fighting alongside General Herbert Plumer's Second Army.

The following day, Haig told Robertson he was going to close down the Arras offensive and start another in Flanders at the same time as the Italians and Russians began theirs. On 3 May, Haig asked General Pétain to take over part of the British front, so he would have more divisions for the Arras offensive. Pétain refused to commit the French to anything. The following day Haig and Robertson met Nivelle and Pétain and they concluded that the British had to take responsibility for the main operations because the French were exhausted. They also determined that the Allies had to stop looking for a breakthrough on the Western Front and return to a war of attrition once again.

The generals further agreed that future planning had to be carried out complete secrecy. The Nivelle offensive had been compromised because the politicians had discussed the details, making it easy for the Germans to find out about the attack. In future the British and French GHQs would keep details of offensive operations to themselves.

The Assault
Each corps had divided its artillery into three groups and they were given specific objectives. The Trench Groups would target the wire and trenches; the Counter Battery Groups would silence the batteries; the Super Heavy Groups would aim for long range targets. They began their work with an all-night bombardment on 30 April. The Super Heavy Group hit the villages with short intense barrages, starting at dawn, to interfere with the reliefs. The Trench Group opened fire as soon as the observers could see and three 60-pounder batteries covered the gaps in the wire to stop the repair parties. The Counter Battery Group spent all day working with the aerial spotters to knock out enemy batteries. The artillery programme on 2 May followed a similar pattern.

Meanwhile, the Royal Flying Corps were again busy. Six Nieuport fighters of Tenth Wing flew low over the German lines, covered by an artillery barrage. They shot down four observation balloons and damaged another four opposite Third Army.

All three army commanders wanted a different time for zero hour. General Allenby wanted a surprise night attack with no artillery while General Gough wanted a night attack supported by artillery. Haig thought the British infantry were too inexperienced to advance at night. The original plan was for the experienced Australians in Fifth Army to advance at 3.30 am while it was still dark. Third Army's British troops would move thirty-five minutes later, in the half-light of the dawn. Haig then changed his mind, probably worried that Fifth Army's early attack would alert the Germans opposite Third Army. Instead, he instructed all three armies to attack at 3.45 am. The compromise pleased no one, particularly General Allenby.

GHQ's last-minute change of heart proved to be a disaster when it came to the tactical aspects of planning the attack because advancing at night required special preparations. Useful items such as message boards and direction posts marked with phosphorescent paint had to be made while the officers needed to see the ground and check their compass bearings. There was no time to do any of these things.

To make matters worse, the staff officers had chosen large distances between the objectives, as was normal with a daylight attack. There was no time to replan the advance with short bounds between the objectives, as was usual during night attacks. The sun was not due to rise until 5.22 am and the last-minute change would literally result in a leap into the dark. Despite the concerns of many senior officers, there was a buoyant mood amongst the troops, as reported by the 10th Argylls in 9th Division: 'Everyone was confident of success; the men are very fit and fresh.'

The troops spent a long night marching up to the front, aware that the full moon setting behind them would silhouette them against the dark sky. On the other hand the black sky up ahead made it impossible to see far. The artillery was firing blind into the darkness and the exploding shells were stirring up clouds of dust which drifted into the faces of the assault troops.

At zero hour a double barrage hit the enemy trenches with a mix of high explosive and shrapnel. The creeping barrage moved fast while the 6-inch howitzers pounded the trenches. Other howitzers targeted potential strongpoints, such as Roeux Wood and the chemical works. But many Germans had moved into no man's land to avoid the barrage. They found shelter in shell holes and their machine gun teams were waiting as the advancing waves of troops groped forward through the dust clouds.

First Army
Canadian Corps, Fresnoy

General Byng had to capture the Méricourt–Oppy Line. Both 2nd and 1st Canadian Divisions had received replacements to bring them up to strength. The Canadian drafts tended to be older and fitter than their British comrades and had also had more training. The German infantry were surprised by the early hour of the assault but the batteries were not; they immediately opened fire.

2nd Canadian Division, North of Fresnoy

Major General Burstall's men had to clear the junction of the Arleux Loop and the Méricourt–Oppy Line. The wire had not been cut in front of 6 Canadian Brigade and the barrage moved on as Brigadier General Ketchen's men cut through.

On the left, 31st Canadian Battalion was hit by enfilade fire from the trench junction on its north flank. They then stumbled on a new entanglement and trench in no man's land and found it unoccupied. Some followed it northwards into the sights of the machine guns in the Arleux

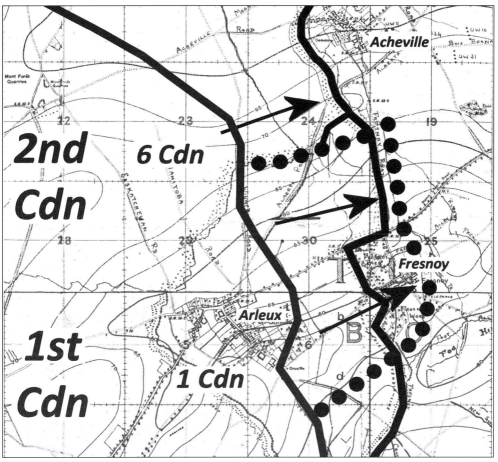

The Canadian Corps' capture of Fresnoy on 3 May.

Loop but the rest reached the German front trench. The senior officer realised he had too few men to hold on so he withdrew them to the trench in no man's land.

In the centre, 27th Canadian Battalion cleared the trench alongside the Acheville–Fresnoy road and pushed onto the support trench 200 yards beyond. Lieutenant Robert Combe led his company through the German bombardment but only five men reached the objective. They bombed along the trench, collecting men and German bombs along the way until they had captured eighty prisoners. Combe stopped the counter-attacks until he was shot by a sniper; he was posthumously awarded the Victoria Cross.

1st Canadian Division, Fresnoy
It was difficult to negotiate the wire in the dark but the Germans could not see the gaps either, so 1 Canadian Brigade were on top of them before they

knew it. As 1st Canadian Battalion's left advanced to the support trench north of the Lille road, the right encountered resistance in the chateau grounds. In the centre, 2nd Canadian Battalion outflanked and silenced three machine guns protecting Fresnoy before pushing through the ruins to the objective, 250 yards beyond. They then put their prisoners to work, collecting and evacuating the wounded. Meanwhile, 3rd Canadian Battalion 'combed the wood south of Fresnoy like beaters in a pheasant shoot'. But casualties had been heavy and only twenty-five men of one company reached Fresnoy Trench, 500 yards beyond.

The capture of Fresnoy was one of the few successes on 3 May. It had cost the Canadian Corps over 1,450 casualties but they had captured nearly 500 prisoners.

XIII Corps, Oppy and Gavrelle
General Congreve faced the Oppy Line between Oppy Wood and Gavrelle. He had instructed 31st Division to relieve 63rd Division and the right half of 2nd Division. But the left half of the division had to stay in line.

<u>2nd Division</u>
General Pereira said, 'the only way that the division could do anything, now that we are so weak in numbers and so many men are unfit for further operations, was by forming a composite brigade out of the remnants of the other three brigades.' Four battalions, identified as A, B, C and D, were organised but Brigadier General Kellett still only had 1,600 rifles to clear the rest of the Arleux Loop. Things did not go well, even before zero hour. A feint barrage was fired to confuse the German infantry but all it had done was alert the German gunners. Their counter-bombardment disrupted the deployment, making some of the assault companies late.

Lieutenant Colonel Weston's A Battalion was spotted assembling in no man's land, a move made necessary because the assembly trenches were under heavy fire. The creeping barrage threw up dust which caused the men to bunch up as they advanced. The captured trenches soon became overcrowded so many men had to take cover in shell holes in no man's land, leaving them unable to help during the counter-attacks. Weston's men withdrew as soon as they ran out of bombs.

Meanwhile, Lieutenant Colonel Vernon's C Battalion reached Fresnoy Trench along with Captain Bannatyne's B Battalion company. Captain Bland's men were shot down on the right flank while the rest of B Battalion had been delayed. Lieutenant Colonel Norris's men 'caught the full blast of the enemy's artillery and machine gun barrage and they were forced to take shelter in shell holes'.

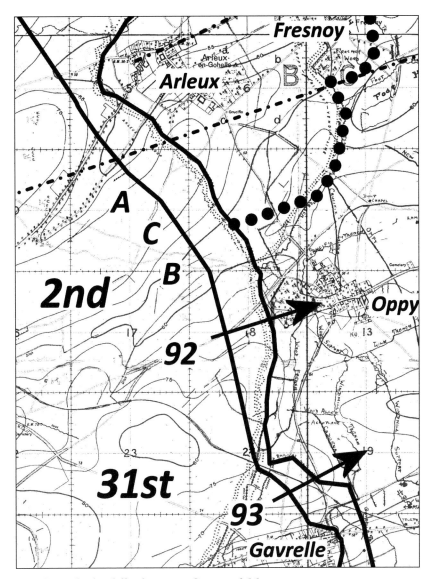

XIII Corps had a difficult time at Oppy on 3 May.

A counter-attack along Oppy Support Trench and Crucifix Lane was stopped but B Battalion had to withdraw when it ran out of bombs; both Bannatyne and Bland were reported missing. The Germans were pushing C Battalion's right back until Captain Anderson's company reinforced the position with the help of Canadian troops. A new line had been established close to Fresnoy but it had reduced 2nd Division to 3,750 men and few of them were riflemen.

31st Division, Oppy Wood

A German plane flew low over no man's land during the night and the crew spotted the assault troops assembling in the bright moonlight. A German patrol also spotted movement and it withdrew to report the news. All the men could do was take what cover they could as the shells rained down.

Brigadier General Williams' 92 Brigade faced Oppy Wood, a 200 metres square patch of smashed trees and shell holes. The 12th East Yorkshires moved past the north side, the 11th East Yorkshires entered it and the 10th East Yorkshires advanced to the south. Or at least that was the plan, because no one could see any landmarks nor judge the creep of the barrage:

In the darkness which had succeeded the setting of the moon, murderous machine-gun fire swept the whole front and rockets and Very lights of every colour shot up from the German lines, but the attacking waves moved steadily forward, although the enveloping blanket of mist and fumes made the keeping of direction an impossibility.

Captains Addy and Carlisle were killed leading the 11th East Yorkshires through Oppy Wood but Second Lieutenant Jack Harrison charged the machine gun team shooting at his platoon. The weapon fell silent but Harrison was never seen again; he was posthumously awarded the Victoria Cross. Only Lieutenant Akester led a few men into the village on the far side of the wood but he too fell. Many East Yorkshires were cut off in the wood and while some were captured, others had to lie out in the open all day while German snipers climbed the wrecked trees to shoot at them.

Visibility was also bad as 93 Brigade advanced north-east of Gavrelle. Captain Parker saw Germans approaching the 16th West Yorkshires and he thought they were surrendering until they opened fire. Coincidently they too were attacking, so the Yorkshiremen shot as many as they could and then withdrew. Lieutenant Colonel Carter reported the 18th West Yorkshires' leading companies were 'mostly wiped out by machine gun fire before they reached the first objective'. The Germans holding Gavrelle had been willing to surrender until they realised how few Yorkshiremen there were. Captains Blease and King were killed leading the 15th West Yorkshires. They were just two of the 400 Yorkshiremen hit around Windmill Trench.

Although Brigadier General Ingles' battalions had made good progress, they had all suffered badly. The Germans counter-attacked from Oppy Wood, driving all three back and Lieutenant Colonels Carter and Croydon (of the 16th West Yorkshires) had to rally the stragglers along the British parapet to stop the counter-attack. The fighting petered out with a fight for

Gavrelle windmill which was retaken by a company of the 18th Durhams. British artillery fire forced Second Lieutenant Hitchin to withdraw but the Durhams retook the observation post later on.

Third Army
XVII Corps

General Fergusson was again tasked with capturing Greenland Hill and the Roeux area. He objected to advancing over the same ground in the dark but had to conform with the rest of Third Army. The double creeping barrage was timed to advance at fifty yards a minute and it was too fast for troops moving in the dark.

9th Division, Greenland Hill

Brigadier General Maxwell had a staggered front, with 27 Brigade's left 250 yards ahead of its right. The brigade had just received many inexperienced men, replacements for those lost on 9 April, and they struggled to find their way through the clouds of dust.

The 6th KOSBs were supposed to wait for five minutes so the 9th Scottish Rifles could come into line. Unfortunately, the Rifles did not see the lamp lit to guide them because of the dust and the two leading companies veered right in the darkness. The KOSBs went forward alone at the set time and while the platoon covering the left flank was wiped out, three companies reached the first objective. Meanwhile, the Rifles had stumbled into Cuthbert Trench, where they faced a hard struggle. The support companies went in the right direction and found the Germans waiting for them.

The Scots had made progress but the Germans infiltrated behind their flanks. The KOSBs came under fire from all sides and a badly injured Lieutenant Colonel Smyth could do nothing to help them. Lieutenant Colonel Fulton came under fire from Wit Trench when he went forward to investigate, proving that the two battalions were cut off.

Brigadier General Maxwell arranged another attack at 8 pm but he only had six platoons of the 12th Royal Scots available. Captain Ritchie was killed leading the gallant rescue attempt but it allowed some of the KOSBs and Scottish Rifles to escape. Even so, the KOSBs suffered over 400 casualties, many of them missing; few would rejoin Major Innes-Browne that night. Only thirty of Ritchie's men returned.

Captain Taylor and Lieutenant Mackenzie became disorientated moving over the broken ground on 26 Brigade's front and only a few of the 8th Black Watch reached the German trench. The disorientated 9th Scottish Rifles charged the second wave of the Black Watch; they had to redeploy

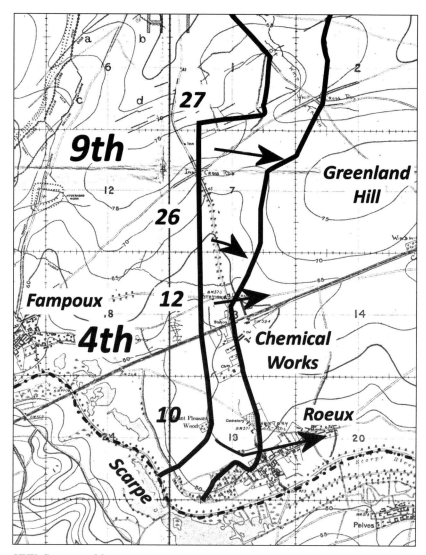

XVII Corps could not capture Greenland Hill or Roeux on 3 May.

so they could advance in the right direction once they realised their mistake. The Black Watch also became disorientated. This time they mistook the British front line for the German trench. They proceeded to advance along it, firing from the hip.

The 5th Camerons were misled by flares fired from the maze of trenches on Greenland Hill and they swerved right into 4th Division's area where they opened fire on the 2nd Essex. The 10th Argylls headed in the right direction in support and advanced straight into the waiting Germans. Two companies were pinned down but one went through a gap in the enemy line and reached the first objective. They were soon surrounded and few escaped.

Brigadier General Kennedy was disappointed that his men had gone to ground as soon as they lost the barrage. They had become dependent on the artillery to protect them and it was a consequence of having so many inexperienced replacements in the ranks. Kennedy instructed the Black Watch to try again and this time they cleared Charlie and Cuthbert Trenches. But they soon had to withdraw, under fire from the railway embankment and the chemical works.

4th Division, Roeux

Major General Lambton was another one who objected to the plan of attack. He thought there were too few guns and the creeping barrage was too fast. He also thought there were too many objectives and that the moppers-up would not find all the dugouts in the dark. Lambton would prove to be right but he also had to conform to Third Army's plan.

Brigadier General Carton de Wiart's men were tasked with forming a flank along the railway line. The 2nd Essex were supposed to dig in along the railway which crossed 12 Brigade's front but the 5th Camerons (9th Division) swerved into them and they ended up shooting at each other in the dark. The 2nd Lancashire Fusiliers advanced astride the railway but Captain Gregory had to fall back on the north side under heavy fire. Captains Slingsby and Martin advanced through the chemical works but they failed to clear the chateau on their right flank. The Germans then used the railway cutting to infiltrate behind the Lancashire Fusiliers and not a man returned.

The counter-attack also cut behind the 2nd Duke's holding the trench in front of Plouvain. Captains Heale and Cunningham had been wounded, their subalterns had been hit too, and the leaderless men were overrun. Only thirty men answered Company Sergeant Major Bamborough's order to fall back while Sergeant Reid sent a desperate message back asking for reinforcements. Another counter-attack overran the small groups of men at around 2 pm and only sixteen men (excluding the headquarters staff) answered the roll call that night. A few stragglers raised the numbers to the strength of two platoons but the Duke's had suffered nearly 400 casualties.

Brigadier General Pritchard had wanted the 1st Irish Fusiliers and Household Battalion to clear the area north of Roeux but only a few men reached the first objective. One machine gun team waited behind a wall as 10 Brigade approached the edge of Roeux. It opened fire at point-blank range as the Household Battalion walked into their sights. The 1st Warwicks and 2nd Seaforths were supposed to advance through Hausa and Delbar Woods but few reached the first objective and even fewer returned.

The 1st Somersets advanced towards Roeux twenty minutes after zero, only they advanced in the wrong direction. There had been no time to check the ground and the map showed some trenches facing north-east rather than north. So the troops advanced towards the river rather than the village until Captain Codner and Second Lieutenant Marler realised the error. They both lost their lives organising the redeployment and their men struggled to find their objectives in the dust. They had lost the barrage and while the left company could not clear the village the right one struggled in the wood on the river bank.

A late-night attack by 1st Rifle Brigade was made against Roeux chateau but it too failed. It brought to an end a disastrous day which had cost 4th Division over 2,000 casualties.

VI Corps

General Haldane had to advance his line between the Scarpe river and the Cambrai road. On his left, 12th Division had to reach Pelves, 3rd Division had to clear Bois du Sart in the centre, while 56th Division was expected to reach the Saint Rohart Factory east of Guémappe. The problem was all three divisions had been engaged in the fighting on 9 April and all had received many replacements.

12th Division, Pelves

A preliminary attack was made at 1 am on 2 May to bring 36 Brigade into line with 37 Brigade. Livens projectors fired gas across no man's land but the wind blew it back into the faces of the advancing troops and only a small section of Rifle Trench was taken. The Germans retaliated when the British artillery opened fire by smothering the batteries with gas shells.

Brigadier General Owen had told Lieutenant Colonels Elliott-Cooper and Overton to watch for green Very lights across the river, indicating that Roeux chemical works had been captured. They never saw any signals through the smoke and dust, so the officers warned their men to watch for the barrage to start. Some shells fell short on their trenches when it did and the heavy guns were firing so slowly that it was hard to see the barrage moving in the dark.

The 8th and 9th Royal Fusiliers reached their first objective. Machine gun fire from Roeux killed Major Coxhead as the 9th Royal Fusiliers approached Scabbard Trench. They kept advancing to Devil's Trench but many dugouts were missed in the dark and the Germans were able to confront the support companies. A bombing attack drove all the Royal Fusiliers back and many were taken prisoner.

In the confusion, one mopping-up party threw a bomb into a dugout

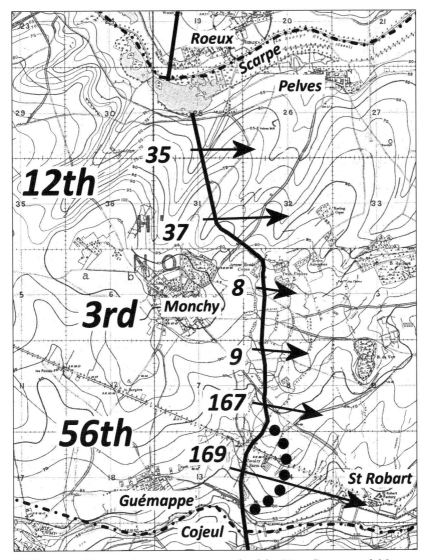

VI Corps could not make any progress south of the River Scarpe on 3 May.

where Corporal George Jarratt and other 8th Royal Fusiliers had been left by their captors. Jarratt stood on the bomb to save his friends; he was posthumously awarded the Victoria Cross. Another group of prisoners saw their guard dive for cover when they came under shellfire, so they ran back across no man's land.

A second attempt to take Devil's Trench was made by the 7th Sussex and Essex at 12.10 pm and they both reached Scabbard Trench, taking nearly one hundred prisoners between them. A third attempt after dusk failed to hold any ground.

On 37 Brigade's front, the 7th East Surrey and 6th Buffs reached their first objective but many officers were hit, including Captains Kitchin and McDermott. The leaderless men found it difficult to keep in contact and a counter-attack cut off many in Devil's Trench; only a few escaped. Lieutenant Colonels Baldwin and Cope were unable tell Brigadier General Cator any news for some time, so the artillery could not help. Around forty Buffs under Second Lieutenants Cockerham and Gunther were trapped in Keeling Copse. They stopped all counter-attacks and Cockerham shot a German officer who called on them to surrender. Only ten men, many of them wounded, were fit enough to withdraw when it was dark. Major Dawson was wounded leading 6th Queen's Own in an attack against Devil's Trench after dark.

3rd Division, East of Monchy

The Germans seemed to know an attack was imminent and they shelled Major General Deverell's front line and Monchy with gas and high explosive shell. They also smothered the field batteries with gas, so the gunners had to work with masks on and it affected the creeping barrage. No man's land was also hit with gas shells and the fumes made the men sick as they deployed.

Some Germans had hidden in shell holes to avoid the British barrage and they shot at the 1st Scots Fusiliers and 2nd Royal Scots as they struggled to keep formation. They then discovered that the artillery had missed some trenches and they were pinned down in no man's land until dusk. Captain Tuck had to lie close to the German trenches, listening to how they wished to finish him off. Brigadier General Holmes reported that 8 Brigade was back on its start line by dusk.

The 13th King's and 4th Royal Fusiliers advanced under enfilade fire from Bois des Aubépines and Bois du Sart. The King's suffered particularly badly, and Captains Byng, Coates and Hunter were all wounded. They stopped the first counter-attack but the second one drove 9 Brigade back and many men were left behind. Calls for help took time to reach Brigadier General Potter because the 'runners were greatly handicapped, getting through the barrage with difficulty. Brave fellows, theirs was an unenviable task.'

The attack was a disaster even before the start. The guides took too long to find the 1st Northumberland Fusiliers and 12th West Yorkshires. Everyone had to put on their respirators as they moved forward under a gas barrage. They then found men from 12th Division holding their assembly trench rather than the objective. The crowded trench was under enfilade fire and many were hit before zero hour. The two battalions suffered 350 casualties between them in just ten minutes and they had not gone beyond the British front line.

56th Division, Cavalry Farm and the St Rohart Factory

Star shells and explosions lit up the dark sky above no man's land at zero hour, creating a confusing spectacle. The support waves moved too fast, worried they would lose contact, and the battalions merged into a mob, making them an easy target for the German machine guns.

The German artillery was on target as it shelled the Londoners at zero hour but the British gunners missed Tool Trench because it was beyond the crest of the hill opposite 167 Brigade. The 1/7th Middlesex and 1/1st London Regiment were pinned down while the few men who reached Lanyard Trench were taken prisoner. The 1/9th London Regiment captured Cavalry Farm on the right and then bombed up Tool Trench.

The 1/2nd and 1/5th London Regiments reached the first objective around the St Rohart Factory in 169 Brigade's sector. But the withdrawal of 167 Brigade and 14th Division around noon left General Coke's men exposed and outflanked in Cojeul Valley. The Germans drove them back and Coke's plan to rally back was disrupted by a second counter-attack up the muddy valley.

VII Corps, Sensée stream

General Snow's men had to advance over the Hump and towards Chérisy and Fontaine on the Sensée stream. The artillery barrage was scheduled to move fast in the open and slow through the villages and woods. The troops found it difficult to deploy in the darkness but the Germans seemed to have no problem working out that an attack was imminent.

14th Division, East of Guémappe

General Couper's men had been in action on 9 April and again since 25 April, so the exhausted survivors had been kept busy training the replacements. Both of 42 Brigade's battalions, the 9th Rifle Brigade and 5th Ox and Bucks, were hit by enfilade fire from the St Rohart Factory. Captains McKinsty and Letts of the Rifle Brigade were just two of the many hit as they cut through the wire. Again many dugouts were overlooked in the dark and the Germans came above ground to engage the second wave when there was enough light to shoot accurately. Meanwhile, the 8th KRRC and 8th Rifle Brigade captured the first objective on the Vis-en-Artois spur in 41 Brigade's sector.

Success had come easy but it had come too easy. The Germans had left a few machine gun teams and snipers behind in their front trenches while the rest withdrew when the bombardment started. They then counter-attacked, forcing most of Major General Couper's men to retire.

Some Riflemen dug in near Triangle Wood on the outskirts of Vis-en-

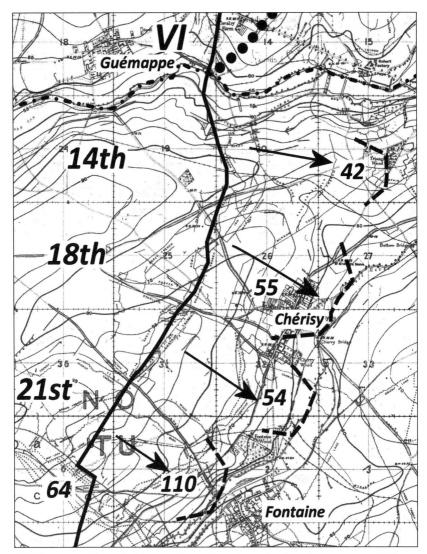

VII Corps could not hold any of its gains along the Sensée stream on 3 May.

Artois, where they would hold out all day. Brigadier General Dudgeon ordered them to withdraw from the isolated position when it was dark. It took time to find Second Lieutenant Round's company. He refused to come back until he had rescued all his wounded men and it took him twenty-four hours to fulfil his promise.

18th Division, Chérisy
Major General Richard Lee's men had just taken over the sector facing Chérisy. The 8th East Surreys and 7th Buffs advanced over the north end of the Hump and down the slope into Chérisy in 55 Brigade's sector. Some

Germans emerged from dugouts to attack their open flank and Captain Black was unable to organise an effective defence in the mist. By mid-morning Brigadier General Price had to report that most of his men were back on their original trenches, but parties were still fighting on in Chérisy.

On 54 Brigade's front some of the 12th Middlesex drifted into the path of the 7th Buffs in the darkness and they ended up in Chérisy. The rest of the Middlesex and the 7th Bedfords were pinned down in front of the wire covering Chérisy Trench until a tank came crawling back towards them. Someone shouted 'retire!' and they began falling back.

The 6th Northants and 7th Queen's were supposed to capture Chérisy at 7.15 pm but it was too late because the East Surreys, Buffs and Middlesex had already surrendered. A second attempt by the 7th Bedfords also failed to get into Chérisy Trench and Lieutenant Reiss was forced to make his men dig in close to the German wire.

21st Division, Hindenburg Line

Major General Campbell's division had absorbed many replacements since the attack on 9 April. Three tanks had been sent to assist the attack but one broke down, the second broke a track and the third ditched trying to find the infantry.

Brigadier General Hessey had been directed, against his will, to send 110 Brigade into a cramped area which was being watched by the Germans. The 8th and 9th Leicesters deployed at the last minute to avoid being shelled and then found the 7th Bedfords moving across their front as they followed the slope. The assault waves became mixed up and while most became pinned down in front of the trench protecting Fontaine, dozens of the 9th Leicesters reached the Chérisy road.

Hessey planned to push the 6th Leicesters through to capture Fontaine Wood but a counter-attack cut off the troops holding Chérisy Trench. The 7th Leicesters were sent towards Fontaine Wood during the evening but they were too late to save the situation. A counter-attack had already driven back 54 Brigade out of Chérisy and they had taken 110 Brigade with them. Hessey issued a withdrawal order but hardly anyone received it. Nearly 390 Leicesters were reported missing and most were taken prisoner along the Sensée stream.

Meanwhile, 64 Brigade had made little progress down the Hindenburg Line or beyond the Sensée. On 6 May Private Michael Heaviside spotted a comrade from the 15th Durhams laid out in no man's land; he had been there for four days and nights. He crawled out to him, dressed his wounds, gave him water and then returned with stretcher bearers when it was dark. Heaviside was awarded the Victoria Cross.

Chapter 20

It Was All a Bloody Mix Up
Bullecourt – 3 to 16 May

General Gough wanted to wait until Third Army had reached the Sensée stream before he tried to capture Bullecourt again. But VII Corps was struggling to advance towards Chérisy and Fontaine and Fifth Army's operation was postponed several times. By the time the attack took place on 3 May, GHQ was bringing the main offensive to an end, but another attack against Bullecourt would convince the Germans to keep a reserve opposite Fifth Army.

Lieutenant General Edward Fanshawe's V Corps still held the line west of the village while I Anzac Corps continued to hold the area to the east. Tanks were allocated to 62nd Division but General Birdwood had refused them after the fiasco on 11 April. This time 2nd Australian Division would rely on the artillery to prepare the Hindenburg Line and more heavy batteries had been moved into its area.

The bombardment had started the day after the first attack but the delays meant it had continued for three weeks, reducing Bullecourt to nothing more than a pile of rubble. Again the final objectives were the villages of Hendecourt and Riencourt and this time the attack would be better prepared. But the Germans were determined to defend the village and had burrowed deep beneath the ruins. They had also been reinforced by the 1st Musketeen Battalion, a unit armed with Swedish automatic rifles which fired twenty-five-round magazines. The battalion had three companies and each one had thirty machine gun teams. The Bullecourt area was going to be covered by machine gun fire.

Bullecourt, V Corps, 3 May
62nd Division, West of Bullecourt

General Braithwaite deployed all three of his brigades in line and had 22 Brigade from 7th Division as a reserve. Ten of D Battalion's tanks would accompany the infantry into the Hindenburg Line. The Germans could see the ideal jumping off line in the bright moonlight, so the jumping tapes had to be placed further back, along the Croisilles–Bullecourt road. The night turned dark when the moon disappeared so the Yorkshiremen faced a long walk across no man's land. The German artillery still suspected something and they shelled the deployment area just before zero hitting many including Lieutenant Colonel Blacker of the 2/4th York and Lancasters. The exploding shells churned up the dry mud, filling the air with dust. It became thicker when the British field artillery started the creeping barrage at 3.45 am, hiding the few landmarks in the area.

On the left, 187 Brigade was supposed to form a defensive flank in the Hindenburg Line. The 2/5th York and Lancasters crossed the battered first trench without realising it and Lieutenant Colonel Hart reported his men were pinned down near the second trench. Some of the 2/4th York and Lancasters had veered to the left in the dust, joining the 2/5th York and Lancasters advance. But some stayed on course and they reached the support trench.

Disaster struck when the York and Lancasters fell back, taking the 2/5th KOYLIs and two companies of the 2/4th KOYLIs with them. The officers tried to stop the retreat but Lieutenant Colonel Watson was killed as he rallied his men. After hearing his men were holding out in the first Hindenburg trench, Brigadier General Taylor organised for the artillery to renew its barrage on the second German trench at 9.30 am.

In the centre, 186 Brigade was tasked with advancing west of Bullecourt. Lieutenant Colonel Ford's men could not find a way through the uncut wire and wave after wave of the 2/6th and 2/4th Duke's went prone as a few men bravely tried to cut gaps through the entanglement. But the 2/5th Duke's negotiated the smashed wire on the right and they cleared both Hindenburg trenches, followed by the 2/7th Duke's.

The reports reaching Brigadier General Hill said there had been no cooperation between the tanks and the infantry; some had crawled ahead of the infantry while others had lagged behind. Lieutenant Colonel Ford and Nash also confirmed that the left of the brigade was falling back from no man's land. Meanwhile, Lieutenant Colonels Best and Chamberlin knew their men had broken through but did not know how far they had gone. The two Duke's battalions advanced past the north side of Bullecourt, followed by the 2/8th West Yorkshire, but they were losing casualties every step of the way. Little is known of their fate but they soon became isolated and a spotter plane saw them holding on around a factory 1,000 yards north of the village.

On the right, 185 Brigade also had some success as the 2/5th West Yorkshire picked their way through the smashed entanglement and passed through the west side of Bullecourt. Some of Lieutenant Colonel Josselyn's

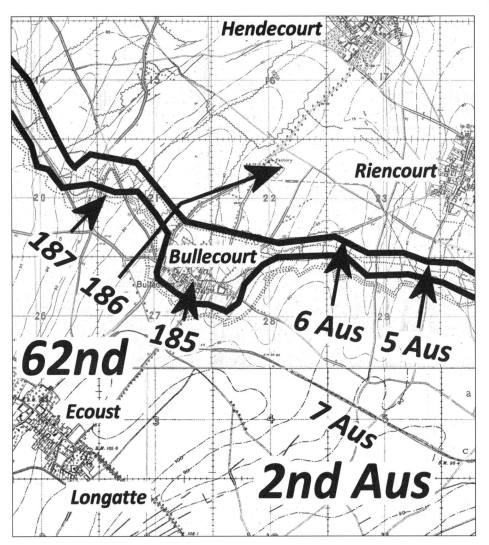

Fifth Army's battle for Bullecourt on 3 May.

men dug in around the church on the north side of the village, but the rest had been hit by the machine guns and automatic rifles of the Musketeen battalion. One German machine gun team held on in the south-west corner of the ruins, stopping the runners taking messages back and forth. A pigeon would deliver the first news of the advance to Brigadier General de Falbe's headquarters at 5.15 am.

The 2/6th West Yorkshires became disorientated in the smoke screen covering the right flank. Many were hit by machine gun fire as they blundered into the path of the 2/5th West Yorkshires but some men made their way into the village. Lieutenant Colonel James learnt that one company had occupied the first trench while another had joined the 2/5th West Yorkshires around the church but casualties had been high. Captain Knowles and Second Lieutenants Wilson and Annely had been killed, and all twelve subalterns had been hit. One junior officer was wounded fourteen times crossing no man's land but he still kept cheering his men on.

Three tanks had also crawled towards Bullecourt and they helped the Yorkshiremen claw their way through the ruins. One reached the south edge of the village but the infantry refused to acknowledge the commander's calls for help, so he took wounded men on board and headed back across no man's land rather than risk entering the ruins alone. Second Lieutenant Knight handed over his wounded crewmen to medics and took on board the crew of a broken down tank so he could return to Bullecourt. The other two tanks crawled around the ruins until they had to return for fuel but one was set on fire as it headed back to the action.

The Yorkshiremen had taken part of the village but they were struggling to hold it. Captain Green twice led groups of men loaded with bombs through the ruins, being wounded twice on the second run. A company of the 2/7th West Yorkshires was sent forward around 7 am, only to be pinned down in front of the wire. The Yorkshiremen then saw 186 Brigade retiring on its left and some fell back to the railway embankment.

Divisional headquarters heard nothing for some time and the barrage was kept on the second objective until another advance was organised. But the second attempt by a mixed group of York and Lancasters and Duke's at 9.30 am failed. General Braithwaite had no more reserves to reinforce the men in Bullecourt and about 'how long the posts held out or what was their ultimate fate, no news could be procurable'. The Yorkshiremen found themselves running short of ammunition by late morning and they began to withdraw. Around one hundred men of the 2/6th West Yorkshires returned from Bullecourt but no one came back from the factory. Altogether 62nd Division had suffered nearly 3,000 casualties.

7th Division, East of Bullecourt

Lieutenant General Fanshawe ordered Major General Shoubridge to take over part of 62nd Division's line so it could attack Bullecourt from the south. Brigadier General Steele was supposed to attack at 6.30 pm but the artillery did not have enough time to cut the wire, so zero hour was delayed until 10.30 pm by which time it was dark. It still only allowed 22 Brigade's 'company commanders time to get their horses and ride forward as near as possible to a point from which they could get an idea of the ground, but even so it was a very inadequate reconnaissance'. The Germans spotted Steele's men rushing to deploy and they shelled their assembly trenches.

A few moments before zero hour, Captain Stevens of the 1st Welsh Fusiliers reported that the 2nd Honourable Artillery Company were still not ready, so Lieutenant Colonel Holmes told him to advance slowly so they could catch up. Stevens' men struggled to get through the smashed barbed wire and an injured Lieutenant Soames was the only officer to reach the south edge of the village.

The delayed HAC reached the centre of the village but they lost a lot of men en route. Many dugouts had been missed in the darkness and the Germans climbed out to drive both battalions out of the ruins. Another attempt at 3 am on 4 May failed because a heavy artillery barrage hit the assembly area just before zero hour. A few of the 2nd Warwicks entered the ruins but Colonel Smalley could not gather enough of the 20th Manchesters together to make an attack. It later transpired that ten men of the HAC remained hidden in a dugout for three days and nights until they were rescued.

I Anzac Corps
2nd Australian Division, East of Bullecourt
Major General Smyth's division was to attack a narrow section of the Hindenburg Line east of Bullecourt. A 300-yard gap had been left between 62nd Division and 2nd Australian Division because the Australians wanted to stay away from the east side of Bullecourt. The plan was for the creeping barrage to move quickly across no man's land and then slow down across the trenches, as the bombers spread out to the flanks.

A searchlight scanned no man's land as the Australians deployed under bright moonlight and 22nd Australian Battalion was swept by enfilade fire from Bullecourt. A German battery accidently fired short, right in front of the German trench, and the battalion split into two to avoid the exploding shells. Lieutenant Garton led a few men into the German trenches but the rest were pinned down in no man's land.

An embankment protected the rest of 6 Australian Brigade and flares over the German trenches indicated that Captain Kennedy and Lieutenant Grieg were bombing their way along the trenches. Meanwhile, Lieutenant Smythe saw a disaster unfolding on 24th Australian Battalion's right and he led his bombers along the trench in front of 5 Australian Brigade. Machine gun fire hit the Australian advance towards the support trench and Captain Maxwell complained he had been 'lobbed here absolutely on my own'. Meanwhile, 23rd Australian Battalion had taken shelter in shell holes in no man's land and Captain Pascoe had difficulty getting his men moving again.

There were reports that the second line had been reached, but less than an hour after zero around 400 unwounded men came streaming back on 5 Australian Brigade's front. They were 'depressed and disappointed' and when asked what had happened, the answer came back, 'I don't know, it was all a bloody mix up.' They regrouped along the sunken Bullecourt–Quéant road and Brigadier General Smith wanted to send them back, unaware that the attack had failed.

The problem was the Australians had taken cover in shell holes while the barrage stopped on the first trench for two minutes and it split them into small groups. The German infantry took the opportunity to line their parapet and they fired at the officers and NCOs as soon as the barrage lifted. One Australian officer allegedly shouted, 'pull out; retire; get back for your lives,' and while some ran back, taking the rear waves with them, others stayed in their shell holes. One observer noted, 'they looked like a crowd rushing across a football ground to cheer the players and you could see they were being cut up by the barrage and by a machine gun, which was playing on their backs.' Only Lieutenant Flockart and a few men entered the German trench and they soon had to retire.

Brigadier General Gellibrand's left was pinned down in no man's land while his right was fighting in the trenches and running out of bombs. Brigadier General Smith insisted that his troops held their objective but Gellibrand could see that 5 Australian Brigade was in trouble. He sent Captain Gilchrist of 6th Australian Field Company to rally the retiring troops in the sunken road. Gellibrand also obtained General Smyth's permission to deploy Major Thorn's company of the 26th Australian Battalion. He led it forward at 5.45 am followed by 200 men led by Lieutenant Davies of 18th Australian Battalion. There was no artillery barrage and they had to advance past their mates huddling in shell holes. The result was inevitable. Major Thorn was one of the many casualties and only a handful of men under Captain Gilchrist reached the few survivors of 24th Australian Battalion.

A German battery was firing short on 6 Australian Brigade's front, forcing 22nd and 21st Australian Battalions on the left to split into two. The left was hit by machine gun fire and Lieutenant Garton led a few men into the trenches but Captain Kennedy's men used a sap to enter them on the right. As Kennedy cleared the front trench, Lieutenant Grieg worked down the support trench.

As 24th Australian Battalion struggled to get through the wire, they could see the disaster to 5 Australian Brigade on their right. Lieutenant Smythe reached the tramway while Lieutenant Pickett secured Central Road on the right. Captain Maxwell led the 23rd Australian Battalion while Captain Pascoe took some men to the second objective. Captain Parkes could see the Germans were firing into the Australian flank so he made his men line Central Road and return fire.

A ferocious bombing battle followed in which the Germans always seemed to have more bombs. Brigadier General Gellibrand asked for a new barrage to help his men clear the trenches, but it was delayed for over an hour because General Birdwood had wanted the advance to continue. He cancelled the order as soon as he heard about 62nd Division's failure and understood the Australian situation. At 6.30 am General Smyth instructed 25th Australian Battalion to attack the south-east corner of Bullecourt over the top. Brigadier General Gellibrand asked Lieutenant Colonel Norrie to see if it had any chance of success but the two platoons sent into no man's land came under heavy fire; the attack was cancelled.

The Australians were struggling to hold on when a counter-attack from the north struck around the same time as they were hit by their own artillery. They fell back to the Hindenburg trenches where Captain Gilchrist rallied and then led them back to the Hindenburg front trench. He was joined by Major Thorn's company of the 26th Australian Battalion and Lieutenant Colonel Murphy with some of the 19th Battalion. They were pinned down near the wire and the snipers picked off the officers one by one.

Gilchrist made it into the trenches where Lieutenant Smythe explained, 'these men are all right, all they need is a leader.' So Gilchrist led them; 'None of the other officers and men present knew who their leader was, but for half an hour or more he would be seen, bareheaded, in grey woollen cardigan, his curly hair ruffled with exertion, continually climbing out of the trench to throw bombs or to call to the men in shell holes, begging them to charge. But at some stage the grey cardigan and curly head were missed, they were never seen or heard of again.' The leaderless men fell back to the support trench.

General Smyth had given 28th Australian Battalion to Brigadier General Smith so he could secure the Hindenburg Line immediately east of Bullecourt. Major Brown and Captain Montgomery led their men up Central Road into the Hindenburg trenches around 2 pm and they began bombing in earnest. They fought all afternoon until a heavy bombardment hit no man's land at dusk, prompting the men who had sheltered all day in the shell holes to withdraw. Some observers thought they were Germans outflanking 28th Australian Battalion in the half-light. General Smith then heard that 6 Australian Brigade was falling back so he instructed Lieutenant Colonel Read to withdraw his men. Fortunately, Brown and Montgomery knew the report was false and they continued fighting along the Hindenburg Line into the night.

I Anzac Corps, 4 to 6 May

7th Division, Bullecourt

Bullecourt was shelled incessantly and the men lived underground in cellars and dugouts. They waited on the stairs of their lairs when the shells were falling and ran out when an attack began. It was difficult to get supplies forward so they searched the dead for food and ammunition; the village was strewn with bodies. There were reports that British parties were holding out in Bullecourt so Major General Shoubridge called for patrols to enter after dusk on 4 May. Wire stopped the 1st Welch Fusiliers and 2nd Warwicks entering the Red Patch at the south-west corner (so called because it was marked red on trench maps). The survivors were relieved by the 8th Devons.

2nd Australian Division, East of Bullecourt

The Australians were dreading a long-drawn-out battle and they blamed Fifth Army's mismanagement for their predicament. Brigadier Generals Smith and Gellibrand had remained in control of the front even though their infantry had been relieved.

The 3rd and 1st Australian Battalions filed up Pioneer Avenue and into the Hindenburg trenches early on 4 May. On the left, 3rd Australian Battalion encountered a flamethrower which engulfed several men in flames when it was hit. On the right the 2nd Australian Battalion came under attack as it occupied a trench filled with bodies and then it was 1st Australian Battalion's turn to face a flamethrower.

Lieutenant Richards led 1st Australian Battalion's bombers west along the front trench at 1 pm and Captain Eliott led 3rd Australian Battalion along the support trench an hour later. To the east, 2nd Battalion had to wait until 3.40 pm when the artillery fired a barrage which moved sideways along the trenches. Lieutenants O'Connell and Moy then pushed forward, keeping close to the Germans so their bombs went over their heads. They 'fought practically stripped to the waist, revolvers in hand, beside their sweating team in the foremost bay, Moy throwing bombs with his disengaged hand and pulling out their pins with his teeth'. O'Connell and Moy were reinforced by the 4th Australian Battalion and they held over 1,000 yards of the Hindenburg Line by evening.

The 11th and 12th Australian Battalions took over the line when the fighting died down and they spent 5 May consolidating under a terrific bombardment. During the evening the Australian gunners mistook the German flares signalling the fifth counter-attack for SOS flares. They immediately fired at no man's land, scattering the advancing German infantry.

General Smyth wanted the two battalions to expand their position at 5 am on 6 May but Major Darnell refused because the men had suffered too much. The German barrage reached 'an unprecedented intensity' at 5 am and a few minutes later they counter-attacked again. But, as luck would have it, the Australian bombardment had not been cancelled and it scattered the German infantry moving over the top. The bombers could not advance along the support trench from the east but two flamethrower teams forced Company Sergeant Major Fletcher's men back along the front line.

Captain Newland and Lieutenant MacNeil stopped the Germans at the top of Pioneer Avenue. Both 12th and 11th Australian Battalions rallied once the flamethrowers had been silenced. Major Darnell launched a counter-attack in which Lieutenant MacNeil ran forward in the open, pelting the Germans with grenades before he picked up an abandoned Lewis gun and drove them away. Sergeant George Howell called for reinforcements when he saw the men on his right were retiring. Captain Alexander MacKenzie organised a group of non-combatant soldiers from the Welsh Fusiliers' headquarters to help him. Snowy Howell then climbed onto the parapet and ran along the trench throwing bombs into a trench while Lieutenant Thomas Richards followed him, firing bursts from his Lewis Gun at the Germans as they scattered. Howell used his bayonet when his bombs ran out, but he eventually fell into the trench; he had suffered nearly thirty wounds. Howell would be awarded the Victoria Cross.

Bullecourt, 7 to 17 May
7th Division, Bullecourt, 7 May
Lieutenant General Fanshawe wanted to attack the south-east corner of Bullecourt as quickly as possible, so he brought zero hour forward by twenty-four hours, leaving insufficient time to check the wire. It did not give Major Generals Shoubridge and Smyth enough time so they agreed to coordinate their efforts, starting at 3.45 am on 7 May.

The plan was for the infantry to advance past the west side of the village while the heavy artillery bombarded the Red Patch at the south-west corner of Bullecourt. The 2nd Gordons' bombers and rifle grenadiers worked in relays and an officer stood waving on the parapet when they contacted 1 Australian Brigade. They were reinforced by Captains Fergusson and Raffin of 9th Devons but artillery fire drove them out of one trench while Second Lieutenant Holdsworth was killed by a shower of grenades. Second Lieutenant Drew decided to counter-attack and his men rounded up over one hundred prisoners.

Shoubridge told Brigadier General Green he had to capture the Red Patch but the 9th Devons could not take it because it had been reinforced. The only consolation was that the 24th Manchesters had dug a communication trench, so ammunition could be carried into Bullecourt.

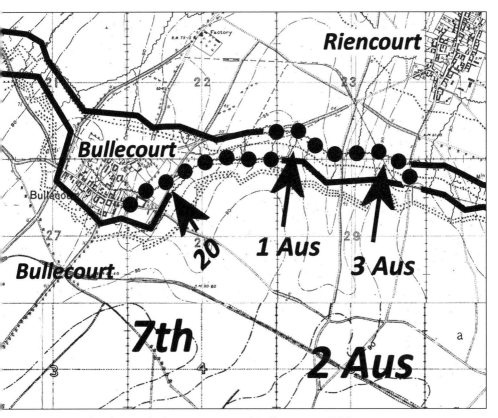

Fighting for the Hindenburg Line east of Bullecourt on 7 May.

The following morning, the 8th Devons bombed towards the Red Patch, reporting they had 'got off well, full of buck, mud very bad'. But the Germans were always able to throw their lighter bombs further than the British ones; a common complaint. The 2nd Border Regiment established a post at the north-east corner of the Red Patch later that evening.

At noon on 9 May the 8th Devons forced their way into the Red Patch and while Company Sergeant Major Heal could not hold Tower Trench, Lieutenant Marshall held off a counter-attack with his Vickers machine gun until Lieutenant Drake's reinforcements drove the Germans out into the open so they could be shot at.

62nd Division, West of Bullecourt, 12 and 13 May

At 4 am 185 Brigade advanced west of Bullecourt to the Crucifix north-west of the Red Patch but was bombed out again. There was no news for a long time but an aerial observer reported the West Yorkshire men 'were well dug in around the Crucifix'. Whether they were or not will never be known because none returned and an attempt to reach them later that night failed.

The Crucifix position was rushed by the 2/7th Duke's at 3.40 am on 13 May but a heavy bombardment forced them to retire.

<u>5th Australian Division, East of Bullecourt, 12 May</u>
On the evening of 8 May, 5th Australian Division relieved 2nd Australian Division east of Bullecourt. The plan was for 58th Australian Battalion to bomb west to contact 7th Division. Lieutenants Dawson and Moon started fourteen minutes after 91 Brigade to avoid the British barrage and they contacted the 2nd Queen's. Dawson forced many Germans to take cover in a large dugout and 186 prisoners were taken. Lieutenant Mick Moon was twice wounded but he shouted 'come on boys, don't turn me down' as he fought off counter-attacks. He only went back to the aid station after he was wounded for a fourth time; he was awarded the Victoria Cross.

<u>7th Division, East of Bullecourt, 12 to 15 May</u>
Brigadier General Cumming's men advanced behind a slow barrage at 3.40 am. Lieutenants Bell and Penketh were killed when the 1st South Staffords came under fire from the village but the rest of Colonel Beaumann's men reached the north side of Bullecourt. Lieutenant Colonel Longbourne's 2nd Queen's moved rapidly, clearing the east side of the village. Machine gun and artillery fire prevented reinforcements reaching the two battalions but Second Lieutenants Woof and Livingstone held on for another three days and nights with the few surviving Staffords and Queens.

An exhausted Brigadier General Cumming wanted 91 Brigade to attack the Red Patch again from the east but Major General Shoubridge disagreed and replaced him with Lieutenant Colonel Norman of the 22nd Manchesters. Shoubridge's plan was for the 2nd Warwicks to attack from the south-west while two 22nd Manchester companies advanced from the north-east.

It proved too difficult to coordinate the two barrages and reports that the Germans had abandoned their trenches turned out to be untrue. They shot down the 2nd Warwicks to the south and the 22nd Manchesters to the east. Colonel Norman abandoned a plan to deploy the HAC because they could not get into positon in time, so he called it off 'rather than risk the casualties bound to be occurred.'

Colonel Norman was given the 1st Welsh Fusiliers and they tried again to take the Red Patch during the early hours of 14 May. Two companies attacked the south-west corner at 2.10 am but the other two failed to capture Tower Trench at 6.15 am. A second attempt was going well until their bomb store was blown up and a counter-attack drove them back. The third attack at 2.30 pm was going well until another explosion destroyed the Fusiliers' bomb dump. The battle for the Red Patch was becoming difficult to coordinate so Lieutenant Colonel Holmes took control of the 21st Manchesters, the 2nd HAC and the 20th Manchesters, as well as his own Fusiliers.

The German Counter-Attack, 15 May
A heavy bombardment started early on 15 May and the Red Patch was reported to be 'alive with Germans' around 4 am. The 21st Manchesters and HAC were driven from the north half of the village but Major Wright held on to Tower Trench. Captain Bower secured a line through the centre of the village while the Welsh Fusiliers held on to the south-east corner. The 20th Manchesters fought on east of the village, as did the 2/4th and 2/3rd London Regiment, both in battle for the first time.

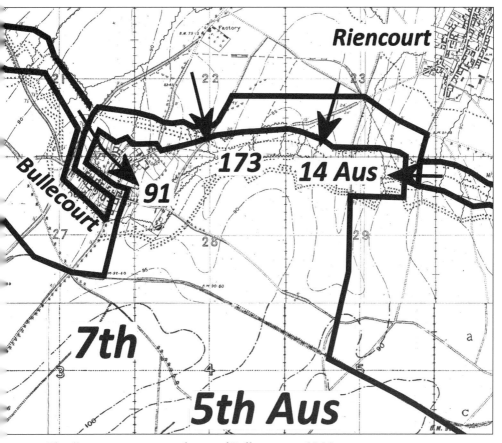

The German counter-attack east of Bullecourt on 15 May.

One company of Lieutenant Colonel Midgley's 54th Australian Battalion had been wiped out by the bombardment and Major Lecky had been unable to recover part of the Hindenburg support trench east of Central Road. Lieutenant Colonel the Rev Beresford sent his reserve companies of the 2/3rd London Regiment forward to help Midgley 'win back as much as he can', but they failed to do so.

A second attack drove the 21st Manchesters and HAC away from the church, so Captain Bluck used every man of the Welsh Fusiliers he could find to hold the crossroads until the 20th Manchesters restored the line around the church. The situation stabilised with the Germans holding the west half and the British holding the east. But it had been too much for 7th Division. After twelve days continuous fighting, General Shoubridge's exhausted men withdrew from the heap of rubble that once was Bullecourt.

58th Division, Bullecourt

Major General Hew Fanshawe's division took over Bullecourt and the area to the east, the first time the 2/1st London Division had been in a battle. At 6.30 pm on 16 May a company of the 2/1st London Regiment captured the Hindenburg support trench in 173 Brigade's sector. At 2 am the following morning there was a two-minute bombardment and the Londoners charged into Bullecourt. The 2/5th London Regiment rushed the Red Patch while the 2/8th London Regiment cleared the east side of the village. The easy capture came about because the Germans had evacuated the ruins. It was a welcome end to the battle of Bullecourt. The capture of the village and the adjacent Hindenburg Line had cost over 14,000 casualties; an average of over 1,000 a day.

Chapter 21

The Final Actions

First Army
Canadian Corps, La Coulotte, 5 to 10 May
On the evening of 5 May, 4th Canadian Division captured forty prisoners in the trenches covering the power station north-west of La Coulotte. More trenches were cleared near Colliery Number 7 late on 9 May. The trenches were lost the following evening but 44th Battalion retook them during a surprise attack on the afternoon of 11 May.

XIII Corps, Fresnoy, 5 to 9 May
On 5 May, XIII Corps took over part of the Canadian Corps line either side of Fresnoy. General Congreve used 5th British Division to relieve the 1st Canadian Division and the 2nd British Division in the salient. The capture of Fresnoy had given the British a great observation point over the Méricourt–Oppy Line and the Wotan Stellung to the east. It had also knocked a stone 'out of the German defensive wall which had to be replaced without delay'.

A counter-attack was inevitable and the Tenth Wing of the RFC took action as the German heavy howitzers began registering their targets. On the morning of 6 May, Nieuport fighter planes flew low over the German lines and shot down seven balloons, only losing one machine in the raid. The German bombardment began in earnest later that evening and over 100,000 shells were fired at Fresnoy in thirty-six hours, an average of over forty-five shells fired a minute. The shelling was particularly heavy against the British batteries on the night of 7 May and many gunners were casualties. The survivors were then subjected to a gas shell bombardment during the early hours.

All Major General Reginald Stephens could do was warn his subordinates to prepare for the onslaught. They all knew what was coming and 'psychologically the atmosphere was charged with premonitions of some swiftly approaching menace.' Just before 4 am German troops began deploying in no man's land, interrupting a relief in 2nd Canadian Division's

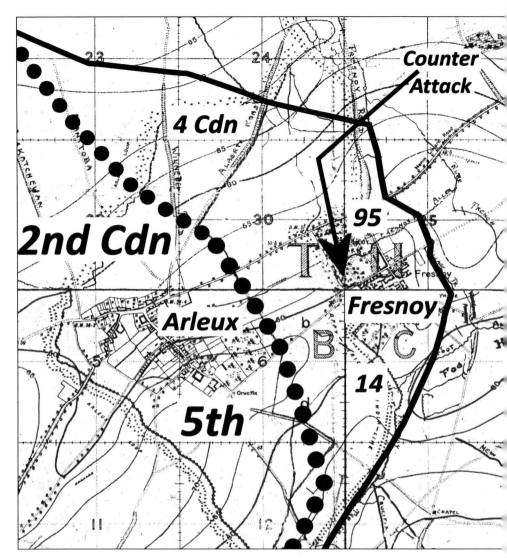

The Germans recaptured Fresnoy from the Canadian Corps on 9 May.

sector. The outgoing 29th Battalion drove them off with the help of the incoming 19th Battalion.

The 12th Gloucesters and 1st East Surrey stopped the first attack against 95 Brigade at 6 am. More than forty German batteries supported the next attack at 8 am while the British field batteries were still suffering and they failed to see 95 Brigade's SOS flares. The 19th Canadian Battalion's right company was overrun while the 12th Gloucesters were practically annihilated as they tried to retire from the village. The Germans then drove the 1st East Surreys back to the east edge of Arleux. General Stephens sent the 1st Norfolks forward to help but they could not retake Fresnoy. Neither could Captain Kendall of the 1st DCLI and it was left to Captains Taylor and Hughesdon to hold the line with the rest of the battalion.

An immediate counter-attack may have succeeded but it was delayed until 2.30 am on 9 May. The 19th Canadian Battalion was supposed to take part of the left flank but the orders only reached one company because the telephone wires had been cut and the runners had been killed. Two Canadian officers ran into the 1st Devons' trenches five minutes before zero to beg them not to advance because they could not help.

The attack still went ahead and Captain Hallé and Lieutenant Wonnacott led the Devons north of the village. The 15th Warwicks passed through the chateau grounds and village and a few of the 1st Norfolks entered the wood to the south. Meanwhile, Captain Sleeman and forty Devons had been cut off and a wounded Sergeant Carleton crawled back to ask Captain Maton for more ammunition. Sleeman fought on even after a German prisoner begged him to surrender. He eventually withdrew his men from what became known as Devon Trench after dusk.

Third Army Operations, 5 to 24 May
On 7 May Haig met his Army commanders at Doullens to explain his plans for the summer. He wanted to capture the Messines Ridge south of Ypres at the beginning of June and he would only send enough divisions north to carry out the operation. He would then move another four divisions to Flanders, to attack east of the town at the end of July. The Cavalry Corps would take over parts of the line, to allow the infantry to rest and train. Third Army would have to relieve Fifth Army, so General Gough could move to Flanders. First Army would also extend its front as far north as the River Lys, so Second Army could concentrate east of Ypres. It would leave First and Third Army with tired divisions and much less artillery.

<u>4th Division, Roeux, 11 May</u>
Major General Lambton was given the task of taking Roeux chemical works even though his division had been in the line since 30 April. He had less than 2,500 infantry left and they were tired but Lieutenant General Fergusson still arranged for an attack on 11 May; he gave one of 51st Division's brigades to help. The attack would start at 7.30 pm so the men could consolidate the ruins during the night but it meant the assault troops would have to wait in their assembly trenches all day, a tiring prospect. Anti-aircraft guns were deployed to stop German planes flying over the assembly trenches and it was fortunate no one spotted them sitting huddled together in the shallow trenches.

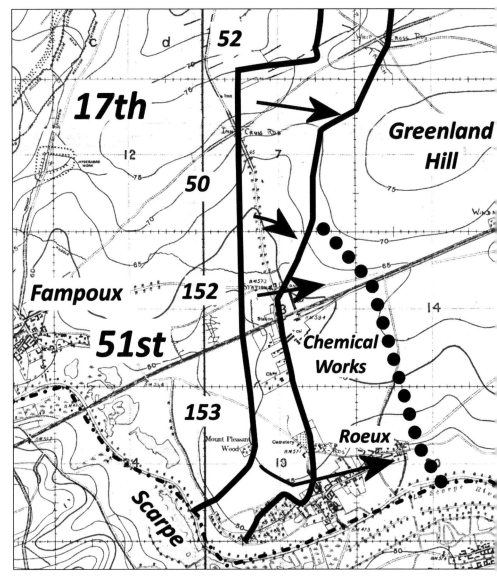

XVII Corps finally captured Roeux on 11 May.

The artillery rehearsed the creeping barrage and aerial spotters noted the locations of the German batteries so they could be shelled at zero hour. The heavy artillery then carried out a slow, methodical bombardment of the buildings either side of the railway, so as not to alert the Germans. The infantry commanders had been concerned about the men's morale but the large concentration of field guns (one 18-pounder every seven yards) gave them confidence. They put down a double creeping barrage with shrapnel following high explosive with each gun firing four rounds per gun per minute. It meant a shell was exploding every minute on each two yards of front.

Two 6th Dorset companies from 17th Division captured a redoubt on the north side of the railway while the 1st Rifle Brigade entered the chemical works in a fight which lasted all night. The 1st Hampshires captured 150 prisoners and seven machine guns around Roeux chateau in 11 Brigade's centre. The 1st East Lancashires captured Roeux cemetery, on the right, making the German position in the village untenable. The 1st Hampshires and the 1st Rifle Brigade advanced north of the Douai railway the following day.

Major Earle's Hampshires had discovered a concrete structure with 'walls six feet thick and seven feet of roof cover' near the chateau. Fortunately, they had silenced the crew before they could bring their machine gun into action but it was an interesting development. Large pillboxes were a common sight in Flanders but they had not been seen before during the Arras campaign and many officers went to look at it.

17th Division, Greenland Hill, 12 to 16 May

Major General Robertson's men assembled opposite Greenland Hill under cover of darkness and waited for zero hour. A German plane flew low overhead as soon as it was light and dropped flares so the artillery could shell the crowded trenches. They also bombarded no man's land as soon as the first wave went over the top at 6.30 am, three hours after sun rise.

The 9th Northumberland Fusiliers could not get through the wire on 52 Brigade's front. The first wave on the 10th Lancashire Fusiliers' left was pinned down but Captain Barrow's second wave carried them forward. A few of Major Comyn's men reached Charlie Trench in the centre but Captain Harriss's men were pinned down on the right. One by one the officers were hit until only Barrow was left standing and he ordered a withdrawal because ammunition was running low.

A machine gun team hiding in no man's land in front of 50 Brigade caused many casualties before the 7th Green Howards and 7th East Yorkshires silenced them. The Green Howards entered Curly Trench but could not bomb the Germans out of the trench in front of the East Yorkshires. Meanwhile, Private Tom Dresser was wounded twice carrying a message forward for Lieutenant Colonel Cotton but he still reached the Howards before they had to withdraw. Private Dresser survived and was awarded the Victoria Cross.

A counter-attack at 3.45 am on 16 May drove the 6th Dorsets and 10th West Yorkshires out of Cupid Trench north of the railway before dawn. The 7th Border Regiment were too late to take part in an attempt to retake 50

Brigade's lost trenches that evening and the 1/5th Gordons could not hold Cupid Trench.

51st Division, Roeux, 16 May

Major General Harper's Scots returned to the Roeux area only to find the Germans had evacuated the east end of the village early on 14 May and their artillery started shelling the Scottish front line in earnest. The Germans penetrated the Scottish line west of the station during the night of 15 May. The 1/8th Argylls, with the help of Lieutenant Colonel Campbell's headquarters staff, killed or captured all the Germans north of the railway before dawn. Colonel Campbell climbed the railway embankment and saw that two 1/6th Seaforths companies had stopped them south of the railway. The Argylls then gave covering fire from the embankment while Second Lieutenant Bliss led the Seaforths towards the chemical works. The 1/5th Gordons helped them clear the complex.

Brigadier General Burn had moved his men away from Roeux during the same attack to avoid casualties from falling brickwork. A number of Germans infiltrated the village because they were misidentified for returning Scottish troops in the darkness; they were driven off as soon as the mistake was realised.

VI Corps

Following a brief bombardment on the evening of 12 May, three battalions, two from 12th Division and one from 3rd Division, charged towards Devil's Trench. The Germans had not been affected by the creeping barrage and were all pinned down in no man's land.

56th Division, Tool Trench, 11 May

A practice barrage was made on 10 May but it drew a lot of fire from the German batteries. The following evening only the heavy artillery fired at a slow rate until just before zero hour. The field guns joined in when the 14th London and 4th London Regiments advanced at 8.30 pm and they took the Germans holding Tool Trench by surprise. A mile of trench was captured between the summit of Infantry Hill and Cavalry Farm on the Cambrai road.

31st Division, Gavrelle, 16 May

The 18th Durhams made a night attack against Gavrelle Trench but both company commanders were wounded early on. The left company could not get through the wire but the right company captured the battered trench. A shower of hand grenades stopped the advance and a counter-attack forced them to withdraw.

29th and 56th Divisions, Infantry Hill, 19 May

Lieutenant General Haldane wanted to capture Infantry Hill because it overlooked VI Corps trenches around Monchy. He also wanted to capture the Bois des Aubépines because it was an ideal assembly point for attacks. Major General de Lisle's 29th Division had to capture the two objectives with 87 Brigade while 56th Division cleared Tool Trench on the right flank.

The 2nd SWB moved into no man's land at 9 pm but the German machine gunners were waiting for them as they charged towards Devil's Trench. Captain Davies and Lieutenant Jones were killed but Sergeant Albert White and Corporal Nowel silenced the party covering one machine gun. White was riddled with bullets as he turned his weapon on the gunners; he awarded the Victoria Cross. Only half of the SWBs returned.

The few men of the 1st Border Regiment and 1st Inniskilling Fusiliers who reached Hook Trench were all killed or captured. More were ambushed when they entered the wood at the north end of the trench and few returned. The 1/8th Middlesex also failed to reach Tool Trench on 167 Brigade's front. The survivors complained that the Germans were waiting for them and Captain Gillon of the Inniskillings believed a deserter may have told them.

29th Division, Hill 100, 30 May

Major General de Lisle was instructed to make another attempt to capture Infantry Hill and this time he wanted to make a surprise attack at night with no artillery barrage. Zero hour was set for 12.40 am on 30 May but then came the news a soldier had deserted and had been taken prisoner. A concerned de Lisle postponed the attack until 11.30 pm the following night, but there was a problem: the moon would be up. So an artillery barrage was used to keep the Germans under cover.

The change in plan resulted in a confusion over orders because the men left their trenches fifteen minutes before zero hour and deployed in a moonlit no man's land. They were spotted, flares alerted the German artillery, and most of the troops were pinned down near the wire. Brigadier General Williams reported that the few men of the 16th Middlesex who had entered the trenches on Infantry Hill opposite 86 Brigade had been captured.

General Allenby had expected the men to leave their trenches at zero rather than before it and he blamed the failure on the inexperienced troops. Lieutenant General Haldane suggested banning night operations because the replacements had no battle experience and they needed extra training in trench warfare.

VII Corps

33rd Division, Hindenburg Line, 20 to 27 May

Lieutenant General Snow had assembled over 600 guns to shell the Hindenburg Line with a slow bombardment. Major General Pinney was hoping Fifth Army could attack the Hindenburg Line north-west of Bullecourt but it had no reserves after the prolonged battle for the village.

At 5.15 am on 20 May the mine laid to destroy the barricade blocking the trench was detonated so 98 Brigade could bomb down the Hindenburg Line towards the Sensée stream. The frontal attack by Brigadier General Baird's 100 Brigade against the Hump surprised the Germans in the fog and smoke. The 5th Scots Rifles, 9th Highland Light Infantry and 2nd Worcesters advanced across the Hindenburg Line trenches but they could not hold onto the support trench.

Brigadier General Heriot-Maitland organised another attempt on the north bank of the Sensée at 7.30 pm and another section of the Hindenburg support trench was taken. The 5th Scots Rifles and the 20th Royal Fusiliers passed through 100 Brigade's line on the Hump but they mistook a line of dugouts and shell-holes for the support trench.

The final attempt against the Hindenburg Line was made by 33rd Division at 1.55 pm on 27 May. It had been timed to hit as the Germans relaxed after their lunch. On the right, 19 Brigade's attack over the top failed to take any trenches on the Hump but the 4th King's bombers crossed the Sensée and contacted 19 Brigade.

Chapter 22

Conclusions

The British Expeditionary Force had learnt a lot about combined arms warfare during the Somme campaign and it had many veterans in its ranks by the end of the four and a half month long campaign. But the Germans had learnt a lot about defensive warfare too and they also had an experienced cadre who could teach and train replacements in the art of trench warfare.

The Central Powers started 1917 with the admission that they were not strong enough to fight an offensive war. It was also doubtful they could win a war of attrition. While the Austro-Hungarians seriously considered suing for peace, the Germans chose to make it as hard as possible for the Allies to win an offensive war. They decided on unrestricted submarine warfare at sea and choosing the ground where they wanted to fight on land by building the Hindenburg Line. The Allies would have to fight at a disadvantage against a fortified line which had been prepared without interference. It is argued that the shortening of the line created a new reserve of German divisions but it also created an equal surplus of Allied divisions for their offensives. The Hindenburg Line would mean that the Allies would have to pay dearly if they tried to fight an offensive battle or engage in a war of attrition.

So what did the Allies know about the Hindenburg Line? The first signs were spotted as early as November 1916 and its full extent was known by the end of February. They knew it was a trench system but pilots had not been able to photograph it in detail for several reasons. Firstly, it was a long way behind the front line and difficult to fly to in the changeable winter weather. Missions deep into enemy territory were also dangerous because British pilots faced superior machines in the sky. But the RFC were given many other important tasks, particularly when the Germans started withdrawing from the Somme area during the last week of February.

The British first heard about the grand scale of the withdrawal from a prisoner over two weeks before it began in earnest. But they could do little to check the information and were often slow to react when it was clear the Germans were pulling out. Time and again the German rear guards interrupted the Allied advance either at defensive positions or in villages. But we have to remember the Germans were moving back at a steady rate, never giving the British time to make plans, check out the ground or bring up their artillery. No one was in a hurry to attack a fortified village when it was in all likelihood going to be abandoned a few hours later. The evidence shows that hasty attacks were usually punished while well prepared actions rarely failed. The Germans skilfully withdrew their guns, their transport and their men stage by stage and were never caught in the open. They also carried out widespread destruction and booby-trapping, making the Allies even more cautions.

More than two years of trench warfare had left the Allied soldiers with a cautious, and sometimes sluggish, attitude towards offensive action. But it has to be remembered that only the small number of Old Contemptibles, veterans of 1914, had experienced open warfare before. Everyone else had to get out of the habit of digging in and waiting for an artillery barrage to support them. They also had to learn that rapid movement and taking acceptable risks was usually the best way of gaining more ground at the cost of fewer casualties. They learned quickly, taking on fortified villages, one after another, with surprise attacks and outflanking movements. Then, just when the British and Australian troops were getting used to moving in the open, they were in front of the Hindenburg Line.

The seizure by Canadian troops of the document entitled 'Experience of the Recent Fighting at Verdun' just before the capture of Vimy Ridge illustrated German thinking on defensive tactics. General Ludendorff and Sixth Army's chief of the staff, Colonel von Lossberg, were also looking to use an elastic defence which could absorb and then break up enemy attacks. They wanted a lightly held outpost zone which relied on strongpoints and machine guns to disrupt an advance. A second fortified line would serve a dual purpose: it would be used to rally units and as an assembly point for reserves to counter-attack from; it would also protect the battery positions if there was a breakthrough. Again it was not about holding ground it was about defeating the enemy when he was at his weakest. It would prove to be a successful tactic but there had not been time to build enough strongpoints on Vimy Ridge to make it work.

The withdrawal to the Hindenburg Line illustrated that the Germans were not concerned about giving up ground if it improved their strategic position. They made a similar rearward move following the loss of Vimy Ridge, waiting only long enough to prepare a new defensive line. They made more tactical withdrawals, especially from boggy areas. They would, if they were able, wait until the British had the advantage before pulling back to another position. It made sense to give up useless ground and choose a new place to fight to put your enemy at a disadvantage. But the German High Command recognised that rearward movements were bad for morale.

The weather's effect on the terrain was a constant source of trouble. The ground beneath the men's feet changed quickly as the temperature hovered above and below zero. Below freezing and the mud was too hard to dig through and the ice was difficult to walk on. Above zero and the landscape was covered in soft mud which slowed movement to a crawl. It made it difficult to judge the correct speed for a creeping barrage; too fast and the infantry were left behind but too slow and the Germans had time to exit their dugouts.

Visibility was often an issue and was difficult to predict. While the troops liked the protection of a smoke screen as they moved in the open, early morning fog, evening mist and dust caused problems. Men became lost, the barrage was obscured, objectives were missed and dugouts were overlooked. Equally, too much visibility was a problem at night. Moonlight made it difficult to deploy in secret while snow on the ground could turn night into day, as it did at Bullecourt on 11 April.

There had also been studies into the effects of the weather on the firing of artillery shells. Regular weather bulletins detailing wind, air pressure and temperature were issued to the gunners so they could adjust their guns. Ammunition was far more reliable than it had been nine months earlier but frost could still affect how shells reacted.

The organisation of the artillery had settled into a routine by April 1917. Each corps divided its guns into three groups, each with a specific objective. The field artillery and mortars formed the 'Trench Groups' which targeted the wire and trenches. The heavy artillery formed the 'Counter Battery Groups' which silenced the batteries. The largest calibres formed the 'Super Heavy Groups' which aimed at long range targets.

The heavy artillery was encouraged to fire short, intense barrages at random intervals because it was believed that the anticipation of a violent period of shelling was more effective than a prolonged bombardment. Generals often preferred a short, sharp bombardment to increase the chance of taking their enemy by surprise. Some wanted to go without a barrage altogether because they believed their men had a better chance of taking their objectives by stealth.

The artillery had learnt many lessons during the Somme campaign. Many gunners were becoming experts at conducting accurate barrages which could advance at the optimum speed for the terrain. But it was also acknowledged that the recent rapid increase in the number of heavy howitzers meant there were many inexperienced gunners in the field and they had a lot to learn. There were standing barrages, creeping barrages which moved at different speeds, barrages which jumped back and forth, and feint barrages to test the Germans reactions. It was noted that feint barrages could also alert the German gunners and the counter-bombardment could cause more problems.

The main bombardment prior to 9 April was a massive affair and the Germans referred to the days before the attack as the 'week of suffering'. Allenby had argued for a short hurricane bombardment but the artillery experts had had their way. Horne had done away with the intense period of shelling before zero, starting it on zero hour to maximise the shock and increase the chances of catching the Germans underground.

The double barrage became a regular feature and the first mention of it is at Le Transloy on 27 January. Half the batteries bombarded the German front line while the rest hit the area in front of the trenches. They moved forward together in the hope the Germans would leave their dugouts after the first barrage passed over, only to be caught by the second line of exploding shells.

Controlling the speed of a barrage had also become more flexible. Sometimes half the gunners followed a fixed programme, moving forward at an agreed rate while the rest responded to signal flares fired by the infantry. It gave the infantry a degree of control over their support, resulting in a flexible approach to the advance. It meant they could respond to unplanned events or unseen enemy positions.

An innovative way of referring to targets had been introduced for the heavy artillery. The German-held area had been divided into small coded areas, each one a definite target; the effect was to cut out indiscriminate shelling. Zone fire was also introduced, with batteries aimed at inner and outer zones, aiming to catch troops as they escaped from an intense barrage on a lucrative target.

The gunners used the coded areas to help them respond quicker to SOS calls. Rather than relying on lengthy map references, they used a new power buzzer to send the code. The one-way message code identified the target area and the gunners were able to fire at the target immediately.

The importance of monitoring the progress of a destructive barrage had also been recognised and there were regular pauses in the barrages so that aerial spotters could inspect the damage and take photographs. It was also impressed on intelligence teams to forward the results as quickly possible.

The introduction of the 106 impact fuse was important. It meant the artillery could hit ground targets with confidence, particularly the wire. No longer would gun crews have to guess the timing of a fuse because they now exploded the instant they hit the ground. The only problem was there was a shortage of the valuable devices, so the artillery and trench mortars often had to resort to traditional methods to cut the wire.

The German howitzers soon had their own version of the instantaneous fuse and the first mention of it was in the Lagnicourt area early in April. The 5.9-inch howitzers caused havoc amongst the Australian guns and they would have to be dug in to protect the crews.

The way the infantry fought in the spring of 1917 had been decided on the Somme. New weapons, like the Lewis gun, the Stokes mortar and the rifle grenade had all been integrated into their tactics. Troops usually advanced in waves but they were adept at tackling strongpoints, with the Lewis gunners and rifle grenadiers providing covering fire while the riflemen and bombers moved in for the kill.

Tanks were a regular feature on the battlefield in April and May but the infantry were still wary of them. Some of the teething troubles which had surfaced during the Somme campaign had been ironed out but the tank crews were often driving old models. The much improved Mark IV would not appear until after the campaign. The machines struggled with the mud and craters and, more than once, artillery support was reduced or dispensed with so as not churn up the ground. First Army's front on Vimy Ridge was simply too much for them and the few that were deployed did not go far.

There were never enough tanks to make a strategic difference but they could create tactical opportunities. It had been recognised that they were useful for ripping up wire, particularly the wire beyond the range of the field artillery. The problem of how to integrate tanks with the creeping barrage was bypassed by not including them during the early part of Third Army's advance on 9 April. The plan was to save them for the deeper advance; only a few made it due to the bad ground, engine trouble and enemy action.

Infantry and tank coordination was still poor but we have to remember that many troops had not worked with them or seen them in action before. Generals and privates alike were wary of tanks and they contributed to the disaster at Bullecourt on 11 April. The Germans had also worked out how to reduce their effectiveness with armour-piercing bullets and wide trenches; what we would know as tank traps today.

After the success of 9 April, attempts to capitalise on it or replicate it ended with disappointing results. Problems were often attributed to tiredness or inexperience of the men. Haig went as far as wanting to ban night attacks because he did not trust the replacements. The bad weather had adverse effects on man and animal alike. The guns were also wearing out and they never had enough time to establish their positions or register their targets.

The biggest failure was the final attack on 3 May. The three army commanders had chosen different times for zero hour but a last-minute compromise resulted in them advancing while it was still dark, which pleased no one. It left no time to make the necessary preparations while the creeping barrage and objectives had been set for a daytime advance. The light wind drove dust into the faces of the assault troops in the darkness, resulting in a disaster.

One major problem which grew during the Arras campaign was a shortage of troops. Field Marshal Haig refused to commit extra divisions because he wanted to save them for the summer Flanders campaign. Instead, divisions were used time and again until they had been bled dry. Battalions were reformed as companies and brigades as battalions until replacements were sent forward. The veterans then had to teach the inexperienced newcomers in the rudiments of trench warfare on the battlefield. It was noted that the men went to ground too soon, resulting in unnecessary casualties and poor results.

The BEF had come a long way in the nine months between 1 July 1916 and 9 April 1917. The 3½-mile advance on 9 April was the longest in a single day since trench warfare had begun. With proper preparation the BEF had proved it could smash through defensive positions, capture ground and take prisoners. But what came afterwards proved that they could not always sustain that advance. Both sides had learnt many lessons on the Somme. They had learnt more around Arras but the British sometimes forgot them and paid the price. The question was, could they now breakthrough in Flanders?

Index